THE GOLDEN LAMP

THE GOLDEN LAMP

PORTRAIT OF A LANDLADY

Alasdair Alpin MacGregor

With 28 Illustrations,
21 of which are reproduced from
Photographs by the Author

ὁ βίος βραχύς, ἡ δέ τέχνη μακρή
"The lyfe so short, the craft so long to lerne"

London
MICHAEL JOSEPH

First published by
MICHAEL JOSEPH LTD
26 Bloomsbury Street
London W.C.1
1964

© *copyright 1964 by Alasdair Alpin MacGregor*

Set and printed in Great Britain by Tonbridge Printers Ltd,
Peach Hall Works, Tonbridge, Kent, in Plantin ten on
eleven point, on paper made by Henry Bruce at Currie,
Midlothian, and bound by James Burn at Esher, Surrey

MISS JANE AITKEN

(1854-1938)

Minded

by

yin o' her laddies

Preface

WHEN FOR the purposes of a volume such as this, I fail to recollect what I should readily remember, I cannot but rebuke myself for not having kept throughout the years some sort of diary, setting forth observations on people met and places visited, recording points from conversations heard or participated in, comments upon books read, impressions of interesting situations and occasions, and the thoughts and philosophisings running through one's mind over the years.

For my having omitted to do this, it used to be my plea that a man or woman, whose pen is his or her means of livelihood, has enough to do with it apart from encouraging the habit of committing to a diary a few hundred additional words each day.

However, when I discovered that prolific writers like Arnold Bennett, during the most strenuous decades of their lives, and wholly unaided by secretaries and typists, had set down in journal form, in their own diligent longhand, as many as a million carefully chosen words as a sort of sideline to their immense literary output, I found myself not only regretful that I had not built up a similar reservoir of material in this way, but also bereft of my pristine pretext for *my* not having done so.

As the concluding chapters of this book deal with at least *some* of the trials and tribulations of authors, to which most readers throughout the centuries have contrived to remain insensible, you may allow me to enter a not altogether inappropriate and unjustifiable caveat.

The man whose pen is his livelihood, whilst happy to hear from the readers of his works (even those obtained through libraries, and therefore perused for nothing so far as he is concerned) cannot cope with long, rambling, and usually egotistical letters from correspondents, especially when some sort of answer is expected without even assisting the hard-pressed recipient by the inclusion of a stamped, addressed envelope.

This applies, likewise, to people who write to authors as though they conducted travel-agencies enabling them to supply particulars as to where the readers of their books ought to spend their holidays, or might find suitable hotel or boarding-house accommodation . . . just in case they might decide to go here, or there, or for that matter anywhere. I don't know how other authors deal with this sort of request; but I do know that I cannot undertake to cope with it any longer!

You realise that authors give generously, and for very little. If not, you certainly will, by the time you have read our concluding chapters! The dustman and the busman make five times more a year under

7

welfare-state wage agreements than 90% of authors make on serious books. Does that startle you? Or does it perhaps shame you a little?

Authors are constantly being written to, appealed to, and even phoned to, by people seeking, free of charge, their hard-earned knowledge and information about this or that, about matters relating so often to their groundless genealogical claims and suppositions, even about the placing of literary works they one day intend publishing, *but never even write!*

All too many people in all too many walks of life get from authors, for nothing, what no other professional class, except, perhaps, the clergy, would supply but on a professional or commercial basis. From artists and musicians, from doctors, surgeons, dentists, specialists, lawyers, accountants, architects, and mercenary consultants, the public doesn't expect anything without having to pay a fee of some kind in respect of professional time absorbed and professional services rendered.

Why, then, should it be taken for granted that authors, who work exceedingly long hours over long years, and for the merest pittances, are at anybody's disposal, free? This is fairly universally assumed; but that makes it no less monstrous, thoughtless, presumptuous.

I append a hint to my caveat. If you simply *must* have the information you know a particular author possesses, never preface your written request for it by mentioning, as do so many, that you made this discovery while reading this or that book of his, *borrowed from some library.* Be subtle enough to keep that to yourself, even although the recipient of your request may well have reason to *suspect* it. If an author receive a royalty of 10% on a book published at 25/-, he earns exactly 2/6. If his royalty be, say, 12½%, which comparatively few ever achieve, he earns 3/1½. For this shameful sum, hundreds may well read the same library copy.

* * *

Finally, of our 28 illustrations, 21 are reproduced from my own photographs. The most delectable of the remaining seven is surely that facing page 40, showing Rupert Brooke in the garden of the Old Vicarage at Grantchester. Until fairly recently, it belonged to the Stevensons, with whom he lodged at The Orchard. It was given to me in Grantchester the other day by Sydney Wells, who, a few years ago, succeeded them at The Orchard.

ALASDAIR ALPIN MACGREGOR.

48, *Upper Cheyne Row,*
  Chelsea,
    London, S.W., 3.
      October, 1963.

Contents

Illustrations

CHAPTER ONE

Go Not, Happy Day!

Go not, happy day,
From the shining fields!
—Tennyson.

WHEN I ask myself whether there has been any period of my life, howsoever brief, during which I experienced unqualified, unalloyed happiness, I recall unhesitatingly one particularly felicitous interlude, and also the circumstances that, as it were, conspired to create it.

I write at the moment of the early summer of 1919, just after my return to Edinburgh, following upon a few blissful months at Cambridge and at Grantchester with friends to whom I had gone, partly to restore, in a setting I already knew intimately, that measure of sweet reasonableness which the war had destroyed in me, partly to recuperate from the injury it had done my mind and body, and partly to occupy agreeably at least some of the time intervening between my discharge from the army and the beginning of my first session at Edinburgh University.

The closing weeks of that interim period, I should perhaps mention, found me engaged not too enthusiastically at Skerry's College, ostensibly learning shorthand, typing, and a little book-keeping. I cannot imagine why! In any case, I didn't get very far with them. Where shorthand is concerned, I have always regretted this because the acquisition of even a little proficiency in it would have been immensely helpful throughout the copious note-taking years which were to follow. So I have had to invent a form of shorthand of my own, which is disadvantageous in that nobody can decipher it except myself; and even *I* have difficulty in doing so at times! I do not appear to have been endowed with the type of intelligence which makes such training easy. In admitting this, I derive a *soupçon* of consolation from what the famous C. P. Scott of *The Manchester Guardian* said to Neville Cardus at their first interview. "It doesn't really matter on the M.G.

Besides, Cardus, I am of the opinion that some men are born to short-hand: others achieve shorthand: others have shorthand thrust upon them."

My associations with the Cambridge scene the previous summer and autumn, although curtailed by wartime restrictions, as also by my very recent recovery from rheumatic fever, due to exposure on the Western Front during that holocaust, the Battle of Menin Road, had sent me back to it in poetic mood, chiefly through my having participated in the widespread interest then being shown in the poems of Rupert Brooke—particularly, of course, in *The Old Vicarage, Grantchester.*

In the autumn of 1918, when that frightful slaughter was being in-tensified on battlefields just across the Channel, I was getting to know my Cambridge in a quiet and unobtrusive way. I wasn't well enough to do so in any other way, for rheumatic fever had left me in a very debili-tated condition. Having by this time acquired the first volume of poetry I ever voluntarily purchased (the school-book collections of earlier years having been obligatory), I found myself adequately possessed of just the guide I required for my frequent excursions to Grantchester, awheel by Trumpington, or afoot by way of the water-meadows. This volume, now well fingered and a bit tattered, was the first series of *Poems of Today,* sponsored by the English Association, published in 1915, a few months after Rupert Brooke's death in the Aegean, and containing his poem, *The Old Vicarage.* It went with me to Grant-chester the afternoon I had tea with Mrs. Dudley Ward at the Old Vicarage itself, in the blood-stained autumn of 1918. It returned with me there when the lilacs were in bloom the following spring, and I went to tea again while staying with my friends, the Winters, at the Old Mill House, just over the vicarage garden wall.

By the time I got back to Edinburgh, a couple of months later, to settle down in lodgings at 12, Gladstone Terrace, with Miss Jane Aitken, the finest of Scots landladies, already sixty-five years of age, I was thoroughly familiar with the topography and toponomy of the Grantchester scene. Indeed, in the context of Rupert Brooke's verses it had made upon me so deep an impression as to have influenced the course of my life. The Muse, stimulated by the Golden Lamplight with which Miss Aitken endowed me, was now to ensnare me as never before, and, unfortunately, at a time when I ought to have been giving serious attention to the more urgent matters of the University cur-ricula upon which I was soon to embark.

Several years prior to this, Miss Aitken and I had seen quite a lot of one another through my visits in boyhood to Frederick Victor Branford (frequently referred to hereinafter as Victor) when *he* lodged with her. He was then studying Rhetoric and English Literature at

Edinburgh, under the celebrated Professor George Saintsbury, who predicted for him a brilliant career in these fields. That was in the days when Miss Aitken's home in Gladstone Terrace, situated in the Sciennes locality of our city, first became known to a literary circle of University students as Liberty Hall.

"Ay, ma certie!" Miss Aitken might be heard to say in the course of her many memorable spates in the Lowland Scots tongue. "This is Liberty Ha' wi'oot a doot! Ye wudna cairry on wi' thae capers ony ither place. An' fine ye ken it!"

It was in the days, moreover, when 'once, upon a midnight dreary,' I sat, entranced, in Victor's sittingroom, while his dramatic outbursts of rhetoric placed Edgar Allan Poe's raven so ominously, so terrifyingly, in our midst that I was too afraid to look up, lest I should find this ghostly bird perched on the door, too uncomfortably near me. Victor's midnight application to his sonnets,[1] with no sound but the creaking of his pen, and of its being dipped repeatedly and impatiently in the inkwell, were punctuated so often by these dramatic exercises of his that I knew Poe's macabre verses off by heart long before I ever read them. Ever since then, they have been inseparably associated in my mind with Victor and his sonnets, with Victor and that creaking pen of his, with the eloquent ink-stains he bequeathed so liberally to Miss Aitken's sittingroom table-cloth and carpet, and with that sittingroom door:

"Take thy beak out of my heart!
Take thy form from off my door!"

For some years before my first contact with Miss Aitken, she had been obliged to let rooms as a means of supporting herself and her agéd and crotchety mother. Apart from the few shillings' pittance of an old-age pension payable each week in respect of the latter, and the little Miss Aitken herself earned spasmodically at dressmaking (she had been employed for some years by an Edinburgh court dressmaker, but had been obliged to abandon this to look after her old and improvident parents), no cash came her way except what she made by letting rooms to University students, and received as a Gillespie Pensioner. In connection with the latter, she had been awarded in 1915 an annual pension of £10. Ten years later it was increased to £15. This she continued to receive throughout the rest of her life.

When James Gillespie of Spylaw died in 1797, he left the bulk of

[1] Many of them, reprinted from *Athenaeum, The English Review, Voices, Today,* and *The Cambridge Magazine,* were included in *Titans & Gods* and *The White Stallion,* collections of his poetry which Christophers published for him in 1922 and 1924, respectively.

his estate to the Master, Treasurer, and twelve representatives of Edinburgh's Town Council, and the Minister of the Tolbooth Church, for the endowment of James Gillespie's Hospital, founded "for the aliment and maintenance of old men and women". In 1801, when the Trustees were incorporated by Royal Charter, the Hospital was built in Gillespie Crescent. Many years ago it was amalgamated with other charitable endowments under the Merchant Company Endowments Trust. Beneficiaries must be "decent, godly, industrious, peaceable, sober men and women in indigent circumstances, of at least 55 years of age", except where unable to earn their living on medical grounds. They must belong to the City of Edinburgh, or to the County of Midlothian; and preference must be given to applicants bearing the surname of Gillespie. Miss Jane Aitken, this volume's central figure, amply fulfilled the requirements. Twice or thrice a year, therefore, a Gillespie Visitor called on her in a routine way, to confirm that she was still the deserving recipient of James Gillespie's charity, and that she was in reasonably good health.

Old Mrs. Aitken, to whom Victor and his college contemporaries referred—none too deferentially—as Old Party, or simply as O.P., was already an auld wife, a *crotchety,* auld wife, as I said earlier, excessively so when anybody sought to humour her. She must have been about ninety the year with which this saga of mine begins.

"How old are you now, Mrs. Aitken?" someone might ask, appreciative of her great age. At this she would look up, silently and sullenly, as if disdaining to answer so presumptuous a question. Then would come the invariable reply, like a burst from a machine-gun unexpectedly brought into action:

"Same age as ma little finger, an' a wee bittie older than ma teeth!"

Mrs. Aitken, like her daughter, had bouts of resorting uncompromisingly to the Scots vernacular, even when, without the slightest difficulty, she could have rendered in good, plain English what she had to say. Curiously, this was at a time when so many Lowland Scots folk, in Edinburgh and elsewhere, were striving to discard their native tongue in the belief that it wasn't quite genteel. To the end, however, both Miss Aitken and her mother exhibited their preference for it, never employing a purely English word where a good Scots equivalent was available. With the rich farmlands of Haddingtonshire—of East Lothian—as their ancestral background, why descend to the 're-feened' accents then so much in vogue in the bourgeois districts of the Scottish Capital? Never once did I hear either of them use the word, *child,* or *children,* for instance. Children, to them, were always weans, or bairns. *Little* children were weanies or bairnies. As you will see later, Miss Aitken's speech was sprinkled liberally with unusual words and phrases, many of them not easily netted even by the most indefatigable lexicographer. Her letters, on the other hand, were in the finest English, with the occasional insertion of a Scots word where no English one would have conveyed just the subtle nuance in which 'the Vernacular' is so rich.

By the time *I* came on this scene, O.P., no longer as nimble on her feet as she had been, was largely confined to an armchair by the kitchen fire, except when answering the doorbell which her stone-deaf daughter never heard. Yet, albeit her physical frame now lacked mobility, her keenness of eye entitled her to recognition as an acute observer. Nothing slipped her. Nothing passed unnoticed. There she sat by the fireside, all day long, watching everything that went on, criticising inwardly because her daughter's deafness rendered impracticable any vocal expression of her disapproval. The cat's yawn even was recorded. "Whit ails ye?" she might be heard to ask her fireside companion. The canary's blink was observed too. It justified the complaint that, "if it doesnae get a bittie protection frae that hot sun, it'll be deid by the morn". It promoted the urgent enquiry as to whether it had ample seed and water to be going on with. In like manner, every movement of her daughter, in the execution of her domestic duties, was followed critically, and none too generously commented upon. *Crotchety* she certainly was!

Old Mr. Aitken, already some years deceased, had been an Edinburgh cabinet-maker of some standing, and an active supporter of the Baptist Church. Many a piece of furniture about the house showed his skill as a craftsman. The mighty family scrapbook Miss Aitken had preserved showed him to have been a bit of a rhymester. His printed successes in this field were to be found among the newspaper cuttings punctiliously pasted into it by a dutiful daughter. Most of them were from Haddington's local paper.

"Pity faither hadna paid mair attention tae his lawfu' business!" Miss Aitken used to say, when wistfully recalling modest riches lost to mother and daughter through his neglect.

That scrapbook, by the way, contained many an interesting thing, especially about East Lothian—fragments of local lore and history, such as that concerning the last vicar of Gullane, deposed by King James VI. for "ye high crime of smoking tobacco, a weed which His Majesty deemed only fit for diabolical fumigations".

Old Grandfather Aitken, on the other hand, had been a well known clockmaker in Haddington. The grandfather clock that ticked and rumbled so noisily in the lobby at Liberty Hall as to leave an eerie silence when it inadvertently had been allowed to run down, was his handiwork. Its illuminated face bore, in fancy lettering, the words,

William Aitken
Haddington

and a date which I now forget.

When browsing in a secondhand bookshop in the King's Road of Chelsea the other day, I picked up a volume on Old Scottish Clock-makers. It contained several references to the name of Aitken, among them the aforesaid William, who flourished at his craft in Haddington between 1805 and 1837. Just fancy! That 'grandfather' of his had been ticking and rumbling away before Queen Victoria came to the throne!

But the ancestor about whom Miss Aitken spoke mostly was her maternal grandfather, with whom she spent many of her early years, and through whom she acquired her knowledge of flowers and garden-ing. They lived together in the little lodge at Preston Grange, the property of the Grant-Suttie family, situated between the mining villages of Preston and Wallyford, about a mile from historic Preston-pans. The grandfather was gardener and gatekeeper at Preston Grange. The lodge, known as the West Lodge, had been built for him and his grand-daughter, not so much because its predecessor had fallen into disrepair as because its predecessor's roof was too low to allow of its accommodating the grandfather clock, to which Miss Aitken had now fallen heir. The Grant-Sutties appear to have been good to grand-father and grand-daughter. The member of the family about whom Miss Aitken used to relate the strangest reminiscences "was a bittie daft, but a gey bit o' a lad for a' that".

From all accounts, Miss Aitken's floral displays at the West Lodge were a pleasing feature of this countryside for many a year. "We grew a' sorts o' auld-fashioned things like phloxes an' apple-ringie[1] roond the door an' up tae the window-sills, wi' clematis an' the like clam-berin' up tae the eaves."

When you reach the passage where I describe our window-box dis-plays at Liberty Hall, you will see how they were influenced by horti-cultural ongoings at Preston Grange, so many years earlier. "Och, laddie! Thae nasturtiums are awfu untidy", she once remarked, noticing how we had allowed them to get a bit out of hand. "Grand-faither used to say—." Here would ensue a long dissertation on nas-turtiums as once reared at Preston Grange.

Miss Aitken, during her sojourn at Preston Grange, got to know all the joys and woes of the mining communities in its locality, for she was an active church-worker in those days, thus making with mining families friendships that were sustained to the end of her life. Likewise,

[1] southernwood.

with the fisher-folk at Fisherrow when, on the death of her gardener grandfather, she went to live and work among them, residing at Kildonan Cottage, close to Fisherrow harbour, then a picturesque place of masts and sails, of spars and tarry ropes, of nets and creels.

It was while living at Preston Grange, by the way, that, in the words of a cousin of hers, "she became acquainted with deafness". This was the result of a prank played on her when a girl: the son of the Grant-Sutties' farm-manager discharged a gun at the side of her head. This noble woman, richly endowed with worldly wisdom, actuated by lofty, Christian principles, carried her affliction with fortitude, and even with humour. Nobody ever enjoyed more than she herself did the humorous situations which at times her lip-reading misinterpretations precipitated.

The Liberty Hall I first knew lay immediately beneath that in which, eventually, I was to find myself so agreeably installed with my Golden Lamp. It was situated on the first floor. There, until shortly before the outbreak of war in 1914, Miss Aitken had accommodated a succession of Edinburgh University students, some of them doing Medicine, some Arts, some Divinity, and a few doing Law. The flitting with her mother to the flat overhead followed the death of its tenant, a neat, little septuagenarian of a woman always seen in a brown, high-collared blouse, with cameo brooch to match, her hair tightly drawn back in a bun.

Both flats were the property of the same landlord—silken-whiskered, wheezy Mr. Scott, an elderly gentleman of leisure made to look the more gentlemanly and leisurely by reason of his trilby, and his silken scarf neatly adjusted and expensively pinned. Mr. Scott called in person on rent-day, primarily, to receive due payment, secondarily, to listen politely to any suggestions his tenants had to make in regard to renovations and repairs they considered necessary. Particulars of these he recorded at the back of his old-fashioned rent-book, but seldom attended to, on one pretext or another, the commonest of which was a recurring touch of asthma. That asthma excused many a broken promise, though, oddly enough, it never interfered with his calling to collect his rents on the statutory day.

Never was Mr. Scott known to have left Miss Aitken's on rent-day without getting his due in cold cash, carefully counted out before him on the kitchen table. Once he had slipped it securely into an inside pocket, and re-arranged the scarf momentarily dishevelled in the process of his so doing, he sat down, as was the custom, to sip the tot of whisky expected from each tenant on all such auspicious occasions. He already had had a few warming tots on his rent-collecting rounds before reaching Miss Aitken's; but these were never known to have rendered him other than amiably competent to count his cash, and duly enter in his rent-book such particulars as were necessary. That tot clinched the deal, as it were, in the manner long approved by Lothian custom. Indeed, one might well have believed it was statutorily obligatory on the part of the tenant to provide it.

With a silken handkerchief Mr. Scott wiped away any dampness from his silken whiskers as he rose to bow himself away in the direction of the next tenant on his list.

Never a cheep did Miss Aitken have from Mr. Scott, nor a sight of him, until the next rent-day when, once again, the same particulars of things needing attention were as studiously noted.

The reason for Miss Aitken's ascending from the first floor to the second was a practical one. Whereas the under-side of the spiral stone staircase darkened the front door of the lower flat, nothing of the kind occluded the daylight from that of the upper. In other words, although Miss Aitken couldn't *hear* what any caller might have to say at either door, she could at least *see,* and therefore identify or otherwise, and perhaps even lip-read, the caller standing on the upper doorstep.

This flitting had provided the opportunity for my ingratiating myself with Miss Aitken. It actually laid the foundation of the friendship and understanding, upon the strength of which I returned as a welcomed caller in the summer of 1919, to be invited to stay a couple of weeks as her guest, a temporary situation which was to resolve itself into something in the nature of a permanency. On two successive afternoons during that flitting in 1914, I transported, from the lower flat to the upper, all Miss Aitken's furniture, including even a cumbersome sideboard and Old Party's massive wooden bedstead. I was exceedingly strong and wiry in those days. My task was considerably simplified, of course, by my having to do no more than arrange upstairs the articles of furniture, and a variety of utensils, precisely as I found them downstairs. By tea-time on the second afternoon, therefore, all this had been accomplished; and Miss Aitken, Old Party, and I sat down, rejoicing, to our first felicitous tea in the new kitchen, where, in the years that were to follow my return in 1919, I was to have several thousand meals of one kind or another.

That interlude of unqualified happiness began, then, that summer, with Miss Aitken's invitation. Of the intensity of this happiness, I can scarcely believe myself to have been capable at any time in my life. In my innocence I believed that the First World War, so recently concluded (at all events in the superficial sense), had purified us all of our wickednesses. I little realised then that wicked people like Clemenceau, Lloyd George, and Winston Churchill were laying at Versailles and elsewhere the firm foundations for the Second.

My bedside book was the volume of poetry I have mentioned. It reposed on a bedside dresser by the Golden Lamp, in the light of which Victor had fashioned those sonnets of his in pre-war years. Its contents, in addition to *The Old Vicarage*, enchanted me. I recall Stevenson's lines to S. R. Crockett, W. B. Yeats's *Lake Isle of Innisfree* and *Down by the Sally Garden*, Alice Meynell's *Shepherdess*, John Masefield's *Twilight*, and—very particularly—Edmund Gosse's *Lying in the Grass*, because I had watched, so recently, three such mowers at Cambridge, where I myself had been the fourth. You will understand more clearly what I mean when you have re-read this poem.

Each night, as I lowered the wick of my Golden Lamp, praying that this felicity might never pass, there ran through my mind that line from Tennyson, with which this book opens—*Go not, happy day!*

CHAPTER TWO

The Moth and The Golden Lamp

IN CASTING a backward glance at that little room of mine at Liberty Hall, and all it contained—its simple furniture, much of it homemade, its table-cloth of crimson velvet, its coloured print of the Carpenter's Son at his father's bench in Nazareth, hanging above the mantelpiece —in recalling all this, and the room's scented repose at eventide, in visualising yet again that mighty patchwork quilt on my bed, wrought in many colours by Miss Aitken herself when a young woman, in reflecting on the golden gleam of the lamplight in which I discovered Edmund Gosse and those mowers I mentioned, and so much else that was to heighten my perception and enrich my life, I recall a little incident which had nothing whatever to do with my felicitous situation that summer, but which, quite irrelevantly, occupied my thoughts one evening as I sat up in bed, reading poetry in that first volume of *Poems of Today*, with everything hushed around me.

A moth, attracted by the lamplight, entered by the open window to encircle over and over again my Golden Lamp, and to dash itself as often against its hot globe, learning nothing from repeated trial and error. Watching it as it fluttered and fell, as it crawled a bit with wings vibrating at an incredible speed, as it fluttered and fell again until finally, with singed wings, it dropped from exhaustion to the slightly oily surface of the lamp's reservoir, I began to ponder on that strange aspect of existence known as Chance. What Chance—what *mis*-Chance, I asked myself—had brought that particular moth from the sweet and comparatively safe night-air of Gladstone Terrace into my particular room, there to spin round and round my particular Golden Lamp until defeat and death should have overcome a thing so fragile, so harmless, so innocent?

Ah! Chance!! how much of that moth's painful performance, now concluded with a few last feeble flutterings on the thinnest film of paraffin—just sufficient to contribute all that was necessary to its final enfeeblement—how much of this performance had been a game of chance in which, unwittingly, it had forfeited its life?

This minute and superficially minor tragedy prompted me, there and then, to consider the inherent nature of Chance, and to clarify my own approach to those gaming expressions of it which obsess so considerable a proportion of mankind, and which, certainly since the fate of that moth, have never laid any serious hold of *me*.

With very little money, and with but slender prospects of increasing for some time what I had, beyond what was required for the bare necessities of a young man about to matriculate at a university, I was now approaching cautiously a period of personal freedom possibly fraught with perils and pitfalls which must be eschewed. Alcohol I had never tasted. Nor have I yet. A cigarette had never touched my lips. Nor has it yet. So you see what a crashing bore many people must find me!

I now asked myself whether there was any likelihood of my ever being attracted to betting and organised games of Chance. So many of my friends and acquaintances in those years of post-war recklessness were putting a shilling on here and there, to use a popular euphemism. Would *I*, perhaps, succumb one day?

In the gleam of my Golden Lamp came that quite unexpected flash of insight, as it were, enabling me to resolve the position for myself, and at an age when I might well have been caught up in the post-war wave of chancy enterprises then being stimulated on every hand. In Edinburgh, as elsewhere, dog-racing was now getting a firm grip of the masses. Whippets were steadily acquiring the reverence hitherto bestowed upon racehorses. In many a home "the whupputs'" wellbeing came before that of the bairns. Miss Aitken knew families in the mining localities of Prestonpans and Tranent which had literally 'gone to the dogs' with betting—and, of course, with drink, its wily concomitant, its natural corollary. Her attitude to this sort of thing was identical with my own. This helped to make exceedingly easy and agreeable the years I was to spend under her roof.

Mind you! I do not arrogate to myself anything the least self-flattering in the attitude I had adopted. All I would dare say in this regard is that, having thrashed the matter out with myself one evening, in the gleam of my Golden Lamp, I have never had to contend against temptation in this singularly unrewarding field. In other words, I have never experienced the slightest desire to place a bet anywhere.

Although exceedingly stupid when it comes to matters involving numerical calculations and deductions, I discovered what I still feel convinced is true, namely, that all games of chance and all betting transactions can be separated into two categories:

(1) Those in which the risks are equitable, and

(2) those in which they are not.

I can hardly imagine that the habitual gambler ever asks himself into which category, if any, his speculations fall. As a contributor to a well-known Sunday newspaper put it recently, an equitable hazard is one where both gains and losses are relative to the prospects of success. An *in*equitable hazard, on the other hand, is one in which the speculator receives less when he wins than the amount calculated in accordance with the probability. To me, it has always been too painfully obvious that bookmakers, casino proprietors, and bingo promoters must make certain, if merely for their own survival, that the games of chance they encourage, or the betting chances they professionally declare, are inequitable. And so I agree with those fervent participants who, themselves, have assured me that betting, from which they would simply hate to abstract themselves, is 'a mug's game'.

Having said all this, I must now proceed to remove from the reader's mind any suspicion I may have created of unctuous self-commendation, by confessing to a series of occasions upon which I indulged almost fanatically in a game of chance. This was some years after I had become separated from the reflective influence of my Golden Lamp. It was actually in 1932. I remember this because so many of that year's doings and happenings fell to be recorded in *The Haunted Isles*, published in London the following year. Much of the material included in that book resulted from a prolonged stay the previous autumn with the MacLeods at Scaliscro. Some years previously, my kinsman, Norman MacLeod, then a doctor at Skipton, had availed himself of the opportunity offered by the first Viscount Leverhulme of becoming, in a mild way, a landed proprietor. When Norman's native Isle of Lewis was being offered for sale in 1923, and in lots not wholly unattractive, some of them going for as little as threepence an acre, he sensibly purchased Scaliscro, a moorland property with fishings and shootings, situated in the west of the island, admirably suitable as a family holiday retreat.

Norman and I, ever since our days at The Front, had retained an innocent penchant for vingt-et-un, or pontoon, as we called it in the army. A succession of wet and blustrous days at Scaliscro that autumn, and the encouragement lent by a couple of friends spending a fishing holiday with the MacLeods there, provided a pretext for renewing our acquaintance with this game. Night after night we played 'vanty', and often during the day also, especially when, for one reason or another, Norman and his guests were prevented from trudging the moors in oilskins and gumboots to the more promising lochs on the Scaliscro property. Indeed, we now pursued our pontoon sessions with a fervour akin, to fanaticism, I scarcely can believe to have been possible. In these we were sometimes joined by Norman's three sons—

Iain, who was still at Fettes, and his younger brothers, Torquil and Roderic, both of whom were at school at St Ninian's. A brother-in-law, husband of their only sister, Rhodabelle, completed our pontoon school that autumn.

Torquil and Roderic usually dropped out early in the game, since the few pence at their disposal were soon in wilier pockets. But, somehow or other, Roderic would return in a nonchalant manner a few minutes later, ready to participate in the game once more. We suspected that a little cupboard love in the shape of a little loose change, surreptitiously slipped him by an adoring mother, enabled him to re-instate himself on these occasions.

The only member of our school who, throughout, maintained an air of blasé indifference to our gains and losses was Iain, who, with his prodigious memory, always knew, after a few deals, precisely the order in which the cards lay, upside-down, in the banker's hand, except when a too recent 'vanty' had necessitated their being re-shuffled and cut.

We little thought then that, years before Iain MacLeod entered politics with the distinction he has since attained, he was to be recognised as one of the world's foremost authorities on Bridge! It may well have been Iain whom Lord Hemingford had in mind the other day when he declared that he would prefer a statesman who had mastered Bridge to one who remained content with Nap or Snap!

Reverting for a moment to those frantic pontoon sessions at Scaliscro, how much money would you suppose this orgy of card-playing involved? When we came to a final reckoning, we found that nobody had lost or gained more than two or three shillings. Those of us who were a bit in pocket one evening were usually out of pocket to about the same extent the following evening. You see, the maximum stake we permitted ourselves was tuppence. The banker, of course, could double this if he chose to do so. Even though, it meant that at the end of several highly concentrated hours of play, nobody was ever very much in or very much out.

Innocent enough, so far as it went. Yet, admittedly, not in conformity with the conclusions I had arrived at in the gleam of my Golden Lamp. I must confess, therefore, to having been guilty of a temporary aberration from the commonsense of things. For several days and nights on end, in response to a touch of romantic appeal in a highly romantic setting, I had departed from my disciplined and dispassionate assessment of earlier years. That assessment I believe to have been accurate, and entirely free from prejudice. *Mais revenons à nos moutons.*

CHAPTER THREE

Cheepity
(whose dates are forgotten)

Buckie
(1914–1933)

•••

ALTHOUGH I cannot remember a time when animals did not mean something very real and personal to me, it was not until my Golden Lamp days that my life became inseparably bound up with them, particularly with the feline and canine tribes. It is true that during childhood at Applecross I had had a fox-terrier named Don; but for many years after his death my doggie friends were the property of others.

It is also true that throughout the intervening years my canine interest had been whetted by my father's frequent allusions to the dogs he had had during his many years in India and Burma, and by his reminding one from time to time of the affection shown by Sir Walter Scott toward the various dogs he had owned. When Camp, Scott's very special dog, died in Edinburgh, he was buried by moonlight in the little garden behind his home at 39, Castle Street. "My wife tells me," wrote Lockhart, his son-in-law, "that she remembers the whole family in tears about the grave, as her father himself smoothed the turf above Camp." Scott had had an invitation to dine abroad that evening, but had sent apologies for his inability to avail himself of it, owing to the death of "a dear old friend".

From the first it looked as though my residing at Miss Aitken's was likely to be of as permanent a nature as anything could have been in those days and circumstances. Apart from the succession of theological students who now lodged with her, we had, at the outset of my sojourn, two additional personalities on the permanent strength, as it were. One of these was Cheepity, a melodious canary allowed the freedom of the house for a couple of hours each day, without ever showing any inclination to leave us even when the windows were open, and he found himself at liberty on the window-sill.

The other was Buckie, the cat. Buckie, when still the merest kitten, had been presented to Miss Aitken in 1914 by Dorothy Walker, the school-friend of my sister, Margaret. The Walkers' cat was constantly involved in the occupational hazard of having kittens more quickly than dear, humane Mrs. Walker could find homes for them. So Dorothy suggested that Victor's landlady, as Miss Aitken was at that time, might be willing to provide a home for one of that pre-wartime lot. Miss Aitken's ready acceptance supplied Dorothy with a pretext for visiting Liberty Hall after school each day. She used to arrive ostensibly to enquire for the kitten. This meant two or three of Miss Aitken's fine, Scottish teas in the kitchen every week until Old Party— yon crotchety auld wife!—put a stop to her visits. Dorothy came, very sensibly, at tea-time, rang the doorbell, and waited. If Miss Aitken answered, all was well: if Old Party answered, all was gruff.

Miss Aitken: "Wha wes at the door, mither?"

Old Party: "Need ye ask? Yon Walker lassie, of course!"

Miss Aitken: "Whit way did ye no' invite the lassie in tae her tea?"

Old Party: "Weel, Ah didnae. Ah jist slammit the door in her face!"

Miss Aitken: "Ay, mither! Ye shouldna hae dune that! The lassie cam' tae enquire aboot the kitten."

Old Party: "Stuff an' nonsense! She kens fine hoo the kitten is. She saw it yesterday aifternoon. Ach, Ah cannae be bothered wi' yon cheeky brat. Me havin' tae answer the door tae her ev'ry aifternoon! A'm fair sick o't!"

Although resentful of her agéd mother's attitude toward a mere schoolgirl, Miss Aitken was just a little thankful, since she, too, had been finding Dorothy's visits rather frequent. At all events, O.P. thus put a stop to her calls at Liberty Hall.

In the days when Dorothy arrived with the kitten, O.P. dispensed similar treatment to myself when she, instead of her daughter, happened to answer the door, even although I was some years older than Dorothy, and usually had better reason to call. Placing my ear to the outer door after one of her slamming receptions, I overheard, quite clearly, the following conversation within, for O.P., though aware of her daughter's stone-deafness, still imagined that the louder she spoke, the more likely Miss Aitken was to hear:

O.P.: "Ah went tae the door the noo."

Miss A.: "Yes, mither. Ah see the doorbell's shakin'."

O.P.: "Ah answered it a' richt! Ah did that!"

Miss A.: "Wha wes it?"

O.P.: "Yon MacGreegar laddie. He asked if Branford was in. Ah telt 'um Branford wes *oot*, an' wudna be back till a' 'oors. Ah jist shut the door in his face!"

Miss A.: "Oh, mither! Ye shouldnae hae dune that! Branford's expectin' MacGreegar for his tea. A've set the tea ben for baith o' them."

O.P.: "Och, Ah cannae bide yon MacGreegar laddie. He's an awfie lee-ar [liar] onyway. Whit wes yon story he telt us aboot his faither? Ah didna believe a word o't. Ye mind, he cam' ben an' telt us aboot his faither gettin' a knighthood. Jist a big, big lee tae curry favour. Na, na, Jane! Ah cannae thole 'um!"

How little one imagined then that a few years later I was to be installed here, and to write in these digs my first four books and innumerable articles, in the gleam of the Golden Lamp that had provided the light in which the inspired Frederick Victor Branford had set down the best of his sonnets!

Little Dorothy Walker, after *her* rude reception, did not venture near Gladstone Terrace again until a year or two after the First World War, when my sister, Margaret, shortly before her marriage, came North about Christmas-time on a couple of weeks' holiday. Margaret stayed with Dorothy and her parents at Portobello. Early in the New Year, the theological student Miss Aitken had at the time suggested that he and I should give at Liberty Hall an informal party to which each of us would invite a few guests. I invited Dorothy and Margaret. My fellow-lodger invited, among others, a theological contemporary named James Stewart.

The party was but twenty minutes old when a nice, little flirtation began between Dorothy and James, stimulated by a rollicking parlour game we played—a game necessitating its participants' creeping about in pairs and in darkness under the table. As the evening wore on, it became obvious that a mild flirtation was developing into something less mild. By midnight, when Miss Aitken entered to break up the party in the interests of decorum, things between Dorothy and James were pretty desperate. Indeed, the matrimonial die was—cast! The tying of the conventional knot in due course seemed inevitable.

All this happened on a Saturday evening, early in the wintry month of January. Dorothy and Margaret had persisted in staying so late that public transport had ceased by the time they graciously announced their preparedness to depart. Taxicabs were comparatively scarce in Edinburgh then; and it was doubtful whether, as we were now on the threshold of the Sabbath, even a horse-cab could have been summoned to undertake the long descent to the Walkers' home at Portobello. This meant that Stewart, my fellow-lodger, and myself were obliged to escort them home on foot. Miss Aitken was furious about this. Here was the very situation she had tried to avoid for all concerned. Several times throughout the evening she had intervened to remind Dorothy and Margaret of the increasing lateness of the hour. But they paid no heed. Fortunately, they had arrived properly clad and shod for this wintry occasion, since the flurry of snow accompanying them from Portobello turned out to have been but the prelude to a fall of several inches by the time Miss Aitken, none too politely, saw them off the premises with a parting commentary on Elders' Hours and associated matters which young ladies ought to observe.

That such snow had now fallen, nobody realised until I went to a window to see what sort of night we had to face. Very early that Sunday morning we set forth, the five of us, everything stilled and hushed, the air clear, crisp, and flakeless, the ground covered in untrodden snow, the vigilant street-lamps, lit with gas-mantles, casting upon it lanes and pools of yellow light so enchanting as to have dissolved one's first irritation at having to turn out in order to escort so far, and so late, a couple of young women thoughtlessly reluctant to leave.

Our journey by the King's Park and Duddingston was accomplished in two separate parties, for Dorothy and Stewart, now very much arm-in-arm, travelled by themselves, sometimes romping ahead of us, sometimes lurking behind. Eventually we all reached the Walkers' house in West Brighton Crescent, the escorting trio standing half-hidden behind a leafless lilac-tree in their garden to see that Dorothy and Margaret actually got in. The thud of the door-knocker and the repeated pulling of the doorbell brought no response. Not to begin with, at any rate. Could Mr. and Mrs. Walker, in alarm, have gone out to search for daughter and guest? Were they off to the local police-station to report their non-return? The complete absence of footprints in the snow dissipated any such probability. Were they lying doggo, then, just to emphasise their anger?

At length a glow of light appeared in the fanlight above the front door; and the front door was opened tardily—very slowly and mysteriously. All one could hear were those disapproving tut-tuts of Mr Walker, standing behind it in his night-attire. These brought me forth from my concealment by the lilac-tree to the snowy doorstep in order to explain

"I *am* so sorry, Mr. Walker!" I whispered; "but—."

"No need to be sorry, Alasdair! No need to explain! I realise exactly what happened. You see, *I know Dorothy!*"

As I retreated noiselessly from the doorstep, up went a window, and out popped a large, white, conciliatory mop of a head. It was white-haired Mrs. Walker's. Her voice now issued forth with all the authority of a royal command, breaking the snow-silence my whisperings were endeavouring to preserve at so late an hour. "COME BACK, THE THREE OF YOU, ABOUT TEA-TIME FOR A NEW YEAR'S PARTY!"

It was taken for granted that we would obey this command, since the window was slammed down before we could draw breath and politely signify acceptance.

But what was the explanation? Had Dorothy, in the few intervening seconds, quietly told her mother she had met the man she would like to marry?

Anyhow, no more than twelve hours later, the three of us, in daylight, again trudged through those same snows to Portobello, identifying in the King's Park that afternoon all the foot-tracks there were —five in one direction, three in the other. James Stewart, though unaware of it, was now on his way to meet, for the first time, his parents-in-law. Shortly afterwards, Dorothy became the wife of the Rev. James Stewart, M.A., B.D. She made a remarkably happy marriage. If her previous visit to Liberty Hall, six or eight years earlier, had been rewarded with the door in her face, as the saying is, this visit to our party rewarded her with a husband.

The cat, now in his prime, was the pride and envy of Gladstone Terrace. Nobody ever saw him abroad until he had been properly groomed by Miss Aitken with his own special brush and comb, kept in a tin on the ledge of the sewing-machine. The cat, impatient to be allowed out, used to leap on the ledge and knock the tin over on to the floor in an endeavour to draw Miss Aitken's attention.

For years our splendid puss had been without a name. "What do you call him?" asked a licensed grocer friend who came to tea one afternoon, and upon whose lap the creature instantly jumped.

"Well, Mr. Porter," I replied, "he's never had a name."

"Let us christen him here and now, then! Call him Buchanan! He's Black and White!"

From that day until his death, he answered to the abbreviated name of Buckie. Of all the feline friends I have known in my life, Dorothy's donation, in the shape of the very miniature Buckie, was to become the most endearing and responsive. There existed between the sagacious Buckie and me, right up to the time of his death at the age of nineteen, a bond as eternal as anything in Eternity—if there be such a thing.

In remembering Buckie, I find it difficult not to remember at the same time the Newhaven fishwife who called with her creel every Tuesday, and became a bit of a nuisance when she persisted in calling every Friday as well, on the pretext that, even if Miss Aitken had all the fish she required until the following Tuesday, "the caat micht be gled o' a nice, fresh bittie".

Our fishwife, of course, belonged to that picturesque fisher-folk community at Newhaven, bringing Nathaniel Gow's melody to Lady Nairn's verses to the lips of the Lowland Scot:

Wha'll buy ma caller herrin'?
They're bonnie fish an' halesome farin';
Wha'll buy ma caller herrin'
New drawn frae the Forth?

Newhaven's fishwives are a remarkable race of women. No rouge nor lipstick nonsense about *them*! Weather and the nature of their calling bestow upon them all the colouring they need. No stiletto heels either, for they must needs have their feet firmly on the ground.

A Society of Free Fishermen was established in Newhaven as early as the closing years of the sixteenth century; and it is said that, when George IV. visited Edinburgh, he pronounced the Newhaven fishwives the most handsome women he had ever seen. Their descendants still adorn the streets of the Scottish Capital, clad in traditional costume, and carrying laden creels, usually knitting as they go. See them on a gusty day, battling against the elements, so sure of foot, so fresh of cheek, the leathern straps of their creels slung across the forehead. Their appearance in our midst, with the tang of the briny Forth about them, never fails to prompt that poignant and pregnant line from *The Antiquary*—

It's no' fish ye're buying: it's men's lives.

Miss Aitken's particular fishwife had been calling regularly with her creel ever since she and her ageing mother had flitted up to the South Side of the city. The fishwife's only drawback, Miss Aitken used to say, was her refusal to take 'no' for an answer. "Ye're that thrawn!" Miss Aitken might be heard saying as she left the fishwife and her creel at the door for a moment, while she sought her purse and a plate from the kitchen shelf. "Jist a couple o' thae haddies, an' nae mair. Yer fish is awfie dear. Ah can get it cheaper roond the corner!"

"Ah believe *that*!" conceded the fishwife, as she swung the creel on to her back. "Maybees, ye can; but it's no' sae caller!" (It's not so fresh!)

In closing the door as the fishwife's descending foot touched the top step of the stair, Miss Aitken would say to me, with a volume meant even more for other ears, "Did ever ye ken the likes o' her? She wunna tak' 'no' for an answer, an' jist stands there, stookie-like, wi' her creel, as plausible as ye mak' them."

It made no difference how emphatically the fishwife was told not to return too soon. "Now, mind ye, Ah'll no' be wantin' mair fish for a week onyway!" Miss Aitken would say. But back the fishwife came in a few days, as innocent and plausible as ever.

"Ah telt ye no' tae come back for a week!" one might hear Miss

Aitken screech at her, with an unmistakable touch of annoyance.

"Ah, weel," the fishwife would reply with a pretence of contrition, "maybees, Ah thocht tae masel, the caat wud be wantin' a bittie fish ower the weekend!"

"Stuff an' nonsense!" retorted Miss Aitken. "Dinnae blame it on the cat. The cat's no' finished the last lot o' fish-heids ye left."

While argument of this sort went on, Miss Aitken's heart usually softened at sight of the fishwife's sad and sea-blue eyes; and a fishy whiff might now be wafted through the house as the fishwife dumped her creel yet again on the door-mat with a right, good, creaking thud. The transaction thus completed, Miss Aitken would deposit her wet and flabby purchase on the kitchen table, and then come ben to acquaint me of the details of this conversation at the door, unaware that I had overheard most of it. "Ah've aye telt ye she wunna tak' 'no' for an answer. Ah'll no' be in the next time she calls. *That'll* sort her!"

Buckie, of course, was the member of the household most likely to benefit from the fishwife's importunities.

A bond not dissimilar from that which existed between Buckie and me also existed between me and Cheepity. My return to Liberty Hall after a few days' absence was always acknowledged by Cheepity with a tremendous outpouring of song, a thrilling and trilling ovation Miss Aitken never failed to hear. She heard nothing except a bird's whistle and a dog's bark.

"Ay, Cheepity, he's safely back!" Miss Aitken might be heard to say. "Nae need tae mak' sic a noise aboot it. We ken ye're pleased!"

The joy of that little kitchen at tea-time, with the afternoon sun at its westering, with the singing kettle, with Cheepity alighting every now and then on the hearthrug beside an unheeding Buckie, is something I have never forgotten. Cat and canary respected one another as members of the same household, just as did the cat and the dogs to be mentioned shortly. When Cheepity wearied of his freedom, he retired to his cage, quietly and soberly. All one had to do to start him singing again was to turn on, for a few seconds, a tap at the kitchen sink, over which his cage was suspended, and in which he bathed in a very thin thread of water carefully regulated for his delectation.

One morning, alas! Cheepity lay dead in his cage. The blithesome thing that had filled the house with song had gone the way of all flesh, so unexpectedly. No sickness, no ailing, no decline in his vigorous repertoire. He simply passed away without any warning. Just a case of sudden death, such as every one of us might well hope for as our ultimate lot.

Cheepity's going left an almost palpable blank at Liberty Hall, rendering it songless and sorrowing. We buried him darkly at dead of night in the back-green, the sods with a kitchen utensil turning. His empty cage hung there, at the kitchen window, for a long time, with never a finger reaching up to it, even to dust it.

But one day, while Miss Aitken was out shopping, I smuggled into it a successor, bought at a pet-shop as a whistling cock for seven-and-six. I hate pet-shops, of course, and would do all in my power to prevent people from patronising them, realising that in removing one captive from them, we are simply providing shockingly confined imprisonment for another. All part of this sordid traffic in bird and beast.

For the first hour or two, Miss Aitken did not notice the newcomer. But soon he was to find so pleasant his new surroundings as to warrant an outburst of song so loud and prolonged that Miss Aitken—well, she was startled—'fair dumfoonert'! She could believe neither her ears nor her eyes. There, before her, hopped a yellow thing she instantly declared to be the finest songster she had ever known in half a century's dealings with canaries. To anybody deaf in the way *she* was, the presence in the home of some living thing, whose voice could always be heard, was profoundly acceptable. That perfectly audible canary was company for her when she found herself alone and lonely.

Cheepity the Second had been with us but a few months when something wholly unexpected occurred: *an egg was found lying at the bottom of the cage!* The whistling cock turned out to be a whistling hen. Miss Aitken's discovery of that egg evoked such a shriek from her that I dashed into the kitchen to see what ill had befallen her. By now she was seated in her chair, laughing irrepressibly, wiping her specs on her apron, the tears rolling down her cheeks. "Ye're no' a bird-fancier, I see," she said in her pawky way. 'Ye didnae ken the difference atween a cock and a hen!"

"*Neither did you!*" I replied, "*until a few seconds ago!*"

Cheepity the Second continued to lay an egg every day for about three weeks, and, as Miss Aitken put it, became fair exhausted in the process. On one or two occasions she laid two in twenty-four hours. "Next time ye visit Mr. Porter," she enjoined, "see that he gi'es us something tae revive oor puir canary. He gave us a name for the cat. Maybe, he'll gi'e us a drappie brandy for the canary."

As I have never purchased a pennyworth of alcohol in my life, either for myself or on behalf of anybody else, it was agreeable to have had Mr. Porter hand me, gratis, the smallest quantity of brandy in the smallest of bottles. A drop or two, deftly administered by Miss Aitken at intervals, on the tip of a salt-spoon, soon restored Cheepity the Second to her perch, after she had had her wee behind rubbed with a little olive-oil to relieve her egg-bound condition. Once recovered from this bout of laying, she resumed her quite remarkable singing, and lived happily ever after.

I am told that the ministration to an ill or injured bird of a drop or two of alcohol is a restorative widely recognised. The other day a lady in Evesham contributed to *Country Life* a letter describing the first feathered visitor to her garden during the intense and prolonged cold of February, 1963. It was an unusual one—a woodcock, which had crashed against a window-pane and immediately collapsed. She revived it with a fragment of bread soaked in brandy. Within an hour the woodcock was running about the house. Was it, perhaps, a little intoxicated?

Apart from the diversion Buckie and the two Cheepities provided, it did not occur to us for some time that the keeping of a dog at Liberty Hall was feasible until one summer a friend of Miss Aitken asked whether we could look after her cairn terrier for a week or two while she went abroad on holiday. The cairn proved such a success that we dreaded its owner's return. We discussed the prospect of getting a dog of our own; but the idea of obtaining one at a pet-shop did not appeal for the reason I have indicated. There was another deterrent, however, where I was concerned, namely, the eventual sorrow of his passing. As Sir Walter Scott put it, the misery of keeping a dog is his dying so soon; "but, to be sure, if he lived for another fifty years, and *then* died, what would become of *me*?"

One way and another, Buckie seemed to fill any need for animal companionship. When he sought a change from the warmth and comfort of the kitchen hearthrug, he hollowed out for himself a space on my bed. If I spent more of the midnight oil than he approved of (thus delaying my coming to bed), he would emit a few scarcely audible whimpers of disappointment. The kitchen fire, as well as that in my own room, would be well out by this time, their hearths already cold. So Buckie would step cautiously from the sofa arm to the table at which I sat writing, and stand there a few seconds, waiting for me to clear sufficient of my books and papers to enable him to lie in the warmth of my Golden Lamp. There he would remain for hours, twitching the end of his tail at intervals in contentment and gratitude, and sometimes swinging the entire tail violently for a few seconds, as if endeavouring to insert the tip of it in the inkwell. Fountain-pens were relatively scarce then. Even among professional writers, inkstands and inkwells, pen-trays, blotting-pads, and ink-stains were still, unmistakably, the evidence of their trade.

CHAPTER FOUR

Ruairi
(1923–1938)

Torquil
(1926–1930)

••

WHEN ON a visit to relations in the Hebrides, I happened to call at the Commercial Hotel in Stornoway. There, tied by a bit of string to a leg of the kitchen table, was a young, fluffy, lovesome thing which I greatly coveted—a black-and-tan collie puppy. Having told my cousin, Mairi MacDonald, that she simply must find me an animal of this sort, she wrote me the following spring that Donald Dearg, shepherd at the neighbouring farm of Stoneyfield, had done so, and that the animal was already under her care, and awaiting my return to collect it. I told Miss Aitken nothing of this. As I walked home by the shore-track to Sandwick with my cousins from the mail-boat the following summer, wondering what sort of creature Donald Dearg had found for me, a wild, skinnymalink of a thing came dashing along the tide's edge to meet us. That was my first sight of the puppy upon which we put the name of Ruairi (Roderic), and that within a few weeks was to become the most inseparable and enlightening companion a man ever had. Soon he lost his hobbledehoyhood. His black coat began to grow and take on a sleeky sheen. Withal, he was developing into something that before long would look both handsome and distinctive on the streets of Auld Reekie.

The night I left Stornoway with him aboard the mail-boat, I was obliged to tie him up to a stanchion in that part of the vessel reserved for livestock and sundry cargo of a bulky nature. Regulations forbade the taking of an animal into saloon or cabin. But Ruairi whimpered so much in the cold loneliness where I had left him that, as soon as the vessel was clear of the Arnish Light, I crept out of my cabin and retrieved him, wrapping him out of sight in the folds of the rug in my bunk, with nothing but his nostrils showing. This was at 2 a.m. In those days the mail-boat arrived at Kyle of Lochalsh at an hour necessitating a wearisome wait ere the first train of the day departed for the south, by way of Dingwall and Inverness. So Ruairi and I were in no hurry to disembark. When we did so, however, I explained to him that he was now on the mainland of Scotland, where he wouldn't have quite the freedom he had known at Sandwick. No more scampering over croftland and moorland. No more dashing off with sundry members of his race to plunge and plouter in the sea. Eventually we made for the Station Hotel at Kyle, set so attractively (if also a little expensively) by the tideway separating Wester Ross from the Misty Isle of Skye. We ordered breakfast. The fuss that manageress and waitresses now made of Ruairi I shall always remember. For a while he lay at my feet below the table, a little nervous of his new environment. The wheedlings and coaxings of the hotel staff soon proved such a strain upon his sense of obedience that I had to allow him to follow them off to the kitchen. When train-time drew near, he was as loth to leave as the staff was to let him go. "We thought that, maybe, the doggie might be hungry in the train," said a waitress when I came to paying my bill. "So we've made up a lunch for him." She handed me a bag containing scraps of this and that, and a bone or two. By the time Ruairi and I reached Edinburgh that evening, the bag's contents were very completely consumed. By this time, too, Miss Aitken had received a telegram I had sent her from Kyle:

Arriving suppertime with sleeky acquisition who staying few nights anyhow.

This mystified her. Or did it? She was watching for us at the window as our conveyance from the Waverley—an old horse-cab—rattled over the uneven cobblestones of Gladstone Terrace to draw up at Number Twelve.

The front door was already open to receive us. Ruairi dashed upstairs and into the kitchen. Miss Aitken sat down in her fireside chair, tears of delight already streaming down her cheeks as Ruairi licked this ear and then that, doing his best to explain that he would be taking up permanent residence. "Ah see he'll hae tae stay wi' us, no' jist for a few nichts, but for ever!" was her first remark when the excitement subsided. She was so enchanted by this addition to the establishment—to the permanent strength—as to have been quite unable to dish the supper.

Ruairi's puppyhood by the Hebridean shore, his jumping in and out of boats all day, and his early retrieving sticks flung into the sea, all produced a restlessness in him whenever he came within reach of water, which he would seek permission to enter. He would never do so *without* permission. When we visited my father at Portobello, the little waves breaking in gentle curves but a stone's-throw away from the sittingroom window never failed to induce in Ruairi the notion that he ought to be out there, splashing among them. No spaniel ever took to the water more readily than this collie. His seeing from the window

another of his race swimming out to retrieve something flung into
the sea sent him frantic with excitement. To assuage the noise of his
barking, if nothing else, one had to accompany him so that he, too,
might show his paces.

When he and I were able to swim together in the sea just there, it
was delightful; but, whereas a man may float and, in so doing, rest a
bit at intervals, a dog must keep pedalling away all the time for, otherwise, he would sink. To prevent Ruairi from exhausting himself, therefore, these swimming spells had to be of comparatively short duration.
In the summertime I have counted as many as a couple of hundred
spectators and holidaymakers congregated on the sands at Portobello
to watch Ruairi's aquatic antics.

Returning thereafter to my father's sittingroom, he would open the
wall-cupboard door to drag off the bottom shelf his own very special
towel, drop it at one's feet, and promptly bury his head between one's
knees to get his head and ears well dried. The salt water, of course,
robbed his coat of its sheen; but Miss Aitken's daily combing and
brushing soon restored it.

This recalls an occasion when Ruairi, now about three, was mentioned in local despatches. It had always been agreed between Miss
Aitken and me that Ruairi should accompany her on her annual holiday. One year she answered an advertisement for apartments in Buckhaven, one of the less fashionable resorts of Fife. When so doing, she
indicated she would be bringing a collie-dog with her. In presenting
her credentials, she enclosed an article and photograph of Ruairi which
had appeared shortly before in the *Edinburgh Evening News,* and
which we refer to in a subsequent chapter. As nearly every household
in Fife reads that newspaper, the dog was already known to some
extent in 'The Kingdom'.

One afternoon a family likewise holidaying at Buckhaven, consisting
of three or four young children and their parents, were handling
rather clumsily, and at no distance offshore, a rowing-boat, when an
infant fell overboard. "Ruairi!" screamed Miss Aitken, who was seated
on the sands nearby. She pointed. In an instant the dog had brought
the infant ashore, while the boat's flurried occupants plashed and
splashed madly with the oars in endeavouring to manoeuvre it in such
a way as to allow someone aboard to grab the child. It was indeed a
fortunate accident that the dog had seized the child the right way up,
and thus was able to deliver it into Miss Aitken's hands, little the
worse of its adventure, apart from its being soaked.

The family was immensely grateful. With all manner of gratitude it
crowded round Miss Aitken, as did several others who had witnessed
the rescue. Nobody realised, of course, that Miss Aitken was stone-

deaf, and that this explained how she did no more than acknowledge their felicitations with smilings and bowings while modestly retiring with Ruairi from the scene of all this fuss, followed by dozens and dozens seeking to photograph the heroic rescuer. Ruairi couldn't understand all this to-do. True, he already had received a good deal of admiration in his young life, but never anything quite so overwhelming. He simply didn't realise what he had done to deserve it.

Next morning there reached me from Buckhaven a long letter giving the fullest account of the incident. For years thereafter Miss Aitken carried in her handbag an envelope containing photographs taken by sundry people on the beach that day, given to her before she and Ruairi left Buckhaven, or posted to her after she and Ruairi had returned to Liberty Hall. Only one of these photographs was I able to trace at the time of her death in 1938. A rather indifferent one showing her seated, in her homemade hat, among the sand-dunes by the shore near Buckhaven, with Ruairi not yet quite dry after his rescue. It was taken by a holidaymaker who had witnessed the incident, and had posted it to her some little time later. I wish I had kept the letter she wrote me that same day, describing in detail what had occurred, the admiration showered upon Ruairi in Buckhaven, and the reflected glory in which she retreated with him, supplying neither names nor addresses, as if this were the sort of situation in which she and Ruairi had been involved too often to warrant any particular notice!

There were few things Ruairi appreciated more than being photographed. He was well accustomed to it long before those admirers crowded round him with their cameras at Buckhaven. To some extent this is borne out by the photographs of him reproduced in this volume. Ruairi in front of the camera was an accomplished poseur. His sense of coöperation on such occasions was extraordinary. Frequently, I would get him into position, and then keep him waiting while I adjusted the camera or tripod. During these delays he exhibited interest rather than impatience. If his head were not quite in the correct position, I would ask him to fix his attention on some particular object, just as a professional photographer asks his sitter to turn the head a little this way or that, or to look in the direction of some object in his studio. Ruairi would sit absolutely motionless. Ultimately he became so accustomed to being photographed that he took it as a matter of course, and would not move until he heard the click of the shutter, when he immediately relaxed and quietly went about his own business. He had heard that shutter click so often as to recognise it as the immediate preliminary to my closing the camera and detaching the tripod.

"Smile, Ruairi!" I sometimes said to him when he looked too

serious. He is smiling in the upright photograph facing page 64.

"Ruairi, I want to take a photograph that will demonstrate your comely proportions and your glossy coat. Stand there in the sunshine. Don't look too serious. Try to look a little pensive." The result of this faces the same page.

He carried out such instructions to perfection. I remember that, as I was about to take this particular photograph, his tail hung a little too low for my liking. I knew, of course, that if I mentioned tail, he would immediately begin to wag it. So I went up to him, raised his tail about a couple of inches, and enjoined him in the Gaelic to move not as much as an eyelid until he heard the shutter close.

He always looked most beautiful when in the attitude of listening. He and I were in the habit of passing along a high garden wall in the Mayfield district of Edinburgh, on the other side of which, and always invisible because of the wall's great height, was a dog of some sort. Ruairi knew this—so much so that, when he approached the untrafficked spot beside the black paling separating the right-of-way from some trees, he paused for a moment in the hope of detecting some doggy noise. "Listen, Ruairi!" I often said to him by way of whetting his curiosity as we came to that paling.

Never have I seen anything more wistful than my black-and-tan Ruairi listening in sunlight, just there, for the movements of a dog about whose existence he became increasingly curious, but on whom he never set eyes.

Ruairi was a regular traveller on trams, buses, and trains. No dog of his size ever covered, free of charge, so many miles on public transport systems. Although a dog's fare was but a penny in those days, I could count on the fingers of one hand the occasions upon which an Edinburgh tram-conductor asked for it. When boarding a tramcar, which we frequently did in our athletic way while it was travelling, Ruairi would wait for a wave of the hand that indicated whether we went inside or upstairs. By this time the conductor was probably in conversation with him. There were few conductors in our city who did not know him intimately. His early training had made him the disciplined traveller. Once inside, and without instruction from me, he would proceed as far in as he could, and then lie down, out of the way of the passengers' feet, irrespective of the position of any seat I might occupy. On alighting, he stood a few inches behind me until a pointed finger sent him bounding straight across the street to the pavement. I won't go so far as to say that he could read the numbers of the various tramway routes; but he always knew which tram to take when we stood waiting for one at the West End of Princes Street, or at the G.P.O.

Number 6—the Marchmont Circle tram, as it was in those days—was the one we used most frequently. Ruairi once boarded a Number 6 without me, due entirely to a bit of slowness on my part. I put my finger up to warn him not to attempt to jump off. The conductor let him off at the stopping-place in Marchmont Road where we usually alighted. I found him awaiting me there when I arrived by the next tram a few minutes later. He was immensely relieved when we came together again.

In all the annals of canine travel there is recorded (so far as I know) only one comparable instance of travel sagacity. It was related in *The Sunday Times* some twenty years ago by Mrs. Susan Baird in connection with a Scots collie owned by her late father, Sir James Fergusson, when he lived in London. This dog sometimes missed his master in the traffic. When tired, or when he believed himself to be farther from home than usual, and in a part of the city unfamiliar to him, he hired a hansom. A cabby, waiting on the Fergussons' doorstep on one occasion for the dog's fare, was asked by Lady Fergusson just how it came about that the dog should have been his passenger. "Well, madam, the dawg 'e jumped in an' sat on the seat, sort uv smilin' like, an' waggin' 'is tail. So I just looked at the address on 'is collar an' druv 'im 'ome!"

Trains Ruairi loved, especially those East Lothian ones on which Miss Aitken took him when visiting friends in places like Haddington and Dunbar, where he could squeeze himself into a window-seat to review the scenery, and growl at any of his kind seen relatively close to the line, on this locality's famed farmlands. These excursions were made from the Waverley Station, where the dog was as well-kent to the ticket-collectors as to the city's tram-conductors. Never a ticket did Miss Aitken purchase for him. He was already through the appropriate barrier when she was asked to show any tickets she had. This is where her deafness was such a help. It enabled her to sustain, undeterred, her share of the following conversation:

Miss Aitken: "Ay, he's wi' me a' richt"

Collector: "Ha'e ye a ticket for him?"

Miss Aitken: "Him an' me gangs everywhere thegither! He looks aifter me gey weel!"

Collector: "But ha'e no' a ticket?"

Miss Aitken: "Ye've jist clippéd ma ticket."

Collector: "Ah ken; but it's the doggie's ticket A'm wantin."

Miss Aitken: "Ay, my! He's a clever, wee sodger. He's lookin' forward tae seein' his freends in Dunbar—at Spott. Dae ye ken Spott? A bonnie place."

With Ruairi already some distance ahead, keeping himself clear of

Grantchester: The Old Vicarage from the lawn

By courtesy of Sydney Wells, Esq., Grantchester

Grantchester: Rupert Brooke in the garden at the Old Vicarage

Miss Aitken in
middle life

Miss Aitken in 1927,
knitting by her kitchen
fireside at Liberty Hall

the dispute, the ticket-collector just gave up.

"Ah ken yon auld wifie," a fellow collector might be overhead to remark while Miss Aitken and Ruairi, always in good time, proceeded leisurely and confidently up the platform. "She's as deef as a lamp-post. Doesna hear a thing. Ah ken her fine. Ah jist let the doggie through wi' her. Saves an awfie lot o' bother. Yon's the dog whase life-story and fottie wes in the *News* a while back."

I must confess that the privilege extended to Ruairi on our Scottish railways as a V.I.P. in Edinburgh's canine world was one which I myself—none too honestly, I concede—was happy to recognise. "You know, MacGregor, you could take that dog anywhere with you, free!" a know-all of my acquaintance once informed me. "He's a collie, a real sheep-dog. No shepherd ever pays for his dog on the train, any more than a plumber would be expected to pay extra for his tools. The dog's as necessary to the shepherd as a journeyman's bag of tools is necessary to a travelling plumber."

Encouraged by this plausible reasoning, I had little difficulty in convincing myself that the mere fact of my *not* being a shepherd didn't really matter. It was the *dog's* status that was important, rather than his owner's. Without allowing myself the mental discomfort of examining just where the logical application of this illogical tenet might lead, I thought it quite a good idea. Of course, nobody looked less like a shepherd than Miss Aitken when presenting herself at the ticket-barrier; and I cannot claim that I looked very much like one either, except perhaps for the heather-mixture tweeds I usually wore at that time. They certainly smelt of the moors and of moorland sheep, particularly after a gentle sprinkling of rain. Ruairi, however, smelt of neither, though I always retained in the back of my mind a picturesque account of his adolescent contact with sheep, if ever I were challenged on his qualifications. I could at least claim that, when a few of the crofters' sheep wandered down from the moors to the shore near his birthplace in the Hebrides, and looked as though they might get in among my cousins' cabbages, he promptly saw them off of his own accord. Oh, yes! There was no doubt in *my* mind that he was a sheep-dog within the meaning of the Act, as it were, although I never went so far as to claim dog-licence exemption for him!

"How much does the dog's ticket cost you?" I once asked a Border shepherd accompanied by his dog and travelling in the same railway compartment with me.

"Na, na!" he replied. "Ah never pay a penny for the likes o' him. Ye see, Ah couldna dae ma wark wi-oot 'im!"

I had no difficulty in convincing myself that I was in a similar situation. How could I get my books and articles written without Ruairi?

He at least required that bit of travel and exercise that kept me in good condition for my work. Thereafter, when he and I had occasion to visit Glasgow, we recalled that shepherd's words. No difficulty presented itself at the Edinburgh end of our journey. By now, Edinburgh's ticket-collectors all knew Ruairi, had a friendly word with him, and allowed him to pass through like any other duly authorised passenger. If there happened to be travelling on the train a collector who knew not Joseph, Ruairi was advised to conceal himself under the seat until all danger was past.

Arrival at the Glasgow end of our journey presented no problem whatsoever. A cautionary word to Ruairi as we approached the ticket-barrier saw to that. He would sit down, out of the way of passengers' feet, about ten yards from the critical point. Once *I* had got myself past it, an almost inaudible whistle reserved for emergent occasions brought him dashing through. On returning to Edinburgh, we adopted the same tactic. It never failed. So successful was it that when, a year or two later, Torquil, another black-and-tan collie from the Hebrides, joined us, all one had to do when travelling was to see that he imitated Ruairi in getting under the seat at the right time, in waiting at the same spot on the platform, and in following him through at the required moment.

I trust British Railways, on the strength of these confessions, will not render some sort of account in respect of those canine journeys on the Old North British and Caledonian railway systems of that time. It would be grossly unfair if they did, having regard to the interest, amusement, and picturesqueness with which these collies of mine provided their patrons!

I might add that they travelled in like manner on our S.M.T. buses. Although one was expected to purchase a dog's ticket aboard, never a penny was proffered nor asked for, even when both Ruairi and Torquil were travelling on the same vehicle. Edinburgh's bus conductors knew them and their exemplary behaviour; and, if they did not actually know Miss Aitken, they certainly knew who she was by her bodyguard. This guaranteed her favoured landlady treatment when travelling with them. Great deference was accorded her in consequence on the S.M.T. company's vehicles. This enterprising concern which, in its pioneering days, did so much to open up rural Scotland, brought to shepherds at lonely hirsels the first public transport facilities they ever knew. Shepherds and sheep-dogs from the remoter localities of the Pentland Hills, from the Moorfoots, the Lammermuirs, and the sheep country of Peeblesshire soon became a common sight in Edinburgh. They have been a familiar class of passengers on the S.M.T. bus system since its inception. In the days when comparatively few of those employed in rural areas possessed cars, one seldom travelled on a Lothian bus that hadn't among its passengers a shepherd and a collie or two. They have always been part of the S.M.T. tradition, especially on those routes serving the sheep country to the south and east of Edinburgh.

Much of the territory Miss Aitken and Ruairi covered together by bus was covered by Ruairi and myself by bicycle at various times. To render possible our longer runs, I designed a carrier for him. This was made by a joiner friend round the corner from Gladstone Terrace. It was affixed to the handle-bar and cross-bar of my bicycle by large, clamping thumb-screws, and could be adjusted or removed in the matter of seconds. I trained Ruairi in the use of it by placing him on it for a few minutes twice daily, and then wheeling the bicycle through Liberty Hall from one room to another, until he had confidence in it, and I had sufficient confidence in him to feel that we might try out with safety this mode of canine transport on some public thoroughfare.

Our experimental route lay between the Newington district and Portobello, by way of the King's Park, Samson's Ribs, and Duddingston. As I always lunched with my father at Portobello on Sundays, we travelled this road when it was quietest. Edinburgh at this time was still very much a churchgoing city, which meant that most of its citizens, if abroad at all, were afoot, rather than awheel. As the greater part of our journey to Portobello was downhill, and gravity, with the prevailing wind astern, carried a bicycle more rapidly than a dog could be expected to run for long without ruining himself, there was a particular spot, just by Samson's Ribs yonder, where Ruairi, if he happened to be ahead of me, waited. If, on reaching it, I pretended not to notice this, he immediately began to nose about the pedals to draw attention. I promptly alighted and lifted him into position on the carrier. Had he moved as we now coasted before the wind, it would have been serious. Both of us might have been killed. Roughly three miles farther on, and with little need to impel the bicycle by recourse to the pedals, we drew up within a few yards of my father's doorstep. A snap of my fingers indicated to Ruairi that he might now leap from carrier to pavement.

The homeward journey, for the most part, was different. Against a head-wind, so often reaching gale-force where the Queen's Park road hugs the cliffs' base at Samson's Ribs, the dog could move more quickly than I could cycle—if, in fact, I could cycle at all. Many a time we returned drenched and breathless to Liberty Hall after an hour's battling with the elements on that exposed road in time of equinox or winter.

To Miss Aitken, who watched for us from a window, it mattered little how drenched and dishevelled *I* was on my return—at any rate until the dog's discomfort had been relieved. "Get yer towel, sodger!" she would announce as Ruairi, at her request, shook himself on the doorstep before entering. Into the kitchen he would rush to drag forth that old towel conveniently kept for such occasions on the sewing-machine's treadle. She rubbed him vigorously while he whimpered and whined with delight. By the time this operation was over and he had been fed, I already had lit my Golden Lamp 'ben the hoose', and had laid out my evening's work.

How was it that this dog knew the days of the week? How was it that he resented my laziness on a Sunday morning, and did his best to get me out of bed, often tugging at the sleeve of my pyjamas in an endeavour to do so? That was our Portobello day. The day when he chased rabbits along the whinny hillsides of the King's Park, the day when he swam in the sea.

"'Way ben an' get him oot o' his bed!" I often overheard Miss Aitken say to him. In a trice he had pushed my bedroom door open with tremendous vigour, and was nosing his way under the bedclothes, where by this time I had taken shelter. Once well and truly in there, a pushing contest began. It continued until all the clothes were on the floor, and I was obliged to acknowledge defeat.

How did he recognise Thursday mornings? On Thursdays he extricated the basket which, of his own accord, he carried round to the newsagent's for Miss Aitken's weekly papers, returning a few minutes later with *The Weekly Scotsman*, *The British Weekly*, and *The People's Friend*. With pride and emphasis he dumped that basket every Thursday morning on the kitchen hearthrug. "Well sodger," Miss Aitken would then say, "what has the great Robertson Nicoll[1] got tae say the day?" Ruairi would stand watching her as she scanned *The British Weekly* for a preliminary answer to this. Soon the dog was lying under the kitchen table with one of the other periodicals he had just delivered, as though he felt himself entitled to a little reading-time for all his

[1] Sir William Robertson Nicoll, born at Lumsden, Aberdeenshire, in 1851, was obliged by ill-health to abandon the ministry in Scotland in 1886. That year he moved to London to found *The British Weekly* which, under his editorship, became the most important and influential Nonconformist publication in Britain. In 1891 he started *The Bookman*. For at least a quarter of a century, he was regarded as Britain's leading Free Churchman, writing voluminously under the pseudonym of Claudius Clear, as well as under his own name. He was knighted in 1909, and in 1921 was made a Companion of Honour. He died in 1923, and was buried in Highgate. His influence upon the Nonconformists of Miss Aitken's generation was immense.

trouble. There he lay, watching her intently, waiting for one of her weekly comments before stepping forward to place in her lap the paper held tightly in his jaws. It was usually *The People's Friend*. "What's Annie S. Swan got tae say for hersel *this* week?" one might hear her inquiring of the dog, when alluding to this particular publication.

Several years later, when Mrs. Burnett Smith (better known by her maiden name of Annie S. Swan) used to visit me in Chelsea during her occasional excursions from Scotland, I told her of the avidity with which Miss Aitken read her every week, and of how Ruairi dashed out for *The People's Friend* every Thursday morning. She burst into tears with sheer joy. It was the nicest little anecdote concerning herself she had ever heard, she remarked, during all the years she had been associated with publishers and editors. She died at Gullane, in East Lothian, in 1943, at the age of 83, after a long and highly successful literary career.

And how did Ruairi recognise Saturday afternoons? That was the only afternoon of the week when he deliberately hid himself to avoid my inviting him to go out with me. He was quite willing that Torquil should accompany me, however.

An hour or two before Miss Aitken laid out her shoes, Ruairi had deposited on the hearthrug the big shopping-basket which, every Saturday afternoon, he carried out empty and carried in full. That was the afternoon they did the week's shopping together in the Causewayside, in South Clerk Street, and in Nicolson Street. "Let's awa' ben tae the parlour an' consult the Clerk o' the Weather!" If the weather looked propitious, Ruairi sought to expedite matters by trailing that big basket very demonstratively through the house. On the other hand, when it looked as though rain were imminent, he crept out of sight under her bed, remaining sulkily there until he saw her reach for her hat. He now knew that, rain or no rain, they were going.

I once gave Miss Aitken a birthday guinea to buy for herself any little thing she fancied. A guinea went quite a long way in Edinburgh in the 1920s.

"Ah saw a graund pair o' hoose-shoes in a Nicolson Street windae when Ruairi was oot shoppin' wi' me last Saiturday aifternoon." Addressing the dog lying in another room, she continued: "Where are ye, sodger? Are ye no' comin' oot tae the shoe-shop? Mind yon pair the twa o' us had a look at last Saiturday? Let's gang an' see if they're still available."

Off they went, Miss Aitken with her guinea, Ruairi with the basket in which the shoes would be brought home. In an hour they were back, and Miss Aitken, highly pleased with her purchase, cam' ben the hoose tae show me her cheepers. They cheeped for many a day. Of this she was aware, though she couldn't hear them.

The really big event of Miss Aitken's life was that Graduation Day at Edinburgh University when she and Ruairi went off to the Mac-Ewan Hall to see me capped. She had been there before, of course, when earlier students of hers had been dealt with in this way. "Get yer brush an' comb, sodger!" I heard her say to the dog an hour or two beforehand. "Ye'll hae tae look yer bonniest the day, ma certie! Stick close tae me, an' we'll baith get in on ma ticket. But ye'll hae tae behave yersel, mind! Nae barkin' when the students tegin their capers!"

My father was already seated somewhere in the hall when, from some little distance, I observed Miss Aitken arrive with Ruairi. "Losh me!" she was heard to say to one of the servitors when he told her that no dogs could be admitted. "Can the dog no' be present tae see his maister's graduation? Weel, if Ruairi's no' gettin' in, A'm no goin' in either."

The servitor, recognising my dog rather than my landlady, turned a blind eye as both sailed past him. I knew that Ruairi was present somewhere in the hall, since I detected his joining in the applause which so punctuated the Vice-Chancellor's remarks as to have rendered them unintelligible. When my turn came to approach the rostrum in order to have the Doctor's hat touch the head of my demure and bowing self, I heard a shrill voice from the body of the hall: "There's yer maister at last! Capped an' gowned an' a'!" Being so deaf, Miss Aitken had no idea how audible her observations often were. Ruairi, already seated bolt-upright in her lap, taking note of everything, was now heard to give an ominous growl. He had interpreted the Vice-Chancellor's gentle application of that emblem of learning as an assault upon the person of his master. Miss Aitken immediately explained matters to him, however.

The crux of such a ceremony is, of course, the touching of the candidate's head with a Doctor's hat. *And such a hat!* Do you realise that I was touched that day with a hat said traditionally to have been made from the breeches of that illustrious sixteenth-century historian and humanist, George Buchanan? The more correct and conventional of my Edinburgh friends maintain that I have been 'a little touched' ever since.

At this stage I ought to say something about Torquil.

One day, while on a journey with a friend to the rock fastnesses of Dun Othail, in northern Lewis, I noticed a young, beautiful, and frolicsome thing playing about the feet of an old crofter scything grass by the roadside. It bore so marked a resemblance to Ruairi when a puppy three years earlier that I coveted him greatly. After a little bargaining, it was agreed that the creature should be mine. So we arranged that, when passing homeward later in the day, we would call for him and take him back to the cousins with whom I was holidaying at the time. Miss Aitken, meantime, was having Ruairi all to herself in Edinburgh. When I got back with my new acquisition, my cousin, Catriona Mairi MacDonald, very appropriately suggested that we should put on him the name of Torquil. *Siol Torcuil,* the Seed of Torquil, you may remember, was the patronymic of the ancient MacLeods of Lewis, as distinct from the MacLeods of Harris and Skye, who were known as the *Siol Tormoid,* the Seed of Norman.

The arrival of this stranger in our Hebridean village provoked the resentment of its entire canine population. One dog in particular demonstrated the greatest hostility toward the timid Torquil, and chased him off. Torquil bolted over stream and dyke, through cornfields and croftlands and heather, well out of sight. My heart pained within me. The creature's distress gave me considerable misgivings for having coveted him—for having removed him from his native setting and the old man cutting grass, eight or nine miles away. Some days later the dog of the friend who had accompanied me that day to Dun Othail located Torquil crouching among some whin-bushes and, after a bit of stratagem, was able to lay hands on him and bring him home.

In due course Torquil found himself installed at Liberty Hall, welcomed overwhelmingly by Miss Aitken, but not so overwhelmingly by Ruairi. It took us some weeks of patience and subtlety to bring them together as friends. Eventually they became great allies, always rushing to one another's aid when trouble brewed.

The training of Torquil was the simplest thing in the world. It required a firm hand to begin with, and encouraging him thereafter to follow Ruairi in all he did. Long walks in the country, away from the city's hard pavements and harassments, provided suitable opportunities for this. There was nothing they enjoyed so much as a day's journey through the Pentlands by way of Fairmilehead and Swanston, by way of the T Wood and the steep screes of Caerketton. A bark and a growl at the Swanston farm dogs in passing put them in the right mood for the rest of the day. They reverted from an obedient domesticity to something exhilaratingly primitive. One saw this whenever they imagined themselves trailing a promising scent, or whenever a rustling in grass or bush or bracken quickened their sense of expectancy.

So intense was Miss Aitken's love for these black-and-tan creatures that in course of time she assumed they were hers. This I did not mind in the least. Indeed, there were times when it was highly convenient to let her do so. If for any reason I had to be away from Edinburgh for a few days, she was quite delighted, so long as I left both dogs with her.

On the few occasions when she lost sight of either of them, if only for a few hours, she was quite demented. A mother who had mislaid her baby could not have been in greater distress. The one and only thing she deprecated in regard to them where *I* was concerned was my keeping them out late at night. Her deafness in no way prevented her from knowing the exact hour at which we returned, since she usually insisted that one or other of the dogs should be left with her of an evening. Apart altogether from considerations of fairness, this meant that my arrival on the doorstep with the one, however quietly, was indicated to her by the movement of the other, always lying at the foot of her bed until I returned. She would then put a match to her bedside candle in order to see the time on her bedside clock. If by any chance I happened to be out after midnight with *both* dogs, nothing would induce her to retire until the three of us got home, and she was able to summon Buckie from the sittingroom window, and turn the key in the front door. Her anxiety on such occasions was not for *my* wellbeing, but for the dogs'. Not infrequently she rated me when I kept them out late at night. "Ruairi's no' himsel these days," she would say, ruefully. "He's got that much sleep tae mak' up!"

I seldom allowed myself more than two really late nights a week. One of these I spent with musical friends named Balfour, who lived in Marchmont Road, roughly half a mile away. "Ruairi's no' weel. He's no' been the same since yon nicht ye had him oot sae late at the Balfours'. He's never been able to mak' up his sleep. Yersel an' thae Balfours should be tied thegither! Ye're fair killin' the dog atween ye!"

I cannot but admit in this context that I have always been most wakeful at the wrong end of the day, and consequently a late bedder. Like the ancient Hebrews and, I believe, the modern Arabs, I am apt to regard the evening as the beginning of a new day which closes with the dawn. I once made Miss Aitken very angry when, in excusing myself for this predilection, I quoted from the Old Testament. "Turn to the very Genesis of things," I said; "and there you will read that the evening and the morning were the first day." She, a devout Baptist, thought this savoured a little of profanity. Nevertheless, I have done my best work while others slumbered. That was just when my Golden Lamp inspired me most.

Ruairi enjoyed his visits to the Balfours. They enhanced his philharmonic appreciation. A pair of earphones placed loosely over his head, as he lay in front of their fire, enabled him to listen to many a symphony in those early days of wireless.

*   *   *

Torquil was the first of these collies to leave us. The circumstance of his passing I will not repeat here: they are already recorded in one of my early books. He lies buried these thirty years and more at Hillend, on a whinny slope of the Pentlands.

When I came south to London, Ruairi was already on permanent loan to Miss Aitken, who by this time had given up Liberty Hall, and had gone to lodge with the provost and his wife in the High Street of Tranent. She spent her latter days there, at this East Lothian mining town, in a neighbourhood she had known in girlhood. The miners and their families made a great fuss of Ruairi. Tranent's provost used to say that his local popularity warranted his being given civic recognition—the Freedom of the Burgh, or something of that sort! Ruairi died in 1938, greatly mourned. He lies buried 'neath good Lothian clods in the provost's garden.

These black-and-tan collies of mine were the most edifying, refining, and civilising influence in my life. The epitaph on the monument over Byron's dog, Boatswain, in Newstead Abbey gardens, might well have been theirs, since they, too, possessed Beauty without Vanity, Strength without Insolence, Courage without Ferocity, and all the Virtues of Man without his Vices.

If the animal creation should ever win through in the evolutionary struggle to make itself articulate, what will it have to say about the suffering mankind has imposed upon it all down the ages?

In reflecting on my Golden Lamp years, I recall with an almost morbid persistence those late Saturday evenings when even Miss Aitken was loth to retire. It was the evening when we recapitulated all that had happened during the week then within an hour or two of its end. Any other student lodger or lodgers she had at that time were usually away at the weekends. They had either gone home, or were conducting Sunday services somewhere. So Miss Aitken and I sat alone by the resuscitated kitchen fire, with the companionable teapot on the hob. At our feet lay the dogs, beautiful, youthful, vital, with Buckie, warm and glossy, outstretched his full length on the hearthrug, among their paws, having just been fed after his evening prowl among the gardens and shrubberies of the neighbourhood. Miss Aitken, then approaching her mid-seventies, was still full of vigour and wisdom, still very much in possession of all her faculties except her hearing.

As for myself, I was not yet thirty. As for the canary, if, in our contentment round the fire on a Saturday evening, Miss Aitken had forgotten to cover her in for the night, she would suddenly break forth into full-throated song which ceased only when this had been done. Many a midnight carol she gave us

So there we were, the six of us, but, where *I* was concerned, never without the saddening thought passing through the mind that, in the ordinary course of things—that in accord with some strangely ordered inevitability—five of our happy sextet would have gone years before *I* did. The haunting reality of my being, one day, the sole survivor would have destroyed completely the felicity of our Saturday evening sessions, had I granted it more than occasional accommodation.

CHAPTER FIVE

Memories of Spott
EAST LOTHIAN FLOODS

OF ALL those doggie ongoings related in the last chapter, I was reminded a little sadly in the spring of 1963, while scanning the obituary columns of an Edinburgh newspaper. There I read:

SCAMBLER—At Dunbar Cottage Hospital, Jessie, dearly loved wife of William Scambler, gamekeeper.

Shortly after Torquil had qualified for Edinburgh citizenship, Miss Aitken, giving a thought to her annual holiday with Ruairi, noticed in the *Evening News* an insertion advertising a room vacant for a fortnight at Spott, a small and sequestered place on the outskirts of Dunbar. "A've aye had a notion tae see Spott again," was her comment.

Having known this neighbourhood as a young woman residing with relatives in East Lothian, she promptly answered the advertisement, mentioning that, in the event of her taking the accommodation offered, she would have to bring with her a collie-dog, and that in any case she and the dog would be coming down to Spott one afternoon to see how they liked the prospect of a couple of weeks there together. ("Mind ye! he's gey partic'lar," she used to warn anybody who might assume that Ruairi would put up with anything!)

By return of post came a letter from Jessie Scambler, aforesaid, giving details of situation, terms, strolling amenities, and so on. "We'll welcome the doggie," her letter ran. "We've had doggies aboot us a' oor days; an' oor bairns are quite accustomed tae them."

So promising was this reply that Miss Aitken and Ruairi set off the following day to have a look at the place. They were met at Dunbar, and duly conveyed therefrom to Lake Cottage, the Scamblers' home, set among pines and larches, with a lake close at hand. The lake was then a Dunbar reservoir. Late that evening they returned to Liberty Hall, very pleased with their excursion. They had taken the accommodation on sight, and had agreed the day upon which they would arrive.

Miss Aitken's description of this setting was, in itself, enchantment.

"The bairns were a' roond Ruairi in a jiffy. They took him aff tae the lake, a wee bittie frae the hoose. The sodger wes in the water afore ye could say Jack Robi'son. Oh, it's the place for Ruairi and me! Is it no', sodger?"

A few days later the two of them were off to Spott, leaving Torquil and myself to our own devices. I was busy at the time with my Golden Lamp lucubrations, for I had another book nearing completion. Torquil was fully employed in keeping me company, Miss Aitken having extracted from me the promise that I wouldn't ruin his health, during her absence, with too many late nights!

Before long, we received from Miss Aitken *and* Ruairi a joyous letter which concluded with a pressing invitation. To this letter Ruairi, in the statutory way, had affixed his mark—the imprint of a wet and slightly muddy paw below Miss Aitken's signature! The Scambler family had re-arranged the sleeping accommodation at Lake Cottage in order to make room for Torquil and me during the ensuing weekend. "Ye've never seen onything like the gloss on Ruairi's coat aifter he's been in the lake, and I get him dried, combed, and brushed."

Just in case this might have been insufficient to attract me to Spott, she proceeded to tabulate at least a dozen supplementary reasons why I should accept this invitation. I must see the cat that, a few days earlier, had had kittens in a disused dog-kennel on the fringe of the wood, and that she and Ruairi visited twice daily with food. I must sample the eggs laid by Jessie Scambler's hens: they were far bigger, better, and cheaper than those Miss Aitken could buy in the Causewayside of Edinburgh. I must also sample the honey from Willie Scambler's hives—honey that had a strong, though not unpleasant, flavour of pinewoods. I must meet Willie's well-informed father who kept the provisions shop in the village. I must hear not only the enchanting tittle-tattle left at Lake Cottage by the postie when he called a day or two previously, but also what the Beadle said to Mr. Scambler, Senior, and what Mr. Scambler, Senior, said to the Beadle!

Above all, I must meet the Rev. Lothian Gray, who, as Miss Aitken already had discovered, was familiar with my writings, and who knew literally everything about East Lothian, having been by this time parish minister of Spott for half a century. Miss Aitken, largely through the introductory offices of Ruairi, had met the reverend gentleman more than once, and had told him of my proposed visit. She was subtle enough to ingratiate herself, on my behalf, by mentioning that both she and I were in the habit of reading from time to time authoritative articles of his in a variety of publications. The best of these certainly dealt in the most pleasing and intimate way with Haddingtonshire, which, of course, included his own parish.

It was hard to resist so pressing an invitation as Miss Aitken's letter conveyed. So there, at Lake Cottage, the four of us were installed for a long and memorable weekend, a neighbour in Gladstone Terrace having undertaken to see to Buckie's and the canary's needs at Liberty Hall.

During this wholly agreeable interlude at Spott, I learnt from Willie Scambler much about this historic countryside, especially in Cromwellian times. Close to Lake Cottage stands Spott House, with its commanding view stretching away to the Bass and the Isle of May. There, in September, 1650, on the eve of the Battle of Dunbar, slept David Leslie, while his army of Scots Royalists lay on Doon Hill. On the morrow the Parliamentarians, commanded by Cromwell, Monk, and Lambert, completely routed the Royalists.

According to tradition, Cromwell occupied at Spott House that night the room, and possibly also the bed that Leslie had occupied the previous night. The actual apartment has been referred to ever since as Cromwell's Room; and I am told on good authority that at times Cromwell's Ghost may be seen wandering about this old, Scottish mansion.

Incidentally, it was on the occasion of the rout of the Scots at Dunbar—at the Dunbar Drove of our history-books—that Cromwell, observing the plight of his enemies as the mists cleared from the hills, made his memorable utterance: *Let God arise! Let his enemies be scattered. Let them also that hate him flee before him.* He was quoting, of course, the opening verse of the 68th Psalm, which, along with many another pagan passage exhorting the Christians to violence, is well entrenched in the Book of Common Prayer.

But Spott House has a better known apparition than Cromwell's. It takes the form of a lady in white, and is referred to as the Canongate Ghost. I had it on the authority of Lothian Gray several years ago that it is seen most frequently in the room Leslie and Cromwell occupied on successive nights.

The ways of this supernatural resident were so clearly acknowledged by the late Miss Adelaide Watt, of Spott House, and of Speke Hall, in Lancashire, that she always kept locked the door of that particular apartment, and strictly forbade all mention in the house of anything ghostly in connection with it. The reason she gave for this was that, if such matters gained popular currency, it would be impossible for her to retain servants. But the reason jaloused by the villagers was that Miss Watt found herself sufficiently embarrassed by ghostly ongoings at

Speke Hall, where a ghost that had spoken to her guests at a dinner-party had been observed immediately afterwards to disappear into the wall of one of the bedrooms, close to a window. Subsequent investigations disclosed the existence at this spot of a secret passage leading down through an outer wall.

Miss Aitken, and indeed Ruairi also, took so great a liking to the Scamblers' children that they were loth to return to Torquil and me. They therefore remained an extra week. This was the first of their happy sojourns at Lake Cottage. As some little token of what it had meant to Miss Aitken, from time to time she used to invite Taylor, the Scamblers' eldest boy, to stay with us for a few days at Liberty Hall. She was greatly interested in this laddie and in his future. It was as well that she did not live long enough (she died in August, 1938) to learn of his fate. At the outbreak of war in 1939, Taylor was Clerk of Works at Clydebank. He immediately joined the Royal Engineers. Subsequently commissioned and transferred to the Admiralty, he perished in 1942 when the vessel taking him to the American Naval Base at Trinidad was torpedoed, and everyone aboard her was lost. That would be roughly a quarter of a century after the war in which *my* generation was shattered by the internecine Christians in the War to End Wars, the War to Make the World Safe for Democracy, and All That Sort of Nonsense.

"I have wonderful memories of Miss Aitken and Ruairi," Willie Scambler wrote me from Edinburgh the other day. "They were so happy with us at Lake Cottage; and we were so happy with them. I recall the day Ruairi cut a pad so badly on a broken bottle that I had to cut it completely away with a sharp penknife. He never winced nor gave a whimper. Ever afterwards, when Ruairi and I met, he held his paw up for my inspection. He was so very intelligent, and had such a remarkable memory. A great fellow, Ruairi!"

A year or two ago I thought I would like to have another look at Lake Cottage. Motoring down from Edinburgh, I found Spott easily enough, but had the greatest difficulty in identifying the cottage because I could find neither pinetrees nor lake, although I did find a dried-out hollow where once a lake might have been.

But where were the pines and the larches I remembered so clearly? I afterwards learnt that they had been cut down during the Second World War.

And what of the lake? Do you recall those torrential rains and floods that in 1948 wrought such havoc in East Lothian—in Haddingtonshire—as well as in adjacent Berwickshire, sweeping before them roads, railways, bridges, crops, and livestock? It was then that Spott

Lake burst its banks beyond repair—banks that would probably have withstood the pressure, had those pinewoods bordering upon them not been hewn down for the insensate purposes of war. No wonder I failed to find it!

This locality, of course, has an unenviable record of disastrous floods. Where the ancient and historic town of Haddington is concerned, this certainly goes back to the 14th century, when there occurred one of the most calamitous floodings by the River Tyne, upon which it stands—the East Lothian Tyne, of course, deriving its sustenance almost exclusively from the Lammermuirs, *not* the Northumbrian Tyne. The Spey is probably the only other Scottish river that has wreaked more flood damage than the Tyne. Yet, to see it at Haddington under normal conditions, with St Mary's Parish Church, the historic 'Lanthorn of the Lothians', quietly reflected in it, having survived the wounds received at the vandal hands of the Hammer of the Scots and his marauding army nigh seven centuries ago, one finds it hard to believe that a river so comparatively small can have wrought such havoc.

A plate inserted in a corner-shop wall in Haddington's Sidegate indicates the level to which the Tyne's floods rose on the night of the 12th–13th of August, 1948, the night on which Spott Lake escaped. In the same wall, and but a few yards away, one reads:

On the 4th day of October, MDCCLXXV, the River Tyne,
at three o'clock, afternoon, rose to the plate.
Quod non Noctu, Deo Gratias, Nemo enim periit.

Of these tumultuous and destructive waters roughly a century later, Miss Aitken could speak with authority through her early Haddington associations. One of the objects they have eerily disturbed yet again in recent years lies in the family vault beneath the ruined chancel of St Mary's. It is the traditionally restless coffin of the Duke of Lauderdale, "learnedest and powerfullest Minister of his age," who died at Tunbridge Wells in August, 1682, and whose embalmed body, accompanied by no fewer than two thousand horsemen, reached Haddington for interment seven months later. It cost two thousand eight hundred Scots pounds to get him into his massive, leaden coffin!

The Lauderdale Monument, in St Mary's, is surely one of the most substantial and extravagant examples in Scotland of this seventeenth-century type of work.

This East Lothian countryside bears many an inscription commemorating the Tyne's floods, in addition to those mentioned at Haddington. The most picturesquely placed is at Preston Mill, at East Linton, the property of the National Trust for Scotland since 1950. It was acquired that year from the trustees of the late Mr. John Gray, when a restoration and maintenance fund was raised by public appeal. To this the Pilgrim Trust made a generous contribution. Only the mill and the kiln are owned by the National Trust, which leases the other buildings of the group, and also the haugh—the riverside meadowland—adjacent thereto.

The mill used to be owned and worked by an East Lothian family Miss Aitken knew as a young woman residing with her relatives at Haddington, or at Athelstaneford, a few miles to the north. That family's name, I think, was Draffan. In any case, it was through Miss Aitken's frequently mentioning Preston Mill that my interest in it began. That would be about twenty-five years before it came into the possession of the National Trust for Scotland.

It was operated, single-handed, on behalf of the Trust, by the late George Denholm. When George died in 1959, he had been miller there for 32 years. His son succeeded him briefly, but left. There is now a caretaker in the mill; and, although there is no longer any milling on a commercial scale, its machinery is kept in working order, so that demonstrations can be given. Up until about 1960, then, Preston Mill was rightly regarded as the oldest Scottish mill in use.

In my photograph facing page 128, taken in 1958, the late George Denholm is seen pointing to the tablet inserted under the mill's red-tiled eaves to record the height to which the Tyne's flood-waters rose during that disastrous night in August, 1948, when Spott Lake put an end to its own existence. These flood-waters covered the mill's upper floor to a depth of six inches, which means that they stood eight feet above ground level, thus inundating to a depth of several feet much of the richest grain-growing territory, not merely in the fertile Lothians, but also in Britain. The day I took this photograph, George himself told me that it occupied four strenuous months to repair the floods' damage, and get the mill going again.

Although Preston Mill's age is uncertain, there is no uncertainty about its beauty. Few subjects, anywhere, have been painted and photographed more frequently. On a summer's day, as many as a dozen artists may be found painting it simultaneously, and just as many photographing it.

Reproductions of this historic Lothian mill, showing the red-tiled buildings adjoining it, hang in public galleries and in private homes all over the world.

Edinburgh: The West Side of Gladstone Terrace. The second-floor windows above the boy with the bicycle are the front windows of Liberty Hall

Edinburgh: The Old Mill at Liberton Dams, with Arthur Seat in the background

The Author photographed by himself in 1927 with his Golden Lamp

CHAPTER SIX

Miss Aitken and Her Laddies

••

PRIME favourite among Miss Aitken's early lodgers was a medical student named John Dale, who came from Stranraer, where his father was a doctor. It was John who persuaded Frederick Victor Branford to leave his dingy digs in the mortuary locality of Dalry Road in order to share with him, at Gladstone Terrace, accommodation Miss Aitken could now provide, following upon the recent graduation of an older fellow-student of his. The plan worked admirably. John and Victor had been contemporaries at Dumfries Academy not very long before, and were already leading lights of Edinburgh University's D. & G.—its Dumfries and Galloway, an association then much given over to dialectics.

In the winter of 1917, a year or two after John had got his M.D., and during one of those influenza epidemics, he died at Leeds, in the hospital to which he so recently had been appointed. This saddened Miss Aitken, for he had always been one of her favourite laddies. She used to say that she attended his graduation ceremony feeling herself very much a participant in the honour then conferred upon him. This was but one of several such ceremonies at which she had been present in the MacEwan Hall before my own turn came.

Throughout the years I remained with Miss Aitken, there stood upon my sideboard a framed photograph John had given her, portraying him in his Doctorate of Medicine regalia. His having passed his examinations with distinction, and so soon afterwards submitted a thesis on some very learnéd aspect of medicine, compensated amply for the anxiety occasioned her by the 'stickit' medical student who had preceded him at Liberty Hall. If this 'chronic' passed his finals in the end, she maintained it could only have been possible because of the admitted lowering of examination standards to mitigate the shortage of qualified doctors during the First World War. Apropos the likes of the 'stickit' one, I recall the kind of situation I found in many American universities, epitomised in the question put by the little boy to his mother. "What's the matter, mummy? Has daddy been ploughed again?"

John Dale was Miss Aitken's last medical lodger, apart from a couple of young and lawless doctors who had come all the way from Sydney to attend a post-graduate course of some kind at Edinburgh. She promptly gave them notice when a neighbour conveyed to her, by dummy alphabet, the disquieting tidings that, during her absence from Liberty Hall one weekend, "they had girls in who stayed the night".

The Australians were followed by a series of theological students attending the Congregational Hall. By this time competition for accommodation at Liberty Hall was so keen that Miss Aitken no longer needed to advertise her rooms when they became vacant. Students finishing their curricula usually bespoke their accommodation on behalf of some junior friend or associate who still had a year or more to go.

These prospective clergymen were a mixed bag. It was when referring to the less saintly of them that Miss Aitken resorted to her adage, *The nearer the kirk, the farther frae grace.*

One of them offended her so deeply that both she and he were glad when the completion of his course provided the pretext for his leaving. Their difference arose in the following manner. In order to lighten her domestic toils, I had suggested that we all breakfasted in our cosy and democratic kitchen, before dashing off to our respective classes. Everybody found this arrangement so admirable that such of us as were home for our one o'clock meal were soon having it there also. The menu remained wholesome enough, if somewhat circumscribed, even although Miss Aitken was incessantly bequeathing to the large nail protruding from the edge of a shelf carrying dinner-plates and ashets those recipes she cut out of newspapers and magazines. They dangled there, increasingly, year after year, and were as seldom consulted as the tattered cookery-book they were designed to supplement. The result was that lunch-time became Bird's Custard Time. A big jugful of this went down on the table as regularly as did the necessary knives and forks and spoons, or the cruets. Sometimes it was thick and set: sometimes it would run like water slightly stiffened. One could never tell whether it would be in liquid or in solid form. In whichever form, Miss Aitken dispensed it over the shoulder of each of her seated laddies in turn, whether he wanted it or not.

Came a day when one of her theological lodgers gave this custard Scriptural status by describing it, a little irreverently perhaps, as being "the same yesterday, and to-day, and for ever". Miss Aitken was quite amused when told of this, though it in no way diminished the zeal with which she administered it.

But one day shortly afterwards, as she reached for the Bird's Custard jug, she happened to read this particular student's lips when, seated at table, he made that fatal announcement of his—"The Yellow Peril!" Miss Aitken instantly returned the jug to the table with a sickening thud, and retired to her armchair to weep bitterly into her apron. She was terribly hurt. It took us several days to restore her to her pristine pawky self.

The only other dish she dispensed as a sort of ritual was arrowroot, prepared to her own very special specifications. Every student she had over the years, whether suffering from chill, influenza, toothache, tummy-ache, or lumbago, had to undergo a course of arrowroot treatment, whether he believed in it or not. No refusal could be accepted. Where most Edinburgh landladies would have prescribed a dose of salts, or maybe a drappie o' the bottle, Miss Aitken prescribed arrowroot, made over the kitchen fire, with everybody obliged to stand back in order to allow her unhindered scope in preparing it to the right consistency, sweetness, temperature, and so on. No advice must be proffered. No excuse for disinclination to partake. No interruption permitted. Even the postman tugging at the doorbell with something too large for the letterbox must go on tugging until the arrowroot's perfection had been achieved. I must add that on the occasions when she dispensed this medicine for *me*, I found it remarkably efficacious and soothing.

Meal-times in that kitchen were not without their hilarious interludes. I remember a rather dour 'theological' who, during our amiable but silent breakfast-time, abruptly replaced his porridge-spoon with a clatter and, pointing to the rest of us, blubbed forth "You're all thinking nasty thoughts about *me!*"

That was the next occasion upon which Miss Aitken retired to her armchair to wipe away the tears with her apron. But this time they were tears of mirth. She had read his lips as he made this utterance. Never before had Liberty Hall rung so loudly and so long with convulsive laughter as was precipitated by this wholly unexpected announcement.

For all that, Miss Aitken did not always lip-read so promptly and accurately, which meant that at times her deafness could be a little trying, especially when one wished to tell her something in a hurry. She lip-read best when seated in her fireside armchair, quietly following conversation in which there was no need for her to join. That was when she read people's *characters*, as well as their lips. You could always tell her reactions by glancing in her direction. When some visitor whom she hadn't met before had gone, she revealed within a few seconds her estimate of him or her, whether called upon to do so or not. As the critical onlooker, observing closely a conversation in which nobody expected her to participate, yet noting every gesture and inflection associated with it, she would brush in on some pretext (such as that of putting away the best china in the sideboard, or attending to the fire), muttering sufficiently audibly for me alone to hear, "Jist a lot o' blethers! A lot o' havers! Never heard the like o't! Nae brains! Naethin' but silly conceit, like a' brainless folk!"

You see from this that she was given to speaking her mind, without fear or favour. In later years she had reason to recall the frank things she had said to students and others visiting Liberty Hall, particularly to such as afterwards attained distinction. I recall in this context her observations when a friend of Victor Branford, and indeed of myself in subsequent years, used to come about the place a great deal, mainly with the object of sharpening on Victor his debating wit. That was just before the First World War, when the friend's prowess as a debater was the chief topic of conversation at the University Union, of which he eventually became president. Liberty Hall was his first forum— the battleground where he scomfished his opponents so skilfully that they never dared rise to their feet again.

Though Miss Aitken's deafness prevented her from hearing his rhetorical exercises in that parlour of hers, it did not prevent her from seeing on the face of the kitchen clock the late hour of night—or, as was more usual, the early hour of morning.

"It's time ye went awa' hame tae yer bed, Willie! Thae public platform antics ye're sae fond o' are jist a lot o' blethers! Jist blethers! Besides, ye're keepin' dacent folk frae their beds. Hoo dae ye expect 'um [Frederick Victor Branford] tae get his sonnets doon on paper wi' a' this theatrical cairry-on? Wi' a' them havers, nicht aifter nicht? Ye ken ye didnae need tae stay sae late tae bury michty Caesar all ower again. Ye buried 'um the last nicht ye were here. Caesar can look aifter himsel fine wi'oot a' this palaver! And, forby, wha wants tae ken whit Gladstone said at sic a time o' nicht? Noo, Willie, be a sensible laddie, an' awa' hame tae yer bed!"

It was always something of a disappointment to Willie's Radical associates of those University Union days that, despite the Liberal tradition of his Highland forbears, he should have deserted their ranks for Tory preferment. I remember in this connection the caustic comment of a master at Watson's (whence Willie went straight to the University) when he discovered that I too, had political ambitions, and was friendly with Ramsay MacDonald! "Ah! MacGregor! I'm disgusted with you! I see you're going to be another Shakes Morrison— another twister!" That showed very clearly what *he* thought of politicians!

Willie Morrison in his college days at Edinburgh was popularly known as Shakes, or as Shakes Morrison, because of his Shakespearean oratory. Two interesting things about him might be mentioned, however. Firstly, his fluency with the language of the Gael. Secondly, his considerable literary ability, about which comparatively few know anything. Such of his short stories as have a Highland or Hebridean flavour are so exquisite as to nourish the regret that he should have succumbed to the temptation of ephemeral politics.

From 1951 until 1959, when his health began to give cause for anxiety, Willie was Speaker of the House of Commons. In 1959, as Viscount Dunrossil, he became Governor-General of Australia. He died at Canberra in February, 1961, in his 68th year, and lies buried there, in a churchyard I happen to know—that of St. John the Baptist.

"It's time ye went awa' hame tae yer bed, Willie . . ."

In a ground-floor flat situated in the Melville Drive, just round the corner from us in Gladstone Terrace, lived Mrs. Lamb with her two rather attractive daughters. Mrs. Lamb hailed from Lewis. Contemporaneously with my father, her older brothers had attended their first school at Sandwick, on the outskirts of Stornoway. That would have been during the 1860s, when so many British merchantmen sailing the world's wide oceans were captained by natives of this Hebridean neighbourhood. Among them was George Watt, one of Mrs. Lamb's brothers, whose seafaring exploits are recorded in my book, *The Haunted Isles*. George was chief officer of the *Aldersgate* when she rescued his schoolmate, my father, and a thousand other passengers, from the doomed *City of Paris*, in her day the largest vessel afloat.

Mrs Lamb's flat round the corner was something of a Gaelic rendezvous. There one met from time to time one's own Hebridean relatives and friends. Mrs. Lamb kept open house for folk with Hebridean connections, such as my kinswoman, Johanna Bennett, who lived but a hundred yards away, in Gladstone Terrace, with her studious son, Tony,[1] then applying himself too diligently to his medical studies at Edinburgh University to be able to find much time for Mrs. Lamb's ceilidhs—for her social gatherings. But Tony reminded me recently of an evening when we were all there at an informal Hebri-

[1] Major-General Roland Anthony Bennett, C.B., born in 1899; Consulting Physician to the British Army of the Rhine from 1950 until 1955; Director of Medicine and Consulting Physician to the Army, and Honorary Physician to the Queen, from 1955 until 1959. Since then he has been Physician at the Royal Hospital, Chelsea, within a few minutes' walk of me.

It was Tony who, many years ago now, assured me that, when a boy on holiday with relatives at Port of Ness, near the Butt of Lewis, he and his sisters often clambered over to the Pigmies' Isle to play with the Pigmies' minute chairs and tables!

dean party amusingly, and indeed memorably, interrupted by a tap on the sittingroom window-pane, followed by a few external words in the Gaelic, announcing the tapper's identity. In walked Willie Morrison. In a moment he was holding the floor with a dramatic rendering of one of those favourite Shakespearean passages of his, such as already had earned for him the nickname of Shakes Morrison, or merely Shakes.

"What is your chief ambition, Willie?" asked Johanna Bennett at the conclusion of one of his splendid declamations that evening. "Is it a great actor you would like to be? Another Henry Irving?"

"One day," Willie replied, "I shall be Prime Minister, or something like that. A Cabinet Minister, anyhow. Or Mr. Speaker, perhaps."

Miss Aitken's deafness had its compensations as well as its drawbacks. Yet, what one tried to do in the knowledge that she did not hear was often unsuccessful, for all one's schemings, because of her unusually acute visual observation. Consequently, the best-laid schemes o' her laddies at Liberty Hall went 'aft agley', just as did the fieldmouse's when Burns's ploughshare turned it out of house and home.

In course of time she read my own lips so perfectly that the dummy alphabet, to which we had had to resort when first I went to her, disappeared from our conversations, except when she persisted in putting into my mouth words and phrases I had never uttered. It was sometimes very amusing when, in the course of a discussion, she anticipated one by completing a sentence in a way one had never intended. Her faculty for this was so highly developed that, even when she had thoroughly misunderstood what her impatience had prevented one from explaining in the ordinary way and at the usual tempo, one often had to start again at the very beginning of the matter then under discussion, so as to be certain that she appreciated its proper context and connotation.

If anybody unaccustomed to our ways at Liberty Hall arrived at the front door when Miss Aitken was alone within, he or she often had to go away without obtaining an answer, unless Miss Aitken happened to look up at the row of old-fashioned bells near the kitchen ceiling to notice that the doorbell was moving, even slightly. It was discovered, however, that the readiest means of drawing her attention, if she were not actually looking toward one, was by thumping the table sharply with the clenched fist, or stamping a foot. Old Party, none too mobile in her chair by the fire, drew her daughter's attention by bringing the crook of her walking-stick down with a whack on the kitchen floor. The vibration caused in these ways made Miss Aitken look up or turn round.

Eventually we devised a satisfactory means of letting her know when there was someone at the front door. Behind the kitchen door, and about five feet from the floor, we erected a small, horizontal platform of tin, supported at one end by a longish nail protruding from the doorpost at right angles, supported at the other by a wire fixed to the doorbell wire a few feet above it. On this little platform we placed the quarter-pound weight belonging to Miss Aitken's kitchen scales. It had a ring attached, which facilitated our rendering as perfect as was possible the use to which it now was put. Whenever the doorbell was pulled, the weight dropped to the floor with a thud sufficient to attract Miss Aitken's attention, if she happened to be present in the kitchen when it did so. As this weight, being cylindrical, was continually rolling inaccessibly under the furniture, an improvement upon our invention took the form of attaching to its ring a piece of tape long enough to allow it merely to drop perpendicularly, and strike the floor at the base of the doorpost whenever the bell was pulled. To this day I see in my mind's eye the deep indentation produced in the waxcloth by the incessant dropping of that weight. Its thump must often have puzzled the occupants of the kitchen below.

Few things were more annoying than Miss Aitken's omitting to replace that weight immediately it had functioned. It took me years to discipline her to see that, whenever it fell, she put it back on its tin platform as a matter of routine, *before* answering the door. You may imagine how exasperating it could be when you found you had carelessly left the house without your latchkey, and Miss Aitken happened to be elsewhere than in the kitchen when you returned to pull the doorbell, and heard the weight go thump on the floor to no purpose. It was even more exasperating when one knew her to be in the kitchen without having replaced the weight on its little platform.

Of course, this method of warning fell into desuetude as soon as Ruairi joined us at Liberty Hall. If either Ruairi or Torquil were in the house when the bell went, he always apprised her by barking at her until she answered the door. So now it mattered no longer whether the weight was up or down. As I already have said, she could hear a dog's bark quite well. In any case, I had trained the dogs to follow her into whichever room she chanced to be when the doorbell rang. Not infrequently one or other of them would tug at her skirt if she appeared dilatory about responding to it.

I think I can say truthfully that not once during my Golden Lamp years did I ever hurt Miss Aitken's feelings. I teased her a lot, never failing to do so when she cooked vegetables in that unattractive and wasteful way in which we would seem to have specialised in this country. As a vegetarian, of course, I knew something about the treatment of vegetables. "You may know quite a bit about flowers," I would begin, leaving it to Miss Aitken to complete the sentence, which she always did with an amusing grace—"but you know nothing about vegetables." Yes, I teased her a lot; but never was I guilty—publicly anyhow—of an utterance as acrid and wounding as that relating to Bird's Custard. I sometimes made her angry, however. But this was somewhat different, and short-lived.

She once made *me* very angry about something I have now forgotten. It would have been something quite trivial, I expect. All day long, like the sulky, sullen dame in *Tam o' Shanter*, I nursed my wrath to keep it warm. That eventide, as I sat alone with my Golden Lamp, she entered, very quietly. I pretended not to notice her. And then I felt a gentle hand on my shoulder, and a whisper in my ear: "Laddie, let not the sun go down upon your wrath."

I burst into tears at this. Nothing more salutary has ever been said to me in my life. I felt very ashamed of myself, and only hope that these pages may compensate in some small degree for that day's foolishness and vindictiveness.

I must now record an occasion when Miss Aitken was very angry with *me*. Angry, not in a dour and sulky way, but momentarily—on the spur of the moment. When first I took up residence with her, the big room of the house, usually referred to as the parlour, contained a great collection of ferns and creepers, some of them so large that they resembled tropical plants in jungle places. They grew in outsize flower pots. It took me years to persuade Miss Aitken to perform some drastic surgery on the more massive of them. It took me more years to persuade her to get rid of at least some of them altogether, along with a little of the depressing Victorian junk that went with them as inseparably as a cup goes with a saucer, or a knife with a fork. The house cheered up considerably with the disposal of these sombre decorations, these funereal adjuncts.

One huge aspidistra she simply would not get rid of, nor even curtail in its ever-increasing encroachment upon the daylight. It flourished in an enormous earthenware bowl placed on a tall, ebony pedestal near the window.

" 'Way ben an' bring me the aspidistra!" she said during one of her spring-cleanings. "It's needin' a sponge-down."

I obeyed instantly. Always having associated the word, aspidistra, with feet—with *pedes*—I promptly lifted the massive plant off its massive pedestal, placed it on the parlour floor with an old newspaper

"Try to look a little pensive"

"Smile,
Ruairi!"

"My cousin . . . suggested that we should put on him the name of Torquil"

Torquil, after a scamper through wet grass at Hillend, on the fringe of the Pentland Hills

underneath, and proceeded to carry into the kitchen the pedestal.

"That thing hasna leaves, has it?" shrieked Miss Aitken.

"No," I responded; "but it could do with a sponge-down just the same."

That made matters worse. Suddenly I realised from her wrathful demeanour that an aspidistra was not a pedestal but a plant, and that she wanted to sponge the plant's leaves as a necessary part of her spring-cleaning operations. "Laddie, it's commonsense they should hae taught ye at Watson's, instead o' Laitin!" was her caustic comment when I sought to explain myself.

But how inconsistent we mortals can be! No sooner had we agreed that *indoor* horticulture, in the aspidistral sense, was excluding rather much daylight, than we took it into our heads to try a little *outdoor* horticulture by providing Liberty Hall's wide window-ledges with flower-boxes. The few small, potted plants flowering annually on those ledges gave Miss Aitken too little scope for her love of flowers and a knowledge of them dating from girlhood days spent with a grandfather when he was gardener at Preston Grange. For her own gardening experience, gained at this baronial seat, situated by a gentle encurvature of the Firth of Forth, she had had little outlet in the years which followed her grandfather's death. These window-boxes, made to our own specifications by a joiner round the corner, were now to afford her considerable pleasure in this direction. She and I, between us, produced some quite creditable displays in them. One year we might train sweetpeas up the sides of the windows: another year we might have an array of stocks that scented the entire house. I remember distinctly how passers-by used to halt in Gladstone Terrace to look up at our wallflowers in the month of May; and I remember, too, the special tin in which Miss Aitken collected so punctiliously, each autumn, the nasturtium seeds for replanting the following year.

Though the daylight was again excluded to some extent by our fenestral horticulture, how very satisfying we found it, even when we grew tomatoes that could have been obtained so much more readily and economically at the grocery in Sciennes Road, just round the corner.

Late, late in the evening, when all was subdued and quiet, much of my happiest writing was done when the gleam of my Golden Lamp was suffused with the fragrance of sweetpeas or of night-scented stocks, wafted in at the open window.

For a time there lodged with us a little Chinese student named Gwoa. He came from Manchuria—from Mukden, I think. There he had been

C

engaged in Christian missionary teaching. He had come to Edinburgh for a couple of years' theological instruction. He was one of the most interesting, understanding, and refined creatures it has ever been my privilege to have known. My contact with him did a great deal to undermine in me the prejudice and insularity bred in most of us.

During Gwoa's sojourn with us, I taught him quite a lot of English. I cannot claim to have acquired in return any comparable knowledge of Chinese. Yet, I did learn from him much about the ways of peoples in eastern lands. Now and again, by way of compensating me a little for my wholly pleasurable and often quite amusing tuition, he used to take me off to the Chinese restaurant in Chambers Street, where it was possible to obtain suitable vegetarian dishes, and where he instructed me in the manipulation of chop-sticks. My ultimate proficiency with these, gained under Gwoa's auspices, gave me a pleasing status when, several years later, I found myself among Chinese communities in the East Indies; and I cannot but believe that my frequent visits to this Edinburgh restaurant in his generous company were responsible for that partiality toward Chinese cooking I have exhibited ever since—so long as it is confined to dishes of a vegetarian nature! They afforded me an appetising foretaste of the foods I was to enjoy in Singapore and Penang and elsewhere, during a prolonged stay in Malaya some years later.

Miss Aitken permitted Gwoa the run of the house. She used to say that, in an experience of student lodgers extending over a quarter of a century, never had she dealt with one so courteous, thoughtful, and amiable. Sometimes, as an alternative to resorting to the Chinese restaurant mentioned, Gwoa would take it into his head to cook a meal at Liberty Hall. This was always an amusing and instructive occasion, for Miss Aitken as well as for myself, as we sat well back from the kitchen range and our solitary gas-ring to watch him go through all his weird processes. Even Miss Aitken acquired a liking for Chinese food, despite her declaring at the outset of Gwoa's stay that nothing would ever induce her to place such stuff to her lips.

Roughly once a month, Gwoa would ask Miss Aitken what evening he and a few of his student compatriots might take possession of her kitchen for some hours, and perhaps have the use of the large parlour. She never refused him such a request. One's first indication of the imminence of a mighty evening of Chinese cooking and eating was the arrival, several hours beforehand, of himself and his friends, each laden with foods, spices, and delicacies of the Far Orient. The pending feast always necessitated, in addition, the use of more pots and pans and other utensils than Miss Aitken's kitchen could provide. So these were borrowed from his fellow-students' landladies.

About 5 p.m. on the appointed day, preparations began when Gwoa and seldom fewer than four of his compatriots presented themselves at the kitchen door, ready to set about their co-operative task. All Miss Aitken had to do was to ensure beforehand a good fire and a hot oven. She could then sit back in comfort for the next couple of hours at least, and just watch.

She came to love these Chinese occasions, since every one of Gwoa's companions shared his own splendid qualities. If in the meantime I were closeted with my Golden Lamp, there would come a faint tap at my door. Gwoa would enter to announce, officially, that, of course, Miss Aitken and I were bidden to the feast, that the dogs were bidden too, and that there would be provided for my vegetarian self a couple of splendid dishes. After the feast, while Miss Aitken, now back in her chair, relaxed, the washing-up was undertaken by the entire contingent, and the kitchen left in a spotless condition.

We were both greatly exercised when political disturbances in Manchuria called for Gwoa's return to his own country. My father and he had become friends by this time. He frequently went to a meal with my father, when they discussed parts of China known to both of them.

I remember particularly the pleasant surprises Gwoa sprang upon us now and again. He never bought anything for himself that he did not seek to share with others, certainly with Miss Aitken and me. When he went out on a shopping expedition, he always returned with some little present for each of us. During a Christmas he spent at Liberty Hall, he placed on each of our breakfast-plates on Christmas morning a small memento of some kind, and also one for each of the dogs, and one for Buckie, all neatly concealed in tissue-paper. Each dog's consisted of a tiny, silver disc bearing his name and address. It was made in such a way as to be easily fixed to his collar. Buckie's took the form of a collar bearing *his* name and address. Engraved on a small metal disc attached thereto were the words:

To Buckie, from Gwoa, Xmas, 1927.

The inscription on Ruairi's disc occupied both sides of it:

My Name is
RUAIRI

On the obverse side:

I live at
12, Gladstone Terrace,
EDINBURGH.

Torquil's inscription ran similarly.

I wonder what has happened to this estimable and truly memorable member of human society! What fate has befallen him?

Throughout all those years, I remained firmly entrenched at Miss Aitken's. Indeed, her home was virtually mine during this period of my life. In any event, it vouchsafed me all the care, attention, and simple amenities I then required, and certainly more than I merited. Of all her laddies, I was, unquestionably, the one for whom she did most.

During my long sojourn with her, I never once needed to purchase a pair of socks or of stockings, or a pullover, because her knitting-needles were constantly clicking away on my behalf, even as she sat reading in her armchair. Long after I came south, and indeed until shortly before her death, Christmas-time and Birthday-time always brought from her a neat, little parcel containing a couple of pairs of socks she had knitted for me. Much of her handiwork and industry in this category lies in a drawer here, in Chelsea, most of it still perfectly serviceable.

One or two of the shirts Miss Aitken made for me, nearly forty years ago, I have yet; and, although I have outgrown them, and they look a little the worse for the wear, as the saying is, I just cannot bring myself to throwing them out, or even having them cut up into rags for dusting or cleaning purposes.

Never a stitch belonging to *me* ever went to any laundry during my Golden Lamp years. Miss Aitken's laundry-work would have done credit to the most skilled laundress. Every alternate Monday she undertook a terrific day's washing. Accompanied by Ruairi, she conveyed this in relays to the communal back-green in her creaking laundry-basket. At nightfall she would descend again to strip the sagging clothes-ropes of their load. And this is where *I* came in: I always carried the heavy laundry upstairs for her in one mighty go.

The following day was devoted to starching and ironing. Never did anything exhaust her as did that ironing! By supper-time the finished goods hung so voluminously from the kitchen pulleys that they cast darkness upon this apartment, even on the sunniest evening. "Ma laddie!" she would call out in her high-pitched voice, "Haste ye ben an' pu' up the pulleys. Ma airms is no' able for them. They're gey heavy."

Her task over until a fortnight hence, she would flop in her chair by the fire, completely hidden behind laundry, with Ruairi contentedly at her feet. Reviewing with a sense of achievement and relief that great, dangling array, she quietly dropped off to sleep.

On Saturday evenings came the laying out of my clothes in readiness for church the following morning, and the airing on the little horse before the kitchen fire of my change of underclothes. Promptly at 9 a.m. on Sundays, she entered to waken me, and at the same time to arrange, in chronological order, my Sunday garments, just as fond wives and mothers and sisters used to do for husbands and sons and brothers, in the days when the home was a saner and more integral part of society, and its members, consequently, more thoughtful, selfless, and coöperative.

CHAPTER SEVEN

Lowood and the Borderland

++

"I'D LIKE to help, but I'm a poor hand at remembering incidents and conversations, and even persons, in the years that have receded. I'm sure I couldn't write books like yours to save my life. Mine seems to be a *forward*, rather than a *backward*, type of mind, which may explain how things drop out of recollection all too easily."

Thus begins a letter I received recently from my first fellow-student at Miss Aitken's, one whom I have not mentioned as yet. He enjoys the resounding Highland name of Allan Cameron MacDougall. With this volume in view, I had written him, asking whether he would set down all he could recall of Miss Aitken and her ways during our two years together as students in adjoining room. The letter Allan wrote me was not as unpromising as this preamble of his might have led one to anticipate. Having dealt with the usual observations and formalities, it proceeded to epitomise Miss Aitken in a passage worth quoting:

"Miss Aitken: A very shrewd, independent, elderly Scotswoman of particularly sound mind, carrying with commendable courage the burden of her physical disability, and the problem of making ends meet for her (trying!) old mother and herself. I recall her strong likes and dislikes, and, on occasion, her gift of blunt expression. Alasdair and the cat were her two special fondnesses."

Allan also remembered Miss Aitken's gratitude for small kindnesses, for little, supererogatory acts of consideration, and for the wonderful way in which she could conduct a conversation, once in possession of the thread of it. "When speaking with her, I often forgot she couldn't hear a word."

Allan and I, in addition to our interest in Highland matters, had a common bond. Not long before we settled down to our studies at Miss Aitken's, we had returned from the war. Allan had survived three years with the Seaforth Highlanders at Salonika: I had survived Ypres with the same regiment. Being some years older than myself, he had completed his Arts curriculum at Glasgow in 1915, four years before I was due to begin mine at Edinburgh. So here he was, at Miss Aitken's, quietly pursuing his post-graduate course, equipping himself for the Congregational Ministry. A son of the old Congregational clergyman at Sannox, in the Isle of Arran, Allan was in process of becoming a Congregational clergyman too. "I tried to make a good Christian of you," he once wrote me; "but you seemed more anxious to wrangle with me over the application of words like meticulous, than to listen to my theology. All the same, I liked you fine!"

Our two whole university sessions together at Miss Aitken's were completely amicable throughout. This, I concede, must have been due in considerable measure to Allan's Christian forbearance, since I had returned from the war very intolerant and, indeed, a little embittered about a state of society complacently maintained by so many who, though of military age, had dodged it, had secured all manner of preferment and emolument, and had been able, in consequence, to entrench themselves immovably, while those of us who had experienced another type of entrenchment were, by comparison, of little account. This is always one of the wickedest injustices of war—which can never be just in any case, nor justified.

As Allan's sojourn at Liberty Hall began to draw to a close, a deep depression settled on Miss Aitken and me. True, he had appointed his successor, as it were, in that little room of his; and, although this successor was all he should have been, the scene was never quite the same after Allan's departure.

His theological studies completed, a mood of amusing abandon descended upon him. He gave way to a measure of humour of which neither Miss Aitken nor I believed him to have been capable. "Ah never kent he could be sae droll, sae humoursome!" was Miss Aitken's comment. This change in his demeanour was due, of course, to his relief that he had sat and passed the last of several years' examinations, and was now qualified for ordination.

A day or two ere he left for his home in Arran, he brought to Gladstone Terrace the excellent woman whom he was soon to marry. Jane of the hazel eyes, herself the daughter of an Ayrshire manse, and, like himself, a graduate of Glasgow, sat an entire afternoon and evening with him in that little room, burning papers and old letters Allan would require no longer. "Mind, laddie, ye dinnae pit the lum up!" warned Miss Aitken, as these blazed away. [Take care you don't set the chimney alight!] This little bit of calculated conflagration seemed to make things worse for Miss Aitken and me. It had a frightening finality about it.

That evening Allan and Jane departed together for Glasgow,

leaving Miss Aitken and me disconsolate, despite their assurance that they would be turning up from time to time, and Allan's promise that in a day or two I would be hearing something pleasant from him. An ominous hush had fallen on everything. Something seemed to have gone from life. About midnight, and without a word to one another, Miss Aitken and I went together into that little room of his, bearing my Golden Lamp. The magic of its glow had vanished, Allan, already in the bosom of his family, beyond the sea, appeared to have bereft us of it, just as he had bereft us of himself. The door of the press in which he had kept a few supplies for 'the fly cup' stood open, revealing a partly filled sugar-basin he would never want again, and a fragment of unconsumed butter. The fireplace was full of dead blackness. Every now and then the merest whiff of wind in the chimney brought a ghostly creaking to its burnt-out contents. Still without a word to one another, Miss Aitken and I sat down, looked at each other, and immediately burst into tears. That was the first occasion in my life that I discovered I loved another man deeply enough to sob over his departure.

"Dinnae greet, laddie!" said Miss Aitken, in wiping away her own tears. "He'll be back amang us afore lang!" She remembered that he was due to return to Edinburgh in a few weeks' time for church meetings of some kind.

A day or two later, and in furtherance of his promise, Allan was in touch again when a long telegram arrived from him, giving me detailed instructions to proceed the following day to Arran—by train to Ardrossan, and thence by steamer to Brodick. At the pier there, Kasper would meet me and conduct me to his bus, which, in due course, would travel through Corrie, in the shadow of Goat Fell, and deposit me a few minutes later by the manse gate at Sannox. As the bus pulled up that summer's evening to allow of my alighting, whom did I recognise a little ahead of me but Allan himself in older togs than I had ever imagined him capable of wearing. He had reverted literally overnight from civic convention to rural emancipation, and was actually herding the manse cows across the king's highway and through the manse gate for milking. What a reunion that was! One would have thought we were meeting again after years of separation, whereas Allan had left Liberty Hall but forty-eight hours earlier. Now back in his native isle, he had 'gone native' once more.

My visit to Arran was unforgettable. This was the first Scottish island south of the Hebrides with which I was to become familiar, a matter simple enough through the MacDougalls' knowing, or being known to, every family on it. To climb Goat Fell, of course, was incumbent upon me. This was easy enough from Sannox.

The island of Arran, though even then so closely in touch with Glasgow and its Firth of Clyde resorts, still breathed an air of delightful detachment. Its roads were truly rural. Cars were few, and charabancs fewer. Kasper's local bus service was pleasantly pedestrian. All very different from the Arran of today. Petrol and proletarian progress have altered its character completely.

I had been back in Edinburgh but a few days when Miss Aitken came screaming with excitement to me, holding out a letter she had just received from Allan MacDougall. It bore tidings of great joy for us both: Allan had accepted a call from the Congregational Church at Galashiels, where he had preached more than once during his student days. "Nae distance at all!" exclaimed Miss Aitken, in referring to the map of Tweeddale. "Gala's nae mair nor thirty miles or thereaboots. Branch aff tae the left at Liberton Dams, and cairry on through Heriot and Stow. A nice, wee cycle run for ye!"

Allan and Jane started their married life romantically enough in the romantic Borderland. As the church hadn't got a manse ready for them, they were obliged to spend several months in a wayside cottage by the Tweed, much nearer Melrose than Galashiels. The cottage is actually known as Lowood Cottage. Allan and Jane travelled by bicycle to and from their pastoral duties at Galashiels.

Spring was now upon us. The cottage's garden lay a-bloom with primroses and violets, aconites and grape-hyacinths, with crocuses and daffodils, lilac and flowering currant. The cottage itself had space for a visitor if he cared to avail himself of the divan in the living-room, and could reach Lowood by bicycle. This means of transport would be handy in other ways. The visitor could go a-wheeling with his friends to church on Sunday; and he could accompany them in like fashion on their shopping excursions. Moreover, he could explore the romantic Borderland on his own, leaving his host free to deal with his ministerial affairs. Any day now, as Miss Aitken prognosticated, I would be that visitor. "See you mak' guid use o' yer time noo. And, mind ye, dinnae ootstay yer welcome."

To be sure, Allan and Jane had barely settled in when the former wrote me directions not unlike those he so recently had sent me in regard to my visiting him and his family at Sannox. I have them by me now, after all these years, written on a sheet of notepaper stained and tattered: "You cycle on *beyond* Galashiels, toward Darnick and Melrose, the shining Tweed in the valley below you on the right, the Eildon Hills beyond. On you go till you cross the Tweed by a fine, sandstone bridge. Immediately after you've crossed, turn left to find yourself at the foot of a steep brae. You'll probably have to alight there, after so long a run, and push your bicycle up to a wee house, the way Janie and I have to do. The gable-end of the wee house you'll soon see on your right, with a triangular, flower-filled garden in front of it. That's Lowood Cottage. And that's where we are. And that's where we'll be until our own manse in Gala is ready for us. As the popular saying is, 'You can't miss it!' We're in the angle formed by the road you'll be coming by and a rough cart-track of a road doubling back toward Abbotsford, on *our* side of the river."

With such directions on one's person, how could one have gone wrong?

I was immensely fit at that time, although so few years earlier I had lain weak and debilitated, in a military hospital, completely immobile with rheumatic fever contracted through exposure on the Western Front, and although I had had a bad bout of typhoid in between. Galashiels and its neighbourhood were within reasonable cycling distance of Edinburgh, though road surfaces were still so poor as to render punctures unavoidable. The sharp 'chuckie-stanes' so often deflated progress that one never ventured forth on so long a journey without such accessories as a reliable bicycle pump and puncture repair outfit. It took about five hours, pedalling leisurely, to reach the Mac-Dougalls'; and this was seldom accomplished without at least *one* mishap of this kind. By that ancient pack-bridge spanning the Gala Water on the outskirts of Stow, I habitually dismounted to rest, to eat my sandwiches, and drink my bottle of lemonade or kola.

Lowood Cottage's air of romance befitted its newly-wed occupants. It had been a toll-house at one time. Sir Walter Scott used to visit it then, and have a crack with the toll-wife while waiting there for the mails arriving from Edinburgh by stage-coach. The cottage's little, square, gable window was that from which, according to Border tradition, Scott watched for and waved to the coach as it climbed that steep brae Allan referred to, passing virtually within arm's-length on its journey toward Melrose. A thrilling sight it must have been, certainly in the uphill direction—up that brae from the bridge spanning the Tweed just there.

My memories of those visits to Lowood Cottage, at the commencement of Allan's ministry, are very complete. Allan pursued at Lowood from the outset a habit he had formed in boyhood at the manse of Sannox, namely, that of feeding, and thus taming, the birds frequenting the garden. Soon a robin-redbreast, appreciative of this, took up his abode with him and Jane at the cottage. All day long he fluttered about its eaves, or chirped among its bushes, for the time of the singing of birds had come. Several times a day, and at regular intervals, Allan fed him by hand. After breakfast he would perch outside for a few moments, before splashing vigorously in the little bath provided for him on the kitchen windowsill. When called or whistled for, he would fly in by the open window, alighting on table or mantelshelf. Sometimes he landed on the shoulder or outstretched hand of the cottage's inmates, whom he soon got to know intimately. Permitted the full run of the house, he pried into the oddest corners. The cupboards he knew thoroughly: he inspected them daily. At night he slept in the cottage, sometimes returning early, to sleep on the curtain-rod above the window, sometimes late, finding his way home long after the household had retired. Night and day, a window was left open an inch or two at the top, so that he might come and go as he pleased. When we got back from collecting firewood, or gathering spring flowers in the neighbouring woods, we invariably found robin awaiting us on the kitchen dresser. Seldom was he absent more than a couple of hours. Long before the MacDougalls were due to leave Lowood for their manse at Galashiels, he had become very much a member of the family, demanding—and indeed receiving—more attention than the family dog or cat would expect. His confidence was complete. I remember the day he brought his fledglings for our inspection, arranging them in a row on a rusty rod outside the kitchen window.

That first bicycle journey to Lowood Cottage was my introduction to a region about which, hitherto, I had known little more than what had been derived from schoolbooks and pictorial posters displayed at railway stations. Now its full impact was to be felt when, in pedalling along, my eye, for the first time, caught sight of that tablet which I never pass without paying due homage—without a sob of thankfulness at the heart for the greatness and splendour and incredible industry of the man it commemorates. The inscription it bears is a quotation from Lockhart's biography of his illustrious father-in-law, describing his return home to Abbotsford from Italy, and his gazing on this scene for the last time:

"As we rounded the hill at Ladhope," wrote Lockhart, "and the outline of the Eildons burst upon him, he became greatly excited; and, when turning himself on his couch, his eye caught at length his own towers at the distance of a mile, he sprang up with a cry of delight."

The Wizard of the North had come home to die. There, at Abbotsford, he breathed his last on September, 21st, 1832, in the presence of all his children. "It was a beautiful day—so warm that every window was wide open—and so perfectly still that the sound of all others most

delicious to his ear—the gentle ripple of the Tweed over its pebbles—
was distinctly audible as we knelt around his bed, and his eldest son
kissed and closed his eyes. No sculptor ever modelled a more majestic
image of repose."

Scott's favourite Borderland view, however, was that from the
summit of Bemersyde Hill. Here he always reined up his horses,
that he might imbibe yet again of this wonderful panorama. On the
dark, windy, and lowering day his funeral passed by, on its way to
Dryburgh Abbey, the hearse, owing to some temporary delay, stood
several minutes at this spot.

The roadside memorial tablet I mentioned is but one of many to
The Great Romantic in that region of the Borderland known
popularly as the Scott Country. But, as Miss Madge Elder puts it in
her evocative volume, *Tell the Towers Thereof*,[1] where she discusses
the trees planted at Chiefswood by Scott himself, his true memorial
abides in the minds of men, "for immortal words do live longer than
any tree".

Madge Elder, that devout lover of Scott and of everything pertaining to him, resides in a cot at Melrose. Few can lay claim to knowing the Borderland more intimately than she. When Patricia and I
called to see her the other day, I told her of my initiation so far as
this countryside is concerned—how my acquaintance with it began
with those bicycling excursions between Edinburgh and Lowood
Cottage. They immediately brought me under the spell of the Wizard.

A few years ago Madge Elder and her sister paid a visit to Abbotsford. There they were received by Patricia and Jean Maxwell-Scott.
How memorably Madge records that occasion, particularly as regards
her hostesses! "One felt instinctively they were proud of their heritage,
but humbly proud, prouder than if they had been descended from a
long line of kings."

Was not this as it should have been? Descent from kings is trivial
and meretricious by comparison.

If you would wish to see somebody more like Miss Aitken than
anyone I have ever met, find your way to Melrose, and creep up to
Littlecot when Madge Elder is busy about her garden, wearing a hat
that might have been one of Miss Aitken's. If not kneeling or stooping
horticulturally, you may well catch her standing on her doorstep, as
Patricia and I did, deftly beating the white of an egg on a plate with a
knife, infusing it with air freshly arrived from the Eildons, and meanwhile admiring her blooms, just as Miss Aitken would have done. She
is as accurately informed about the Borderland as Miss Aitken was
about Haddingtonshire, about East Lothian. Like Miss Aitken, further-

[1] Published by Robert Hale in 1956.

more, she knows the ways of bird and beast and flower. Indeed, she's an acknowledged authority on the last mentioned, an expert nursery-woman, having started at Melrose after the First World War a hardy nursery and landscape gardening business of her own. Finally, like Miss Aitken, she is stone deaf. She couldn't understand how I spoke so clearly as to enable her to read my lips quite easily, straight away, and how I so readily helped out in dummy-alphabet fashion with unusual words, until I told her of my Golden Lamp years with Miss Aitken.

Much of historic and romantic interest lay within comfortable cycling reach of Lowood Cottage. Scarcely could one move from it more than a few hundred yards without being caught up in a topography and toponomy engraven as deeply in the pages of Sir Walter Scott as are such in the pages of any literature in the world. Scott does for Scot-land in this respect what the Bible does for Palestine. Of a land swarming with the legends of old Border valour, Border ballad, and Border foray, as one chronicler put it, he assuredly made the most of his knowledge. "I can stand on the Eildon Hill," he said, "and point out forty-three places famous in war and verse."

On the slopes of the Eildons, they say, King Arthur and his Knights of the Round Table lie a-slumbering, awaiting the call that one day will release them from the bondage of enchantment. Just where they lie, the country folk cannot tell one with any precision; but a farmer, in whose company I trod the Eildons some years ago, told me that he thought it was probably on the north side of the central peak. "Three peaks, you see, comprise the Eildons," the farmer related, as I sat with him on the highest of them, contemplating the grandest and most expansive prospect in the Scott Country. "Ay, three peaks. Nae doot, ye'll hae heard tell o' Michael Scot. It was himsel that divided the Eildons in three by nae mair nor the utterance o' a magic word." As Sir Walter puts it in *The Lay of the Last Minstrel:*

> *"And, Warrior, I could say to thee*
> *The word that cleft Eildon hills in three."*

So spake the monk of St. Mary's Aisle while watching with Deloraine by Michael's grave at midnight.

Michael Scot (1175 ?–1234,) was a wizard of great renown in mediaeval Scotland; and popular tradition has it that the Eildons were by no means the only topographical feature of this countryside owing their origin to his magical powers.

Mais revenons à notre Cottage Lowood. Within a stone's-throw of it the Tweed sang its way eastward toward Melrose and Dryburgh, toward Kelso, Coldstream, and the sea. Within an afternoon's walking distance of us lay Darnick and Melrose, Chiefswood and the Rhymer's Glen. Abbotsford itself was no farther. The Eildon peaks required, perhaps half an hour more. At Dryburgh, where Sir Walter Scott lies buried, one is within easy reach of Bemersyde—

> *Tyde, tyde, whate'er betyde,*
> *Ther sall aye be a Haig in Bemersyde.*

The body of Scott, by right of his ancestors, the Haliburtons, lies at a spot in the north transept at Dryburgh Abbey. Close to it is the vault of the Haigs of Bemersyde, where Earl Haig lies.

But a few miles beyond Bemersyde, roughly in the same airt, lie Smailholm Tower and Sandyknowe, reached in those days (unless one travelled cross-country on foot) by farmland ways comparatively unfrequented.

Of our four Border Abbeys, Jedburgh was the farthest from Lowood —a matter of fourteen miles. Melrose, of course, lay but two—conveniently near to enable us to cycle there for our shopping, near enough, moreover, to facilitate one's seeing its Abbey (probably the finest example of Gothic architecture in Scotland) as one first visualised it in *The Lay of the Last Minstrel:*

> *If thou would'st view fair Melrose aright,*
> *Go visit it by pale moonlight;*
> *For the gay beams of lightsome day*
> *Gild, but to flout, the ruins grey.*

Eventually the MacDougalls moved to their manse at Galashiels, leaving Lowood Cottage untenanted. Indeed, it then fell so rapidly into decay that they warned me not to re-visit it if I wished to retain any happy memories of our robin, of our gathering fuel by the banks of Tweed, of tea-time by firelight, of quiet, wood-scented fellowship in the gloaming. The tiny garden was derelict and forsaken. The dust from passing vehicles had smothered and stifled every beautiful thing in it. Jasmin no longer twinkled over the window-lattice. The windowpanes were either black or broken. Gate and palings sagged. No robin twittered in the eaves.

However, when I passed last autumn on my way to Melrose, I was astonished at finding the cottage rehabilitated, though bare and in no way picturesque as I had known it. The garden—well, it was no longer a garden in the colourful, cottage sense.

That the cottage lay in the angle where two roads converge was plainer than ever, now that its sheltering shrubs were gone, and that cart-track of a road I mentioned had been raised to the status of its busy adjunct. The removal of the ivy that long clung to the gable-end I also mentioned now rendered unduly visible the wee window from which Scott greeted the stage-coach climbing the steep brae but an arm's-length beyond it.

Let me conclude this chapter on a little personal note concerning Allan MacDougall and myself. Whatever other afflictions may have tried us during our lives, the dead-weight of material prosperity—the responsibility of physical attachments—has never been one of them. In this regard, at least, we have been happy in maintaining ourselves in a position of exultant freedom. No enslavement to property for us! All our castles have been in Spain, and as high up in the air as the air can manage to support them. They have given us neither fiscal nor domestic worries. We pay no rates nor taxes on them. Neither have we embarrassing situations on their account with tradesmen and contractors, since their larders are easily replenished, and all alterations and repairs we are able to execute ourselves. The servant problem does not effect them; and the only gardener we require is that supplied by clearness of vision, so that we may be able to see from their windows the world as our horizon, without having to cut away dead wood and stifling accumulations.

The view from these castles of ours is simply splendid. It keeps on changing all the time, like some magical kaleidoscope assuming just those dimensions and distances, those colours, scents, and sounds, that one desires. Our castles are peopled at will.

I cannot but acknowledge my gratitude to Miss Aitken for my having established with Allan MacDougall, so many years ago, a fellowship felicitously sustained through our mutual indifference to material success, our distrust of the established monetary system,[1] and the conviction that, whatever may be the functions of war offices, admiralties, and air ministries, the Christian Church is committed to the dissemination of the tidings of Great Joy, the God-spell of the Prince of *Peace*. If this Prince hadn't been the Pacifist He was, He would have saved Himself. Had He done so, there would have been no Crucifixion, no Resurrection, and no Redemption. Those who adjudge such matters according to national, dual-morality standards will, of course, regard this statement of mine as awful nonsense; but it's what The New Testament preaches and teaches all the same. We

1 Allan was largely responsible for the first Report of the Christian Doctrine of Wealth Committee, set up in terms of a remit from the 1960 Assembly of the Congregational Union of Scotland "to examine the financial system from the Christian standpoint". This Report, published recently by William MacLellan, Glasgow, is the first comment for centuries by prominent churchmen on the falsity of our financial system.

see pretty clearly now where our soldier-ridden Christendom has got us.

Allan Cameron MacDougall has just retired, after forty-two years in the full-time Congregational ministry. He and Jane are now living at Sannox, in the manse in which he was born in 1890, within half a stone's-throw of his father's church, where Allan now acts as honorary pastor. While this book is in the printer's hands, I hope to be re-visiting him there.

CHAPTER EIGHT

Swimming Days

++

A VERY substantial part of that happiness upon which my Golden Lamp shone so benignly each evening, after Miss Aitken and I had supped together in the kitchen, was inseparable from the Warrender Park Swimming Baths, situated in Thirlestane Road. To this place of bliss and delight I had been introduced about 1909, roughly a decade before the dawn of my Golden Lamp era. That you may appreciate how I first became associated with it, I shall therefore have to go back to the quinquennium immediately preceding 1914.

The baths concerned lay but ten minutes' hurrying distance from the home of my Edinburgh schooldays in Leamington Terrace—the Leamy of my earlier writings. I hastened to them five afternoons a week, and often five evenings as well. I always left them with a sinking feeling, to dawdle back to irksome homework and an irate father.

That route between Leamy and Thirlestane Road I recall in every detail. I suppose I must have traversed it more frequently than any other in our city, excepting not even that leading to and from school by way of the Meadows. From our terrace it led diagonally across the Links to the top of Warrender Park Road. There one turned right into Whitehouse Loan to follow that high wall enclosing Bruntsfield House and its grounds, pausing a moment, perhaps once a week, to drop an appreciated penny into the cap of the pavement-artist who, throughout my boyhood in Edinburgh, had his own particular pitch there, seating himself longitudinally at the edge of the pavement, his back against the first lamp-post in Whitehouse Loan, a dusty tin of chalks and a rag of a duster by his side, the nearest of his works of art chalked in glowing colours within a few inches of the soles of his upturned feet. A couple of hundred yards farther on lay Thirlestane Road, a street of tenement buildings then comparatively new, the wall of St. Margaret's Convent looming loftily above its south pavement, and ending just where the recessed frontage of the Warrender Park Baths begins.

Round this institution cling many of the happiest recollections of

81

my life, and perhaps a few of the saddest.

Why should a place associated with such felicity also be associated with sadness.? Why this bitter-sweet? My answer, certainly where our Warrender Park Baths are concerned, is a simple one. My early contemporaries there were, for the most part, either at Watson's or at George Heriot's, or had recently finished their education at these schools. Some of them were already at the University. Most of them, moreover, were two or three years older than myself. Just those few older years that ensured for many of them untimely death.

During the years of which I write, these baths were very much a Watsonian affair, due partly to the fact that the homes of so many of the boys at George Watson's lay on the city's South Side, within easy reach, and partly, if not largely, to our having had no school swimming pool of our own when the Watson's of my day stood between Archibald Place and the Meadows, on the site occupied today by an extension of the Royal Infirmary. If Herioters could boast swimming-baths of their own, Watsonians could retaliate by maintaining at Warrender what, for years, was virtually their monopoly. True, we had contingents from James Gillespie's and from Boroughmuir, and maybe a few from Daniel Stewart's; but Watsonians predominated. Of course, the new George Watson's College, in Colinton Road, has the last thing in school swimming-baths.

Why sadness, then? Of a total of well over 3,000 Watsonians, who in one capacity or another, served in the First World War, roughly two-thirds were officers, 1,800 of whom were combatants. Of that 1,800, nearly 600 were either killed or died on active service while serving, for the most part, with Scottish Regiments of the Line—with the Royal Scots, the Argyll & Sutherland Highlanders, the Seaforths, Camerons, and Gordons, the Black Watch and the Highland Light Infantry. This was largely at a time when no fewer than five Watsonians were members of the Coalition Government. Quite big noises in Lloyd George's Wicked War Cabinet, they were!

Those casualties I mentioned left an enormous number of gaps at Warrender. For such of us as survived, the ghosts of that lost generation still haunt our swimming-pond and our denuded gymnasium, still echo in the steamy sprayroom, still call hilariously from the rafters and other lofty places into which their dare-devil originals used to clamber. They are the phantoms of something that by November, 1918, had completely left the world, and that the mighty bombings and bashings and smashings of twenty and more years later made too damnably certain would never return. I must not pursue this matter any further in the meantime, lest in so doing I overshadow with sorrow those happier matters with which I want to deal. Let me

say no more than that I am one of the few who feel very strongly
about Britain's part in the schemings and wickednesses that occasioned
the First World War. If Germany have her responsibility for this
incalculable disaster, so also have we and France. Between us, by our
international machinations, we fractured irreparably pretty well everything Western Civilisation stood for.

So much in life would appear to be chancy, accidental, fatal,
fortuitous, that I would be the last to contend it is designedly fashioned
and fore-ordained in the old theological sense. Certainly, nothing
seemed more accidental than the circumstance in which I slipped into
this watery medium which, for many of my impressionable years, was
to charm me almost fanatically. It was the means of rescuing me from
backwardness and boobyhood, from crying craven at the slightest
threat of opposition or punishment. Within the space of three years it
made me courageous, adventurous, self-reliant, and physically
splendid. Translated into Shakespearean terms, I became bloody,
bold, and resolute, like the witches in *Macbeth*. I felt an urge to
"laugh to scorn the power of man".

These swimming-baths were to absorb so much of my thought,
time, and energy that my father used to say that, were I to devote to
my studies a tenth of what went into various capers at them, I could
be a scholar in no time, and perhaps even a university professor! Of
course, if he had had his way, I would never have attained the proficiency in swimming and kindred pursuits that I did. I would have
been driven off every afternoon to Watson's muddy playing-fields—
chased away to Myreside, where he was anxious I should kick and be
kicked in the hope of my becoming athletic in the approved and conventional sense. However, a few compulsory visits to Myreside (accompanied by my father in order to ensure that I really got there!) were
as much as I could stand. The likelihood of my ever being manly
enough to get enthusiastically involved in rugger, the game at which
Watsonians won world-renown, seemed remote. I didn't like very much
the boys I was expected to play with; and they certainly didn't like
me! I admit to having tried a little footer, however, and to having
found dribbling mildly entertaining, but never for periods exceeding a
few seconds at a time. You see, I was very much what nowadays would
be called a cissy or a softie. During a rugger scrum into which I had
been precipitated, a boy gave me such a dunt that I gracefully with-
drew and returned home.

On my last visit to this celebrated training-ground for manhood,
my cricket-playing contemporaries, in a misguided moment of
sympathy, handed me a bat, which I reluctantly accepted. My per-

formance with it was so hopeless that, after a few minutes' discouragement and jeering, they were glad to relieve me of it. I, of course, was
glad too. Quite thankful, indeed, for the pretext thus afforded me of
quitting the field, even though a little ignominiously. I loitered home-
ward, fearful of arriving there too soon. My father might seek an
explanation.

Cricket, forsooth! I used to hear more about cricket than I wanted
from the authoritative conversations on this game between my father
and Iain, my younger brother. Of C.B. Fry and his kind, I knew nothing, though I had heard the precocious Iain mention C.B. often enough.
The only connection in which his surname suggested anything to me
was Fry's Five Boys! For quite a while thereafter, I didn't even know
what L.B.W. signified; and I well recall Iain's contempt when I asked
him to explain.

My last visit to these none too Elysian Fields was on the occasion
of the school's annual sports, when my father, still hoping to make a
courageous and conventional man of me, dragged me off there. He
hoped that, in company with his enthusiastic self, I might witness a
series of heroic performances such as might inspire in me the ambition
to be brave and competitively athletic in these ways. Never was sixpence in gate-money spent upon anybody less interested.

You may imagine how my poor father felt when, in answer to a
question he put to me, I exhibited but the mildest inclination to emulate
young David Murray Morison, who had cleared the hurdles with such
astounding agility and celerity, and had just won the mile and every
other damned thing open to him! That a lad bearing the historic
Hebridean surname of Morison should quit himself with such distinction on so formidable a field was all the more reason, thought my
father, why I, his retarded son, should be urged to pull himself together and get into some sort of training preparatory to *next* year's
school sports. I was far more embarrassed than encouraged that afternoon when my father, in full view of masters, pupils, and sundry civic
dignitaries, left his seat in the grandstand and marched across the
field to congratulate the victorious David as he lay panting on the grass
by the winning-tape!

David, by the way, has been a doctor in Edinburgh these last thirty-
five years.[1]

[1] For the benefit of Edinburgh citizens to whom, I feel sure, David has
never disclosed his athletic prowess when at Watson's, I have just consulted a volume containing some evidence of it. To begin with, he was
Watsonian Prizeman for Scholarship and Athletics. At the Hurdles, the
Long Leap, and Diving he carried everything before him. He was also in
the 1st Watsonian XV. and the 1st Watsonian XI. A mighty pentathlete
in the Athenian tradition!

When my father despaired of my ever demonstrating a sustained interest in anything he approved of, a boy living round the corner took me off with him to the Warrender Park Baths, his mother having provided him with the requisite admission money for both of us. At the merest remembrance of this quite spontaneous and accidental expression of charity, I could sob with thankfulness as I write these words. It did for me something my young and none too happy life needed very desperately just then. The full import of it I could hardly have appreciated at the time, of course; but I was very conscious of the joy that followed in its train. It was unalloyed delight, sheer enchantment. I shall never forget the impact those early visits to the Warrender Park Baths made upon me. Here I found myself in my element—water, in any form, whether in bath, basin, river, lake, or ocean. Here, in conserved abundance, were 80,000 gallons of it, not to mention the limitless quantities piping-hot in sprays and plunges, and in Russian and Turkish baths.

What is there about water that attracts me so? Of the thousands of subjects in my photographic library, by far the finest and most numerous show as much water as considerations of artistic balance and composition would allow. When wandering the world with my camera, I find myself instinctively setting up my tripod where water is to form an integral part of my camera's field of vision. Scientists tell us that life originated in the dark and slimy palaeozoic waters of Devonian, or even pre-Cambrian, times. So there may well be some atavistic explanation.

That swimming-pool of ours, when the noontide sun of summer fell on it, appeared at one moment tinged with an elusive viridescence. At another it glowed as though shot with filtered rainbow. At times the white tiles enclosing it seemed delicately glazed the iridescent gradations of colour, such as are blent on the surface of shells and pebbles lying still and silent at the bottom of a sea-pool on a very calm day. At times, also, they revealed the loveliest chiaroscuro effects of sunshine and shadow, wherein mother-of-pearl predominated. This was usually at half-light, when the autumn sun at its downgoing sent aureate shafts through the western panes of our sloping roof.

Have you ever observed closely how wonderfully vegetation of any kind whatsoever goes with water? How the colours become vivid? How the meanest flower, the most jaded petal, suddenly lives when it falls into or is cast into water? If so, you may imagine the additional hues lent to this liquid paradise of boyhood and youth when from time to time six or eight luxuriant flower-baskets, each suspended over our pond from a pulley, sent a few petals a-fluttering to the water beneath them, suggestive of something exquisitely delicate in

Chinese or in Japanese Art. Those flower-baskets, filled to overflowing with ferny fronds, with fuchsia and geranium blooms thickset in moss and the brittle bark of birch, lent to the scene a sub-tropical touch, imparting to our pond, during its few really still moments, just that viridescence one associates with a stream running smoothly in sunlight over slabs of moss-covered rock.

The moral effect this setting had upon me was incalculable. It brought me my first elementary awareness of self-confidence, of self-esteem. It inspired in me a sense of cleanliness, a feeling of unencumberedness, of complete liberation, inwardly and outwardly. It established a state of mind. Virtually overnight, the motto, *Mens sana in corpore sano,* writ large above the inner entrance to our baths, became a vibrant reality. Aquatics were now to displace quadratics. Hydraulics, experienced rather than described in textbooks, became an absorbing interest. The ability to rise and fall in deep water with but a minimum of exertion, to move at will in it so noiselessly, fascinated me. I was no longer a tellurian, of the earth, earthy. In no time the stresses and strains required to achieve movement and deportment on *terra firma* were gone. I began to find myself singularly free from such earth-binding influences as telluric gravity and all its associations. Gravity seemed to have given way to buoyancy of spirit, as also of body. The consciousness of a mental as well as of a physical weightlessness emancipated me from the shocks and jars to which flesh ordinarily is heir, so that I felt freed from the usual terrestrial trammels when submitting myself to metaphysical examination. It is my experience that in no better medium than water can one dip into the realm of ontology, can one see more clearly just how and where, in the nature of things, one exists.

It is precisely for this reason that throughout my life I have immediately sought the solace of water when in mental or physical distress. When I am off-colour, see that, in preference to all the pills and potions in the world, I have access to a bright bathroom with water, hot and cold, abundantly laid on, and that I am allowed as much time as I choose to wallow there. Rigidity of mind and body can be dispensed with in this most satisfying of human institutions. Here one may recline in a greater measure of relaxation and comfort than in the downiest of beds. Have you ever been so ill or hurt that the very weight of your limbs pressed painfully on the softest mattress? During that long and painful spell of rheumatic fever, I experienced my first bit of real relief when well enough to allow of the nurses' carrying me to a bath, and lowering me gently into two feet of hot water.

Looking back on my father's spartan regimen, I cannot but recall how he discouraged this sort of thing. To him, it was *effeminate*, as well as enervating. For these reasons, hot-water bottles were taboo. If, during the course of one of his medical inspections of the home, as it were, he found that Iain or I had secreted somewhere an article of this kind, his first impulse was to damage it in such a way as to render it unserviceable.

By the time this volume appears, I will have lived nearly half a century since those spartan days; and I must confess that throughout it I often have had recourse to the hot-bottle without (as I hope) showing any marked signs of effeminacy. When you are creeping quietly to bed in the chilly, small hours, having just completed for a book a chapter such as this, nothing is more consoling, comforting, and sleep-inducing than a rubber hot-bottle. In my view, it is one of the greatest boons suffering and self-destructive mankind has ever invented for its wayward self. It almost ranks with anaesthetics. Its inventor, short of being canonised, should receive an international tribute of some sort. Less worthily lies many a one in Westminster Abbey!

To return to natatory matters, one must be able to swim tolerably well, of course, to be able to experience fully the delights of immersion in deep water, to be conscious of that up-thrust of body, that up-lift of spirit. I suppose, therefore, that I am committing all this to writing in the retrospect of one who, in his youth, was among the best swimmers of his generation. (I trust the reader will overlook this further touch of immodesty.) During the years of which I write, I was closely associated with a team of sprint swimmers of Olympic stature. Our Warrender Baths Swimming Club produced some of the first speed swimmers and water-polo players of the first three decades of the present century.

At the commencement of my aquatic career at Warrender, a season-ticket for a lad under eighteen was—just think of it!—half-a-guinea. Ten shillings and six pennies. Quite ridiculously little! Adults paid no more than twice as much for theirs. As a boy's single admission cost fourpence, my father, relieved that I had found something adventurous and impelling, was swift to appreciate that, if I went swimming but once a week, it would work out at 17/4 a year. Since it now looked as though I would be visiting these baths at least five times a week, a season-ticket seemed inevitable.

Every year until I went to the war, that 'season' was renewed with religious conviction. From every point of view, it was the best money's worth in the City of Edinburgh. For the benefit of those who dislike the idea of their precious little ones attending public swimming-baths, lest they should become pediculous or pick up some infection, let me add that I never had a day's illness, nor even a cold, all the years I went to them. Neither Abana nor Pharpar, the rivers of Damascus, nor yet the waters of Jordan, were more health-giving and health-sustaining.

Fortified with that first season-ticket, I soon became quite muscular, though I must admit that my school examination percentages still remained lamentably low. This muscularity instantly placed me favourably in relation to such of my contemporaries as hitherto had bullied me at school. Those who so heartily disrespected my person on land were now obliged to respect it in water, for otherwise . . . !

I played off many an old score at the deep end of the Warrender Baths, where I felt so safe, so terribly sure of myself. I gave the boy who dealt me that sickening dunt in the rugger-scrum at Myreside a bloody good dooking that sorted *him!* No more nonsense from *that* direction!

You may assess how much my stock had risen by the time I had rescued an elderly gent. from drowning at the deep end, and had dived off the rafters into six feet of water! Of the hundreds of pupils then at Watson's, only two had achieved this latter distinction. After my partner cracked his skull a bit, and had to lie up for months with concussion, the civic authorities proclaimed a special edict prohibiting any repetition of this bravado. Henceforth, the bath attendant's terrifying whistle screeched immediately he observed anybody clambering up to those rafters.

Reverting for a moment to that nice little rescue of mine, during my years with Miss Aitken I saw that elderly gent. occasionally, as he toddled along Princes Street with the kenspeckle and fashionable of those days. As he came toward me, I used to mutter to myself: 'Look here, old chap! I simply must accost you, for you don't seem to appreciate that, had it not been for *me,* you wouldn't now be disporting your complacent self on this 'ere pavement. I'm the fellow who, fully clad, dived into the Warrender Park Baths, dragged you ashore, applied artificial respiration, and set you on you feet again! But for my gallant performance, where would you be today? Certainly not parading Princes Street, you unappreciative old b——!

I had this endearing little speech off by heart, but could never quite bring myself to deliver it.

At this juncture and, as I hope, with not too much Gasconade, I must mention the sphere in which I won acknowledged supremacy, the sphere which was to equip me for dealing with my enemies *on land.* I refer to the rings attached to the ends of long ropes suspended over the pond at regular intervals. I established my acrobatic superiority on these when, in response to a challenge to beat a previous record of 36 uninterrupted journeys along them, I travelled a distance of two miles—non-stop!! As our pond was 25 yards long, this entailed no fewer than 144 journeys to and fro. I might have been travelling along these rings yet, had not one of the umpires suddenly pulled away from my finger-tip grasp the ring at the shallow end, in order to oblige me to drop gently—and sensibly—into three feet of water! My hands for many a day thereafter were torn and painful. Nevertheless, I had succeeded in setting up a record never beaten. Henceforth I became widely known as Kelly MacGregor, King o' the Rings. The Kelly part of this title will be explained when we come to dealing with sundry memories of our sprayroom.

These baths, opened in December, 1887, and deriving their name from that of the estate on which they are situate, were run originally by a private company with a registered capital of £8,000. Attendance and membership had so declined by 1906, however, that they were closed down. Two years later, the City of Edinburgh had the good sense to purchase the entire outfit for £3,000 and re-open them as public baths. The swimming-club associated with them in their private days was now resuscitated, to begin its distinguished record of national and international successes in team swimming, in diving, and in water-polo.

But schism soon assailed its laudable activities, although those of us who were rather young at the time never knew what created it. So in 1913 a rival club, not inappropriately designated the Dunedin, was formed on these very premises. Its existence was short-lived owing to the active hostility of those from whom its promoters had broken away. All I can remember of it is the membership list pinned to its own newly erected notice-board, and including my own name as a junior member at an annual subscription of a shilling; the organised disruption of its trials and matches by leaping in upon them with disconcerting war-cries (sabotage it's called nowadays); the tearing down of anything that went up on its notice-board; the ultimate disappearance of the notice-board itself; and, finally, the filling with broken eggs of its prime mover's overcoat pockets.

Against such resolute opposition the Dunedin didn't last long. At the outbreak of war in 1914, the senior members of our Warrender Swimming Club enlisted to a man. Many of them perished, amongst them the finest swimmers and polo-players of their generation. Their names are graven on the club's war memorial. Several of them were, of course, Watsonians, so that such names also appear in the Memorial Record of Watsonians, published in Edinburgh in 1920.

The Club's revival in 1919 was taken very seriously by those of us who had survived The Trenches, and also by younger swimmers recently qualified for senior membership. Team-racing and water-polo now became our specialities. The polo team waxed so formidable that for a time difficulty was experienced in finding teams to oppose it, and in dissuading visiting teams from failing to keep their fixtures. By 1930 Warrender was quite definitely the premier swimming-club in the country, having carried off every trophy open to it.

The Annual Gala marked the high spot of its year. To this spectacular occasion I usually contributed an exhibition of acrobatics on the rings, and a demonstration of graceful swimming in half a dozen styles. A dinner followed. More than once this sequel, dragging on into the small hours, became so rowdy that local residents complained, with the result that latterly our Gala had to be held without it.

This annual display of our prowess proved a drain on the club's financial resources, largely because prizes had to be purchased. Of course, we had those patrons to whom we were continually appealing for donations, and usually with gratifying response. But the commonest means of raising funds was by watch competitions. Of these we never seemed to have been free. I think we must have had among our patrons a watchmaker always willing to donate a watch for this purpose. The watch was wound, and then placed in a box duly sealed in the presence of witnesses. For sixpence one made a guess at the hour, minute, and second at which it stood when, weeks later, the breaking of the seal was authorised. The award went to the nearest guesser.

Since mixed bathing was still regarded as a little improper, if not actually sinful, three half-days a week our baths were reserved exclusively for female swimmers. *They* also had their swimming-club. Can you imagine our elation at Warrender when, in 1924, there was discovered among its members Miss Ellen King, one of the greatest swimmers of all time? Breast stroke, back stroke, side stroke, overarm, free style—all were equally simple to Ellen. She broke every record, knocking up new ones as easily as most people knock down ninepins. She retrieved for us in the swimming world the place we would have retained but for those casualties at The Front. Ellen King was the only competitor, male or female, ever to win three British championships, each in a different style. In 1924 she represented us at the Olympic Games.

At the following Olympics in 1928 Jean MacDowall, another member of our Ladies' Club, represented Great Britain. So you see that we weren't just paddlers at Warrender.

Our aquatics carried us to the pond's veriest depths, particularly when emulating the *Pleuronectidae* (the family to which flounders and other flat, side-swimming fish belong) by swimming on our sides within an inch or two of the bottom, or when swimming competitively underwater to pick up those thin, metal discs sent a-skidding across the surface of the pond until they sank just as plates do. In fact, we called them plates. Sometimes we hid them from our less adventurous contemporaries by removing at the southwest corner of our pond—its lowest point—the ponderous iron grille through which all those tens of thousands of gallons gushed when the pond had to be cleaned and the water changed. Slipping one's fingers through the bars of the grille, one could just manage to pull it aside sufficiently to be able to deposit a few plates in the rectangular cavity immediately below. Those of us with exceptionally good lungs edged a shoulder into that cavity so as to pass a plate-bearing hand as far as possible down the sloping 12-inch exit pipe which ran from it. Having removed the grille and, like some fish depositing its roe, pushed the plate out of the reach of all but the most amphibious, we usually had to surface for air before descending again to replace it. As the number of plates available for diving purposes became fewer and fewer, one suspected that, when the pond was being emptied, any hidden there were carried away into an underground drainage system, which they might well have obstructed.

The only other recess where we could hide these plates lay deep down under the springboard. It was the large pipe through which steam under pressure came a-rumbling and a-bubbling and a-blurting periodically in order to raise our pond to 72° Fahrenheit, the temperature at which it was maintained throughout the year.

The rumblings this steam created as it entered the pond always tempted us to cluster together under the springboard by hanging on to the handrail, so as to enjoy those quite hot currents sent up just there. The noise accompanying them was mildly volcanic; and the vibration they produced soon gave us a sensation of the collywobbles if we remained hanging any length of time in the vortex, as it were, of those rumblings.

I remember the summer when Big Alick generated more steam than was required for the heating of the pond and, owing to a defective valve, was unable to shut it off completely. For days steam entered the pond in erratic spurts, so raising its temperature that there was no longer any need to resort to the hot sprayroom. Before the city's engineering department rectified the fault, the pond was much hotter than a tepid bath. Far too hot to swim in for more than a few yards, but delightful to lie afloat in. At times the dense blanket of vapour hanging over it made it impossible to see one end of it from the other. It was like a pall of mist reluctant to leave the surface of a lake on a windless morning.

On another occasion something went wrong with the inflow control, with the result that we were able to enjoy a few inches' additional depth. The waves we artificially created in this unusual situation went splashing merrily over the pond's rim, and down the scuppers.

Those underwater exploits I mentioned had a weird quality difficult to describe. One sometimes experienced during them (just as I do at this very moment, in recalling them) an overwhelming sensation of claustrophobia. What if one's fingers got stuck in that grille? What if one's arm could not be withdrawn from that pipe? True, the strongest of us could have brought the grille up to the surface, as in moments of bravado we did, retaining it there until a reverberating blast from Mac's whistle urged us to let it go, to follow it to the bottom and replace it.

Away down in those depths one heard, faintly and intermittently, all manner of strange noises, although as a rule it was as still and silent as the deeps of ocean. The sounds of human activity above and around one reached the ears in distorted form. At times, for instance, one heard a curiously muffled version of Big Alick's stoking the boilers, or striking with a sledge-hammer an inordinately large block of coal. In like manner could be heard the machinery of the laundry, and the wash-tub mangles, and perhaps the voice of a laundress singing at her labours among those countless towels and pants. The rumblings and creakings of massive machinery were always audible underwater, though often originating at some distance from the bottom of the pond where we listened for them.

At times, when deep down there, one felt nostrils and ear-drums being compressed perceptibly by the water's pressure. Of course, it was not until one had had much experience of this strange, watery underworld, and had become thoroughly familiar with its properties, that it could be entered and lived in without apprehension. Ability to experience it depended entirely on soundness of heart and lungs. Any cardiac weakness whatsoever would have placed those nether regions out of reach. Visited in moderation, however, their lure did much to strengthen one's respiratory system, and indeed to expand considerably one's lung capacity. I can vouch for this from personal experience. It equipped me for certain physical exploits I otherwise could never have undertaken. It contributed to my winning two not unimportant army long-distance running championships in France a few years later.

These necessarily brief periods underwater possessed an other-world quality. In swimming along the bottom of the pond into a patch where the water and the tiles enclosing it glistened in sunlight, one felt oneself intruding upon a piscatorial domain, deep among the sunlit pebbles on a river's bed. One was conscious of moving in an iridescent medium for which ordinary air-breathing mortals are so very imperfectly equipped. I have swum more than once among sunlit pebbles at a river's bed in the Highlands, and am therefore in a position to say that, although one cannot do so for any great distance at a time, it is a very lovely experience.

What is there about water that lends to the most mundane of things a nacrous lustre? I have picked up on our Highland and Hebridean shorelands the loveliest stones and pebbles you ever beheld, their colours as remarkably vivid as they were varied and elusive. I have placed them in the palm of my hand to submerge them gently at the edge of a still, sunlit sea-pool to find them instantly transformed into something quite magical.

Since my Golden Lamp days, our Warrender Park Baths have deteriorated shockingly. All the pleasing amenities and finishing touches we inherited from their private owners vanished one by one. The towel-boys and slipper-boys of pre-1914 years have gone long since. The Indian clubs and dumb-bells once filling a couple of racks in the gymnasium haven't been seen these forty years. The rings on which I distinguished myself have been removed. The coconut-matting round the pond's sides went about the same time. The brass boundary-line demarcating the vestibule, and over which nobody dared step except in slippers or goloshes specially provided, lies there, worn and ignored. The Medes and Persians never knew a law against trespass more rigorously enforced, for, after all, you couldn't have people wandering round the pond in their dusty shoon. This explained the cleanly condition in which it was maintained. One could see, through its pellucid depths, the smallest coins, flung in for diving exercises, lying on its shiny tiles at the bottom.

Additional bathing-boxes of the crudest design now crowd in upon the gymnasium of former years. Bare concrete has supplanted the wooden floors once covered with bottle-green linoleum that never seemed the worse of the wear. Clusters of cheap, artificial flowers have displaced the flowering plants that shed so gently, so acceptably, those petals I mentioned.

Sure enough, *tempora mutantur, nos et mutamur in illis.* But why must they always change to conform only to proletarian requirements and standards? Since my Golden Lamp days, this deterioration has become universal, and alarmingly rapid.

CHAPTER NINE

Suspended for a Week

LET ME now recall the occasion when I was suspended from these swimming-baths on account of my wild and reckless behaviour. After school one afternoon, in describing my mighty circles on the rings dependent over the pond, I set a-swinging overhead the arc-lamps placed high up near the apex of the glass roof. I had brought into undesirable contact with the rims of their wide shades the upper parts of the ropes nearest them. In fairness to those who were now to seek a salutary method of curbing these activities of mine, I must concede that I already had been warned in connection with these dangerous heroics. But the man-on-the-flying-trapeze in me couldn't resist the exercise which might—or might not—send those lamps dizzily gyrating again. It could at least be said in my favour that I had never actually got a rope *entangled* in one of them.

Be this as it may, the beastly attendant on duty at the time duly reported me to the superintendent, his beastly old dad; and the beastly old dad thought he ought to call upon my father and lay before him the lawless conduct of his otherwise backward son, and the peril in which he placed the more considerate and law-abiding bathers. Just fancy if one of those lofty luminants came crashing down on somebody's head! The Corporation of the august City of Edinburgh might be sued for damages. And what then?

So beastly old Mr. Hardy called to lay the position fairly and squarely before my father, who, to my immense surprise, even more than to my relief, did not take his part. On the contrary, old Hardy was firmly shown the door.

"I'll have him suspended! *That's* what I'll do!" our baths superintendent muttered as he retreated from our doorstep in anger, resolved to take his revenge in another way. He would report to the Corporation at the City Chambers my lamp-swinging capers and urge the appropriate civic authority to suspend me. This it promptly did. I was suspended for a whole week, one of the longest and most disagreeable in my young life up till then.

As official notification of this quite heavy sentence did not arrive when expected, I presented myself at the turnstile as if nothing had happened. Our cashier looked at me gravely, and then consulted a secret document somewhere out of my sight. It purported to be a sort of black list of miscreants. My name appeared to be there all right!

"Your season-ticket's suspended. It's no' valid until next week," she announced. "Come back next Monday; and well see if we can let you in. But, mind now, no more nonsense, you naughty boy!"

I retired dejected, crest-fallen, defeated. Suspended, with only one ally, and the most unexpected ally—my father, who had taken up the cudgels on my behalf on two grounds, both of which the superintendent appeared to have rejected, and in consequence was shown the door:

(a) *Boys will be boys.*
(b) *Weren't you once young yourself?*

Now, it was during this suspension that there befell another misfortune, the seriousness of which, to a schoolboy provided with pocket-money seldom exceeding tuppence a week, was considerable.

Throughout my writing career I have never felt the slightest desire to descend to the level of lavatories and the like, although I am aware that lavatory literature, like pornography, finds a ready and profitable market. In this country one can be *coarse* in print with impunity, if not also with a measure of approval; whereas one can be *lewd* only at the risk of prosecution. The lavatory aspect of what follows cannot be avoided if I seek to relate a particular incident which now comes to mind, and which I believe to be worth relating. The date of this incident I remember clearly, since it happened to fall on a birthday. It was March, 20th, while I was still an Edinburgh schoolboy.

That morning the despondency due to my current suspension was alleviated by the arrival from the North of a birthday-greetings letter from Aunt Dorothy. I was less interested in the greetings aspect of this missive than in the half-crown postal-order accompanying it, which I very promptly converted into the equivalent coin of the realm. To the schoolboy of those pre-1914 years, half-a-crown in his pocket represented substantial wealth. Recalling the number and variety of things one could do with it, and the comparative cheapness of quite wholesome sweetmeats in the form of boilings and toffees, one remembers how it sustained its possessor in an enviable position of affluence for a week or more, without being too stingy with oneself. The twice-nightly shows at the Operetta House, for instance, or at

The sixteenth-century Nungate Bridge spanning the Tyne at Haddington

St. Mary's Parish Church, Haddington—The Lamp of the Lothians

East Lothian: The Village Postman has his morning rendezvous in passing Preston Mill

the Coliseum, cost the schoolboy as little as tuppence. He could have a cheaper seat at a penny, as hundreds did. A further tuppence expended on a good, fat bag of 'the goodies,' at two ounces a penny, added to the evening's sweetness. A penny bag of chips on the way home rounded off the evening very agreeably. On half-a-crown one could indulge oneself thus for six consecutive evenings! But the great idea, of course, was to retain intact as long as one could this large and significant coin of the realm. Once broken into, its components got themselves spent all too rapidly.

Now, if only I had purchased even a penny bag of 'the goodies' as soon as I had cashed my postal-order, an absurd sequel would have been avoided. Furthermore, the occasion for this particular chapter would never have arisen. Briefly, I forfeited my half-crown in a manner which brings us to the lavatory adumbrated. Putting in as best I could such time as would have been spent at the swimming-baths but for the unexpired period of my suspension, I found myself at a loose end in the vicinity of the Haymarket Station. Suddenly, one of the baser calls of nature assailed me. I rushed for the public lavatory at the foot of Morrison Street, near at hand. In my anxiety to do the right thing in the right place, I inadvertently inserted in the slot of the nearest w.c. door my half-crown. It functioned perfectly; and so did I, if rather expensively.

How could I retrieve my precious coin? I had paid 2/5 in excess of statutory requirements. I explained my painful plight to the lavatory attendant, who informed me that he had no keys for the slotted locks into which pennies were dropped by the less careless, but advised me to apply to the appropriate department at the City Chambers the following day, and report my loss. "The mannie wha empties the locks 'll bee roond again the morrow's morn; an', if ye *did* pit a half-croon in—Mind ye! If ye *did*—ye'll get it back at the City Chambers, 'way up in the High Street."

What a dilemma I was in! Could I wait till the morrow's morn? Or should I just report my loss at the City Chambers straight away? I decided on the latter course, although dreading this first official call at so formidable an institution in the Scottish Capital. I would have to supply my name and address. From these, everyone instantly would identify me as the wayward lad meantime serving a sentence of suspension because his flying-trapeze exertions had set all those arc-lamps a-swinging.

My elementary mind could not conceive it possible that every official at the City Chambers had not been duly informed of my reckless conduct, and of the humiliating penalty arising therefrom. But separation from that half-crown became so unendurable that I resolved to run

D

the gauntlet at the City Chambers without delay. I simply couldn't wait until the morrow's morn.

That afternoon, therefore, I presented myself at the Lost Property Office and stated my case in the fullest detail. Having been allowed to go through the circumstances attending my forfeiture of this considerable coin, I was quietly informed that I was addressing myself to the wrong department. My embarrassment increased as I was passed on from one department to another, stating my case at each, and never doubting, of course, that I was being eyed as the wicked Watsonian under suspension from the Warrender Park Baths.

At length I found myself in the public office of the lighting and cleansing department, where a counter separated callers from a number of very important-looking employees, one of whom lounged about in a jersey such as are worn by professional boxers, jockeys, horsey people, stable hands, and the like. After such delay as children are usually subjected to in such places, lest prompt civic attention should foster in them the notion that they are the least important where courtesies municipal are dispensed, the large, burly man in the jersey condescended to approach the counter.

"Well, what dae ye want?" he asked. His gruff tone made me suspect, even before I had been given an opportunity of uttering a syllable, that he was 'in the know' about my suspension. Yet again I began to unfold my tragic story, and the anxiety this grievous loss had occasioned me.

"Ye had a dose o' the skitters, had ye? Whaur did ye say ye lost the half-croon?" he asked, now leaning heavily on the counter to take down a few particulars.

"I didn't quite *lose* it," I began to explain. "I inadvertently—" He interrupted me, identifying me as a Watsonian by my school-cap.

"Ye what?"

"I inadvertently—"

"Inadvertently? What's that? Can ye no' explain yersel in simple terms like ither folk?"

I made yet another attempt. "I accidentally—"

"Oh, I see! Ye accidentally, did ye? Ye accidentally what?"

"I'm about to tell you," I interposed with as much dignity as a mere schoolboy could command. "I accidentally dropped a half-crown into one of the slots in the public lavatory at the foot of Morrison Street yonder—you know—just where the pavement curves round into Dalry Road—the place in the wall below the railway coal dêpot—near the Haymarket."

His affecting not to know the locality gave me the impression that he suspected me of intent to obtain money by false pretences.

"Ye say ye mentioned the matter tae the attendant. An' what did the attendant tell ye?"

"He told me to come up here."

"He did, did he?"

When I had gone through the circumstances once more, and given him all the details of this truly mighty occasion—everything except the date on the coin in question—he told me to call again the following afternoon. By that time, he explained, the collector would have returned from his rounds with my half-crown—"That's tae say, if ye *lost* it!" Ominous wasn't it?

I did as was required of me, wondering what the situation would be if the collector of lavatory coppers had failed to bring in my half-crown, and denied that he had found one. Suspension from the Warrender Baths, not entirely unearned, was bad enough. But what if I'm now charged with intent to defraud?

I returned to the lighting and cleansing department with increased apprehension. The jerseyed employee of the previous day approached me and, without saying a word, resolved all my juvenile apprehensions by extracting from a drawer a half-crown, and slapping it down on the counter with resounding vigour.

"Thank you," I said, eagerly putting forth a hand to pick it up.

"Na, na!" growled this civic but uncivil employee, laying a big, clumsy hand over it, lest I dashed off with it before he, as a responsible public servant, had subtracted the corporation's due. "Dinnae touch it! Ye're no' entitled tae half-a-croon. Ye telt me yesterday ye had a dose o' the skitters. That means ye're only gettin' 2/5."

There, at that canny counter, I stood, while he and his colleagues searched the pockets of their trousers for such change as I was entitled to. With measured dilatoriness and averted face, he placed 2/5 on the counter before me, and waved me away in disgust.

That half-crown incident would never have occurred but for that suspension; and that suspension would never have occurred but for that beastly, old, nepotic Mr. Hardy. As an unreasoning schoolboy, I naturally harboured resentment against him and his son. But soon I had occasion to rejoice. It was now a case of 'vengeance is ours,' saith the senior members of our quite famous Warrender Swimming Club. Nepotism was going a bit too far!

Some time previously, the promotion of one of our attendants had created a vacancy now very acceptably filled by our beloved Johnnie Baillie, who had been transferred from another Edinburgh swimming-bath. Johnnie, a rotund little fellow of merry ways, endeared himself immediately because of his interest in our life-saving class, to which he promptly appointed himself instructor-in-chief. At that time Johnnie moved in an atmosphere of reflected glory in swimming circles: his brother, Charlie Baillie, held a number of sprint-swimming championships. Some of this glory Johnnie imparted to us. He was our beau-ideal of a baths attendant.

One day Johnnie confided to some of our senior club members that he was about to be transferred in order to make room for the beastly old Mr. Hardy's son. This was carrying nepotism farther than the seniors considered either desirable or just. Since their petition for Johnnie's retention had been ignored at the City Chambers, more stringent measures would have to be taken. We juniors soon jaloused that our seniors were planning to show their resentment in what, now-adays, would be described as 'a big way'. The air of conspiracy was now rife at our baths. Snatches of conversation overheard in the hot, steamy twilight of the sprayroom confirmed the suspicion that some-thing really drastic was afoot. Imagine our disappointment when, at zero hour on the evening decided upon, we—the young, small fry— were hustled out at closing-time by our seniors, so that they might be free to carry through their design unhindered, and without in any way involving us! Our pleading that Johnnie Baillie's removal was every bit as much our concern as theirs was of no avail. Reluctantly, we allowed ourselves to be shepherded out to the pavement of Thirlestane Road, followed by a large and warlike senior member who closed the front door on us. In so doing he whispered, by way of consoling us, "We're going to fling Bob Hardy into the pond with his clothes on."

We waited! We listened! Suddenly all the lights within went out. A master hand at the master switch! Then followed the wildest noises of exultant disorder as seats, armchairs inherited from the private owners from whom the corporation had taken over these baths some years before, duck-boards, towels, mats, coconut-matting, rugs, curtains, trolleys, plants in hanging baskets—as everything movable was being flung into the darkened pond. Meantime, the beastly Bob had escaped into the undergrowth of the ticket-office, where he locked himself in, and promptly telephoned the police. This was long before the days of Flying Squads as we now know them. Nevertheless, the police turned up in no time to quell the disturbance, proudly referred to ever after as The Warrender Riot.

I cannot recall at this length of time exactly what official action was taken. But I know that the participants had to pay about a pound each to repair the damage they had committed. So far as I was concerned, this exhibition of esprit as a protest against an injustice—now so rarely exhibited anywhere except by young people—more than avenged my week's suspension.

Often in my Golden Lamp years, which were to begin roughly a quinquennium later, I set those same arc-lamps a-swinging during our swimming-club evenings at Warrender, regardless of suspension or anything else, though never without recalling my first official contact, in boyhood, with our City Chambers.

CHAPTER TEN

The Bloody Awful Five

MANKIND has a great longing to get itself into clubs of one kind or another, believing them to confer a symbol status. This one realised early in life when a prominent member of our quite renowned swimming-club succumbed to the urge to belong to yet another. So he formed a new and very secret one known as the Half-Moon Club. The maximum membership, according to the Articles of Association as laid down between the covers of a penny notebook, was limited to five. This adolescent cabal styled itself the Bloody Awful Five, or the B.A.F. In no time the waiting-list for membership was a long one; and there was much anxious speculation as to which of the more adult swimmers at Warrender would be invited to fill any vacancy that might occur.

This secret society's meeting-place was underground in the truly subversive sense, as well as in the physical. It convened away down among the dark passages and catacombs underneath the baths. Access to these mysterious parts was obtained by way of the trap-door of the towel chute located in a corner of the gymnasium. If its members hadn't managed to disappear, unnoticed, down that chute just before closing-time of an evening, they had to wait until all was locked up and quiet. Surreptitious admittance might then be gained through an obscure window reached from Thirlestane Lane, the cul-de-sac along which carts and lorries carried fuel for the boilers, and along which, also, Big Alick, our doughty boilerman, might be seen toddling home-ward at nightfall, after he had stoked up for the night, and locked the back entrance. Not until some minutes after Alick had been seen quitting his own particular part of the premises did any member of the B.A.F. venture along the lane to that window.

The club's *raison d'être* nobody ever knew—apart from its sworn duty to see that no Half-Moon conventicle ever dispersed until the hands of the baths clock had been put back half-an-hour in the hope of deceiving the attendant on duty at closing-time the following evening. Thus it would be 9 p.m. instead of 8.30 p.m. ere he blew his whistle and rang the bell that got bathers out of the water and into their boxes.

The club's secret sessions underground were conducted in true sybaritic comfort provided by the divans, cushions, and mattresses temporarily removed from the Turkish Baths overhead. Reclining on these, after the fashion of Eastern potentates, its members smoked the ends of expensive Havana cigars and Turkish cigarettes deposited that day in the ash-trays by the toffs who so recently had patronised the Turkish. The members' beverage was tea. This they pilfered from our laundresses' private caddy in the laundry, and infused with water boiled on their gas-ring. In those pre-frig. days, milk and sugar were kept side by side in an adjoining cupboard.

It was the chaotic condition in which the Bloody Awful Five once left the Turkish that aroused suspicion of these nocturnal ongoings. Its members, in replacing the divans and cushions they had borrowed, thought they heard ominous footsteps. Those of Big Alick, or of Mac, the senior attendant! Perhaps, those of the police! Anyhow, they were too scared to tarry where they might all too easily have been caught. Flinging the borrowed things indiscriminately into the Turkish, they fled to the dark interstices underground, remaining there in palpitating fear until all seemed safe and serene again.

Most of those mysterious subterranean places have gone. When, for auld lang syne, a new attendant escorted me a few years ago through such as survive, I was quite confused because so many of those dark, labyrinthine ways of my boyhood, always strictly out of bounds, are now occupied by the equipment installed in recent years for the continuous filtering process claimed to cleanse the pond's entire capacity every few hours. No more of the laborious emptying, cleaning, and re-filling in which, once a week or so, the more privileged of us were allowed to lend a hand, after hours, following a series of hilarious pranks and antics only possible when no more than a foot of water was left at the deep end.

The Half-Moon Club was short-lived. Its meaningless activities came to an abrupt end the evening its members found in their den a warning note in an unknown hand:

> *Fly before you're discovered!*
> *[Signed] Sherlock Blake & Sexton Holmes.*

Let me now mention the occasion on which the Bloody Awful Five would have given me a mighty scragging, had they caught me.

As two of the more formidable of them stood at the edge of the pond one afternoon, contemplating none too enthusiastically their plunging in, I rushed past and dealt each, in turn, just that wee bit of a push necessary to precipitate him into the water. War was declared immediately. I dashed for refuge. Fortunately for me, I did so in the only safe direction, for I found vacant the little w.c. up the gymnasium steps. It had neither lock nor snib inside, however. But, seated on the w.c. with my wet feet against the door, I was fairly secure, assuming I could hold out long enough. The heftiest of the five, awkwardly heaving themselves against that rather narrow door, made little impression on my muscular legs.

Soon their endeavours to dislodge me were augmented by bathers purporting to require immediate access to the w.c. All I could do was to shout reminders where other such porcelain accommodation was to be found in the building.

How long would my pursuers loiter outside that door in their determination to capture me? That was *one* pressing question. If I hadn't managed to escape by closing-time, what chance would I then have had of successfully running the gauntlet? That was *another*. By that time all my pursuers would be fully clad, whereas I would still have to make for my box where my clothes were.

It was wellnigh impossible to explore the possibility of escaping by the w.c.'s. tiny window so long as I was obliged to remain seated there with my feet firmly placed against the door. The absence of lock or snib certainly restricted my movements. I couldn't afford to be a second off my guard. Very audible and no less rude threats as to what awaited me, when once caught, didn't encourage me to take down my feet, even to keek through the keyless keyhole so as to ascertain how near lurked the nearest of my foes. If any one of them rushed that narrow door whilst I was off my oval perch, I was done.

It never occurred to any one of them that escape by that tiny w.c. window was humanly possible. In any case, it opened in two independent halves, up and down. Moreover, it was too high, too small, and too ledge-less to render escape feasible except in the most desperate of circumstances. There was also the external drop from it to be considered.

Precautions against any attempt on my part to escape *inside* had already been taken, but not *outside*. This I knew from subdued movements and voices beyond. If by any chance I did manage to escape by that window, the Bloody Awful Five realised that I would have to re-enter the baths at the back, since I had nothing on except a sparse pair of pants. I couldn't escape far in those! So they manned the back stairs leading up from the laundry and boilers.

By now I was truly in a desperate plight, realising that the longer I kept my foes at bay, the more painful the scragging I would have to endure when captured. There was no alternative, therefore, but to wait for a lull in the gymnasium, and take a terrifying risk.

Balancing myself upon my hands on the w.c., I raised my body, face downwards, until I succeeded in getting my feet out at the lower half of the window. Pushing myself upwards by the moistened palms of my hands pressed against the wall, I got the greater part of my weight outside the window. The rest was comparatively easy. On my bare feet I dropped on a slated roof, and at no great height above the cobblestones of Thirlestane Lane. In this almost naked state I dashed along to the end of the lane, then round into the busy Marchmont Road, and round again into Thirlestane Road. Entering the baths by the front door, I crept in under the turnstile, enveloped myself in a hanging curtain to spy the land, and waited for the moment when I might be able to skip along the vestibule and down the private passage between swimming-pond and Turkish quarters. A gap in the tiled wall of the passage made it possible to reach any of the three largest boxes from behind. In one of these lay my clothes, wondering whether I was ever likely to return to them. They and I already had been parted four strenuous hours.

Crouching low behind the door of that box, I dressed under difficulties. Leaping back over that tiled wall into the passage-way I have mentioned, I quietly proceeded, quite unnoticed, to the vestibule and the swing-door above the turnstile. My foes, as I could see, were still awaiting me in the gymnasium, some thirty yards away. As I stood and watched them at this safe distance, with the Freedom of the Burgh but a moment's dash to my rear, they spotted me.

'My God! There's that bloody MacGregor, fully dressed!' shrieked one of the Bloody Awful Five. The removal of my clothes from that box was the only precaution against my escape they had omitted to take. It could never have occurred to anybody that such a precaution might have been necessary. After all, sooner or later I would have been obliged to crawl out from that w.c., to plead for such little leniency as my long incarceration might have entitled me to.

I stood on the fringe of the vestibule and gave them a gentle wave of appreciation. At this juncture our beloved Mac interceded on my behalf. It was fitting that we should settle matters there and then, he said, rather than that I should return another day to be given a worse scragging than ever. "Ye must admit he's jinked ye a'. He deserves tae get aff!"

At Mac's suggestion, then, we 'cried a barley,' as the Scots say. We called a truce.

CHAPTER ELEVEN

Fun and Games in the Sprayroom

QUITE EARLY in life, my associations with Warrender enabled me to come to terms very agreeably with what are popularly believed to be the small boy's traditional enemies, namely, soap and water. Up till then, I don't think it had ever occurred to me that cleanliness and godliness stood to one another in any propinquity whatsoever. On the other hand, such grubbiness as I may have displayed *before* these baths absorbed me so absolutely might have been excused on Dr. Henry Flack's pretext (had I but known it in time!) that abnormally clean little boys always filled him with the greatest foreboding.

I was reminded of this the other day when dipping into Ivor Brown's admirable little volume, *No Idle Word*[1], in which he refers to the 'chittering bit' he knew in his own boyhood in Glasgow. "Chittering reminds me of boyhood bathing," Ivor writes. "On cold days we were given a bun on coming out of the water: it was called 'a chittering bit'." This, I think, was the Glasgow equivalent of what we, in Edinburgh, knew as 'a chittery bite'.

Saturday afternoon was the time when one witnessed at Warrender the consumption of this innocent restorative, since that was the time when the premises were crowded out by young people from the poorer parts of our city. Admission was but a few pence—fourpence, I think. They came in swarms to invest their Saturday cash in something that, to *them*, was the highlight of *their* week. In so doing they added appreciably to the baths' revenue.

Once through the turnstile, however, it was doubtful whether they would be permitted to enjoy to the full what they anticipated, and what, indeed, they were entitled to. You must remember that, even then, public servants were beginning to conduct the institutions to which they were attached as though they existed primarily for *their* benefit. As the numbers of visitors so increased at Warrender on a Saturday afternoon that swimming virtually became impossible, instead of displaying at the ticket-office a notice to the effect that the

1 Published by Cape in 1948.

premises meantime were full, these young people were relieved of their pennies despite the fact that steps already had been taken to deprive them of what they rightly were entitled to, with a view to getting rid of them as quickly as possible. The meanest aspect of this fraud was the turning off of the hot sprays, on the false pretext that the water supplying them had run cold, although the temperature of constantly running sprays couldn't have been influenced by the numbers crowding round them. The illogicality of this reasoning—the dishonesty of it—never occurred to the victims. They just took it for granted that this was so.

That's one of the great assets of modern education. It mustn't be permitted to encourage logical, critical examination and deduction. The dates of the battles of long ago, and the unseemly ongoings of kings and their concubines are infinitely more important than one's capacity to sort out irrelevancies and social injustices. I know from personal experience that the education which produces the vaunted scientists of our time also produces men and women lamentably lacking in discernment and in powers of deduction in sociological matters where, quite clearly, the facts of a situation are not in dispute. This inability must be attributable in considerable measure to reading what are known euphemistically as the newspapers.

"And therefore?" one says to one's scientific friends. Well, they can't go further. The Mental Philosophies are so closed to them that they are unqualified to follow the logical implications. I had some shocking evidence of this recently when returning by sea with a friend popularly recognised as "a brilliant scientist". He knew everything about nuclear physics; but—my God!—discussion with him on any aspect whatsoever of human problems was entirely impossible. He wasn't even aware that there are hundreds, if not thousands, of millions of people in the world under-nourished. "If so," he observed, "and I doubt it, they themselves must be to blame." My physicist friend is no youngster. He's older than I am: he's sixty-six, anyway.

But I am straying a little—though not in principle—from those Saturday afternoons at Warrender when, with malice aforethought, the Beastly Bob Hardy was prime mover in turning off the hot sprays. Such cheek, I always deemed it! Obtaining gate-money by false pretences, I call it! Man's inhumanity to young people, over the years, making countless thousands shiver! Never was 'the chittery bite' more in evidence than at Warrender on those heartless Saturday afternoons.

In the heyday of our baths, soap was so plentiful that as much of it lay wasting on the sprayroom's floor, about one's warm, wet feet, as was to be found in the receptacles provided for its retention. Indeed, at times we amused ourselves by smearing the ceiling and white-tiled walls with the soft, viscous lumps into which we kneaded it. So frequently did we compete in sending pieces whizzing through the skylight high up in the roof, and always open a few inches to ventilate this hot and steamy apartment, that gutters and rones became choked with an accumulation not even the winter rains of Auld Reekie could dissolve and carry away. So it had to be scoured periodically with lashings of boiling water, and removed by shovel. Eventually some official, in the course of a tour of inspection, hit upon a brilliant counter measure in the form of a wire tray fitted externally to prevent any object larger than a marble from being expelled when the skylight was open. This simple device is still there. It must have saved many a ton of soap in the intervening years. Yet, I could not but envy certain older lads the skill with which, by a dexterous turn of wrist, they sent slices of our best Sunlight and Carbolic spinning out through the restricted aperture overhead.

The plastering of the walls and ceiling of this cloudy and soap-suddy place continued unchecked, however. So too did the periodic stopping up of the four fishtail gas-burners, one at each of the cardinal points of the bracket suspended from the ceiling in this abode of mirth and mischief. A leg up by one of the taller boys brought the burners within the reach of unruly fingers; and a good dubbing with soft soap ensured that no further light could be expected until an attendant arrived with steps and a bag of tools to unscrew the jets and replace them with others.

Never was there a gas-bracket that stood up more valiantly to so much rough treatment. I remember how we used to drape it with soaking towels, and then birl it round and round from below, having been assured by one of our number, son of a plumber and gas-fitter round the corner in Marchmont Road, that, however much we spun it round, it wouldn't unscrew and fall on our heads, as we sometimes feared. We never failed to give Mac a vociferous cheer when, at dusk, he entered the sprayroom with wobbly chair and blazing taper to light those burners.

At times the atmosphere of this sudatorium of ours was so dense that we saw him as through a mist when he came silently among us in his gum-boots to lighten our darkness. No sooner had the green swing-door banged behind him than we began to aim saturated towels at a specified burner untils omeone succeeded, amid an outburst of applause, in extinguishing it. Escaping gas now added its quota to an atmosphere already heavily charged with saponaceous fumes. And, since we all dreaded asphyxiation by gas, having often read of such tragedies in our local newspapers, a touch of alarm then seized us. Someone would dash out for a box of matches. Someone else, hoisted shoulder-high, would endeavour with wet, clammy fingers to re-light the burner before authority came on the scene. This was always a moment of tension—of anxiety heightened when the matches refused to ignite against the side of a matchbox held in a damp atmosphere by damp fingers. An element of panic was apt to invade the sprayroom on such occasions. Little wonder no bather could commit at the Warrender Baths an offence against public order and safety more serious than that of *taking a towel into the sprayroom!* Yet, to what revered law-lessness those tough towels lent themselves! Today pranks of this kind are a thing of the past: many years ago a protected electric light replaced that old and diverting gas-bracket.

Never did we attend more dutifully to our personal ablutions than when those sprays were hot and soap was abundant. I remember how we lathered our heads until we could fashion the suds into towering turbans, to be dissolved into nothingness, as if by magic, under the spray. We liked this strong soap, so extravagantly supplied for our capers in those spacious days by an indulgent municipality; and with one accord we pronounced effeminate the casual bather arriving in our midst with a cake of some scented variety, and perhaps his own private loofa! The former certainly lent to the sprayroom a perfume more pleasant than did the cheaper brands. But I well remember the scorn with which we eyed those occasional visitors who, ignoring our communal soap-dishes, fearful lest they derived infection therefrom, came with their own soap in metal containers. These they guarded jealously during their cleansing operations, in case any of us should sneak a wee rub of their precious contents. The exit from the spray-room of the 'refeened' possessor of soap too divinely exotic always called forth a very big and prolonged boo, and a volley of 'raspberries'.

There was yet another unlawful use to which soap was put. In our wayward moments, with the sprays still full on, we rubbed it into the interstices of the grating in the floor. Within a few minutes the floor would be standing some inches deep in water threatening to overflow the doorstep to find its sinuous way into other departments. Once or twice, but unintentionally, it was allowed to trickle down the back-stair toward laundry and boiler-house. That brought the boilerman aloft post-haste to see whether a pipe had burst, or something had sprung a leak. His wrath, as he found water oozing toward him from under the sprayroom door, you may well imagine. By this time, of course, the guilty had returned to the pond, and were already swim-ming, undistinguishably, with the innocent. A wet towel, neatly folded and placed over the sprayroom grating produced the same effect, and more efficiently. The towel also had the advantage of being movable. On the other hand, the soap's performance had the virtue of appearing as though it were accidental, whereas the very presence of a wet towel in the sprayroom indicated mischievous intent.

A trickle of water on that back-stair, or a wet footprint left thereon by someone who, familiar with the baths' dark, underground secrets, knew where and how to turn on, for the sprayroom, a better pressure of hot water, prompted frantic investigations on the part of those in charge.

The only other prank known to have brought an attendant as speedily on the scene was our beating the sprayroom floor with wet towels strung together like flails. Even with the door tightly shut, the reverberating slaps thus produced soon brought Mac among us in his waders, and often resulted in someone or other receiving a good, re-sounding skelp across his naked derriere with the very towel in the unlawful possession of which he had been caught red-handed!

Towels firmly knotted together formed an admirable tug-o'-war rope, and also the cordon sometimes necessary when we wanted to encircle and drag away a group of bathers who, in our view, had had more than their fair share of the spray. We also used towels deftly for tying the door-handle of the wee back lavatory, thus imprisoning some unsuspecting entrant who was obliged to remain there until his thump-ings on the door brought authority to his release. In short, we could have compiled a handbook entitled *Towels: Their Uses & Abuses*.

Oh! those days of peace and piping plenty! Plenty of everything. Plenty of soap, of towels, of water, hot and cold, and plenty of time to enjoy them all, and exploit their limitless possibilities. Just after the First World War, and therefore at the dawn of my Golden Lamp Era, we began to experience at Warrender less of everything. To counteract our former extravagance with soap, a special Sumptuary Law was passed. The intending washer of himself now had to ask Mac to be good enough to give him a fragment from his locker. Mac always complied, but never to any greater extent than was necessary for dealing with the surface area of one human body of average size. Strict economy had displaced wilful waste.

As for towels, one per bather, per occasion, became the rule, whereas adults as a matter of course had always been supplied with a white smooth and a coffee-coloured rough. As for hot water, a single spray, somewhat enfeebled, had to suffice where we had known three or four pouring forth, under pressure, their abundance of good cheer, of health-giving and warmth, when one had remained rather long in the chilling pond.

What more soothing than this or, perhaps, a long steeping in one of the plunge-baths round the corner, and in water as deep as the position of the overflow would allow? If not considered deep enough even then, all one had to do was to lie back in order to place the ball of a foot over it until the water rose to the very brim, and nothing but absolute stillness, in conjunction with capillary attraction, prevented its spilling over. The cautious removal of the foot soon relieved this capillary tension.

Lying back lazily in this welter of warmth, and manipulating—*pedi*pulating, if one might coin the word—the taps with one's toes, so that water, cool or bubbling with steam, might be added as desired, without the irksome exertion of sitting up to turn them by hand, one recalled during those Golden Lamp years, as I already have done in these pages, one's lousy, mud-encrusted self in the holocaust of Flanders. Immersed in such felicity, I could not but ask myself whether there existed in Heaven itself anything more desirable than ready access to the warming, comforting, cleansing qualities of abundant hot water. If any reader should have experienced trench warfare, when for weeks on end it rained, and one stood there without ever getting one's wringing-wet clothing off, he will appreciate the significance of this. It seemed odd that so innocent a pleasure, so civilised a necessity as a bath, should have become the thing one craved for above all else the world could offer.

The blitz impressed the truth of this on tens of thousands in this country. Those of us dealing with the blitzed in London soon discovered that, particularly when they were suffering from mild shock, a basin of hot water gave a greater measure of relief and solace than food and a hot drink. Yet, we go on with our wars and our inventions for bigger and better killing and, in our nationalistic strivings for supremacy in this field, subject one another to degrees of inhuman discomfort which even primitive man has never imposed upon himself.

The sprayroom's *place de résistance* in the years I seek to commemorate was the Hot Tub, a large, tiled, rectangular basin about fifteen inches in depth, at one end of which a silvery pipe, its function controlled by a hot and a cold tap readily reached by leaning a little outwards, furnished us with the most delectable facilities for sousing ourselves. When living in Malaya, I watched water-buffaloes behaving just as we did in the Hot Tub. "My word, old chap!" I sometimes said, "I know from experience exactly how you feel, wallowing contentedly there after a day's ploughing in the paddy-fields!"

How many did that Hot Tub hold? The answer to this depends on what you mean. It held at least a dozen little boys, closely seated,

their knees drawn up to their chins. It held, very uncomfortably, eight
adults, after a scramble for places in its warmth. It was at all times
the scene of wild competition, of mirth and hilarity. Not infrequently
it was also the scene of lusty choral exercises. All the contemporary
music-hall ditties were given full recognition there. I remember
particularly the verve with which we rendered Fred Leigh's little song,
Put on your Tat-ta, Little Girlie!

I remember even more clearly our Hot Tub's theme-song, *I used
to sigh for the Silvery Moon*. We had picked it up from the Chocolate-
Coloured Coon himself during one of his appearance at the Empire.[1]
In turning over the pages of our Watsonian War Record the other day,
my eye fell upon the entry concerning a lad named Louis Cowan,
killed at Ypres in 1915, at the age of 19, while serving with the Dandy
Ninth—with the 9th Royal Scots. Louis was one of the most promising
swimmers of our generation.

Such of us as knew him, and are still alive, also remember him for
his sprayroom renderings of *I used to sigh for the Silvery Moon*. To
these he treated us with all the Chocolate-Coloured Coon's mannerisms,
a towel suitably arranged on his head to resemble the Coon's head-
gear. Louis instantly put us right when, in seeking to imitate him in
this rôle, we made mistakes.

The sprayroom was also a sort of phrontistery where we devised
our own variations on Classical themes and music-hall quips. The
former consisted chiefly of Latin and French tags mispronounced and
misapplied; whereas an edifying sample of the latter ran something like
this:

"Good God!" screamed the Duchess, waving her wooden leg.

Years afterwards I accidentally came upon what well may have
been the origin of this. The playwright, Lennox Robinson, had had
a play rejected by Hollywood, because it lacked the five essentials to
popular acceptance as understood in the United States. (One wonders
how many books have been turned down by publishers in recent years
because of these same deficiencies!) The five missing essentials, as
Hollywood informed Robinson, were Religious Sentiment, High-Life,

[1] George Henry Elliott, that charming light comedian of our youth, who
enjoyed many years of popularity on the music-hall stage as the Chocolate-Coloured Coon, was born at Rochdale in 1884, and died in a Brighton
nursing-home in November, 1962, at the age of 78. He was a singer in the
tradition of Eugene Stratton. In his own songs, as *The Times* put it, he
was a memorable and taking artist with a light voice that broke easily into
a yodel. His reddish-brown make-up and white linen suit combined effec-
tively with his agile, if unpretentious, soft-shoe dancing and his tricks of
singing to give individuality to his performances. His repertory of tuneful
songs pleased generations of audiences. The song I have mentioned was,
perhaps, his most popular.

Dramatic Surprise, Sex-Appeal, and Brevity. With these in mind, he promptly devised the following sentence embracing all five:
  "My God!" said the Duchess. "Let go my leg!"

When hoarse with singing the popular ditties, we converted the Hot Tub into a place of conundrums. In this wallow of a setting, we invented our own when the answers to the usual repertoire were already too well known to those steeping themselves there. Our extempore efforts in this field were designed to make things a little less tedious for the smaller boys anxiously and enviously standing by, waiting an opportunity of getting into the Hot Tub. The example I recall best was that propounded by the notable swimmer and trick diver, Willie Porter, the lad whose concussion, as related in an earlier chapter, put an end to our diving off the rafters. I doubt whether even Ptolemy's celebrated Almagest could have provided an acceptable answer to Willie's memorable conundrum:

If it take an elephant three weeks to walk a fortnight, how many grapes are there in a barrel of apples?

The prize offered was admission to the Most Noble Order of the Hot Tub. This was an award too coveted to allow of the riddle's being ignored. Many an innocent laddie stood there, knitting his brows, racking his brains, waiting for inspiration, painfully aware that nothing short of his finding the answer would qualify him for adding his little extra self to the densely packed fraternity already overspilling the sides of the Hot Tub!

A favourite caper, as well as an unfailing source of annoyance, was that of the boy who habitually sat in the Hot Tub with a slightly punctured rubber-ball. By squeezing the air out of it, and holding it under the water, he filled it, and then played a fine jet on the lips or eyes of his companions squatting contentedly there, in this warm and sleep-inducing basin. The ball, trained on the mouth of someone about to speak, usually brought matters to a climax, for a mouthful of bathers' water unwittingly acquired in this manner was tantamount to a premeditated assault upon the person, and invariably precipitated a violent scrimmage in which possession of the ball was the objective. Finally, the ball received the rent through which the offender himself was now soused with gallons of his own medicine.

A jet-player whose propensity demanded sterner measures was a certain Alastair Murray. We envied Alastair the hole he had between two of his front teeth. Through this, while seated among us in the Hot Tub, he was able to squirt long, thin jets from water taken into the mouth for this none too sanitary exercise. He was popular with those who admired the skilful purpose to which he put this dental defect of his, though it earned him many a scragging from those whose unguarded lips received a powerful squirt from his!

The favourite lad among us at this time, I should add, was employed in some quite juvenile capacity in "The Trade". This explained how he was in a position to bring with him to our baths sample bottles of liqueurs—Drambuie and the like. For these, the older swimmers competed, and, in their bravado, affected to enjoy.

My final recollection of our Hot Tub is a personal one. On the very first occasion on which, as a boy of ten, I managed to squeeze myself into it, in face of much hefty opposition, a couple of medical students, intrigued by the Invernessian intonation of my speech, encouraged me to converse with them.

"What's your name?" one of them asked.

"Well, if you *must* know, I'm Kelly," I replied. "I'm Kelly from the Isle of Man!"

Ever after, I was known as Kelly MacGregor, or merely as Kelly. For years this nickname annoyed me—unreasonably, I think. It survived the First World War and, indeed, the Second also. In the nineteen-twenties, even after I had published three or four books, there were people living in Edinburgh who did not recognise me as the author of them. I see from a note in an old diary that I went to a party where my host, as unostentatiously and unembarrassingly as possible, began to hand a couple of my books round among his guests. "My God!" exclaimed one of them, a man I had known for years. "I always thought your name was Kelly. I've never known you by any other!"

"You've done literature and me a vast injustice!" I replied. "How do you propose to rectify it?"

"Are these books in print? If so, I'll undertake to buy them tomorrow."

He actually did so! They reached me by post a few days later for my autograph, with return postage duly affixed. The note accompanying them was brief and explanatory enough: "My God, Kelly! I do apologise for having been so long in discovering that you were Alasdair Alpin MacGregor! Who would have thought that yon daft bastard I've known all these years would ever write a book?"

Let me pursue this theme a little further. A couple of years ago, when living in Toronto, I was interviewed one evening on television. The programme was over but a few minutes when the producer informed me that I was wanted on the telephone.

"Hello, Kelly! How long are you to be in Toronto? Aren't you coming to see us?"

"*Of course,* I am!" I replied, quite instinctively, even before I knew to whom I was speaking. I did know immediately, however, that it was somebody with an Edinburgh background. The accent was unmistakably that of an educated man from Edinburgh.

My caller was Thomas Shirreff Ronaldson, eldest of three Watsonian brothers whom I knew, two of whom, as I also knew, enlisted in the 4th Royal Scots in September, 1914, and fell on the Western Front during the First World War. You know the war I mean —the one we fought to make the world safe for democracy and all that sort of thing. Although Tom Ronaldson and I had seen nothing of one another since he left Edinburgh for Canada forty years earlier, it seemed perfectly natural that he should have addressed me as Kelly. I spent several evenings with him and his family thereafter; and not once did he refer to me except by the nickname I had earned for myself in that Hot Tub, so many years ago.

As might have been expected after so long an interval, those evenings with Tom in Toronto were devoted mainly to Watsonian matters, and the fate of such of our contemporaries as we could recall—among them, of course, Tom's fallen brothers, John and George, both of whom I remember very clearly, for the Ronaldsons were a distinctive family when at Watson's, and their 'old man' a well-known Edinburgh citizen. There were ten in that family—seven boys and three girls. "We were badly messed up in two wars," as Tom put it. "Six of the boys and two of the girls served under fire in uniform."

Our exchange of Watsonian reminiscences brought to mind many of our contemporaries who subsequently attained some measure of prominence. In writing me of them the other day, Tom mentioned three. "A little reflected glory—W. S. Morrison and I were fellow-Sgts. in the O.T.C. at Watson's. We shot at Bisley together. Dave Fyfe of the Woolsack was a recruit in my section. Jas. Robb is also a product of the Cadet Corps of that day. Alas! the glory is verily reflected—and a bit diluted—so far as *I* am concerned.'

The W. S. Morrison referred to was, of course, the late William Shepherd Morrison, Victor Branford's Demosthenic friend and contemporary at Edinburgh University, already referred to in Chapter Six. Willie, renowned in his student days for his rhetoric during debate at the University Union, was born in 1893. Many of his finest speeches were contrived at Miss Aitken's, during rhetorical occasions staged there by Victor and himself, with me crouched in a corner, that they might have as much freedom of movement as Victor's room allowed.

Willie and Victor, in turn: "Friends, Romans, Countrymen, lend me your ears! I come to—"

Miss Aitken, entering to lip-read the line: "Never mind burying Caesar! Ye can leave him a whilie where he lies, till aifter supper onyway. The supper's dished up in the kitchen. Ye'll be better able to deal wi' the corpse when ye've supped, Willie!"

Davie Fyfe is no longer on the Woolsack. They got him off it in 1962! He is now Earl Kilmuir. My early associations with him at George Watson's are recorded in *Auld Reekie: Portrait of a Lowland Boyhood.*

Jimmie Robb is Air Chief Marshall Sir James Milne Robb in more conventional circles. He retired from the active list in 1951, and now lives in Devon, pursuing there his ornithological and archaeological interests.

Tom Ronaldson, born in 1895, was taken prisoner at the Second Battle of Ypres. That is to say, in April, 1915. This was the first occasion on which poison gas was used in warfare. In the spring of 1918, Tom was transferred to Holland whence, after a diagnosis of spinal T.B., he was repatriated in the autumn of that year.

His brother, John, born in 1897, went through the Dardanelles campaign, and afterwards received a commission with the Cameron Highlanders. He fell at Vimy Ridge on Easter Monday, 1917, and now lies buried in a military cemetery at Arras. The Battle of Arras, fought in two stages that April (on the 9th and 23rd) carried to death that bit of the volunteering flower of the nation which had survived the disastrous offensive we opened on the Somme on July, 1st, of the previous year.

George Ronaldson, born in 1899, was transferred from the Royal Scots to the Royal Scots Fusiliers (the Cameronians), and fell near Ypres in November, 1917. He lies buried in Hooge Crater Cemetery, where recently I saw his name engraven.

It was Tom Ronaldson who brought back to mind a rather remarkable contemporary of ours at Watson's—much more remarkable than all the Lords Chancellor, Speakers of the House of Commons, and sundry Cabinet Ministers who received their early education there. I refer to William Gordon Brown, son of a Heraldic Stationer in Edinburgh. Like Tom, Willie Brown was born in 1895. In 1901 he became a pupil at George Watson's, where he remained until 1914, his school years rendered the more pleasurable through his having been the nephew of the beloved Miss Seggie, then on the staff of the infant department.

In 1914 Willie gained the Glass Bursary for Mathematics, and also the George Watson Higher Bursary. At the outbreak of war in August of that year, he enlisted as a private in the Royal Scots, saw service at Gallipoli, and was invalided home. Shortly afterwards he re-enlisted, this time in the Royal Naval Division. In November, 1916, he fell on the Western Front, at Beaumont-Hamel.

"I've always said it was a bloody disgrace that he was ever taken into the army at all," Sandy MacKenzie, a classmate of his, wrote me the other day. "Physically, he was a poor, pale-faced chap, who could scarcely carry a rifle. But what a brain!" When I have told you a little more about Willie, you may feel inclined to agree that it was much worse than a bloody disgrace.

No one who came into contact with Willie Brown failed to recognise something rather remarkable about him, something original, something transcendental about his quality of mind. As was written of him, shortly after his death, by one who had reason to know something of his immense intellectual powers, his school career, from its outset, showed his amazing aptitude for Mathematics. His range of subjects was legion, his knowledge encyclopaedic. In the midst of his preöccupation with the higher branches of Mathematics, he found time to be secretary of the school's Literary Club. Those who knew him at Watson's recall that deferential little stutter with which he ventured to interpose, during the lesson, some awe-inspiring question of his that startled the masters. Quite often he presented the mathematical pundits on the staff of George Watson's with problems beyond their comprehension, with theories wholly outwith their understanding.

While serving as a private soldier, Willie pursued as best he could his mathematical inquiries, and in 1915 had the distinction of contributing to *The Philosophical Magazine* a paper entitled 'Note on Reflections from a Moving Mirror,' and of providing the mathematical theory of a phenomenon in optics. As was said at the time when Willie enunciated his theory, the only two men who, during their undergraduate days, had ever achieved anything quite so brilliant in the field of science were Clerk-Maxwell and Kelvin.

Willie's paper, some little time after his death, was brought to the notice of the celebrated Sir J. J. Thomson, at that time Cavendish Professor of Experimental Physics at Cambridge. Thomson described it as a very remarkable achievement for so young a man. "I feel sure he would have attained eminence in Science, had he been spared."

Willie left behind him other papers, some of which were placed before the Royal Society of Edinburgh. These dealt, *inter alia,* with tubes of electric force in a four-dimensional space. They testify to Willie's having arrived, independently, at the same conclusions regarding Relativity as did Albert Einstein. Indeed, our Willie Brown may well have anticipated Einstein, who did not issue his general theory until 1915, the year in which, quite independently, Willie was busy in that field—the year in which, as we have seen, his startling paper was published. Einstein was then 36: Willie was 20. I think the late Dr. John Alison, headmaster at George Watson's during our time, told me that Willie had been in correspondence with Einstein on fourth-dimensional matters.

William Gordon Brown, dead at Beaumont-Hamel in 1916, at the age of 21! What a waste! War destroys, without discrimination, the strong of sinew and the mighty of intellect.

To some inspiration I wist not of, I feel grateful that this volume should have afforded me an opportunity of recording the foregoing about one whose lot—

The world forgetting, by the world forgot.

CHAPTER TWELVE

The Fantastic Field of Figures

OF COURSE, Willie Brown's uncanny faculty for Mathematics was recognised at George Watson's College even by those of us who were some years younger. I, as a pupil particularly backward in this field, dreading every examination I had to sit, sorely envied him this. By the time I had come under Miss Aitken's care and was deriving inspiration from my Golden Lamp, I realised that the five years' University curriculum upon which I was about to embark would entail a process of planning calculated to ensure the selection of roughly a dozen subjects including certain of the *Mental*, rather than of the *Natural*, Philosophies. The arithmetical solution to any problem assailing me henceforth, I could well leave to Miss Aitken, always a little hesitant about my own calculations until I had seen what results *she* had obtained to such as I was obliged to make from time to time. She was good at figures; and often I would break off my writing to dash into the kitchen, interrupting her reading with a little problem urgently requiring expert supervision. A minute or two later she would enter very quietly to lay by my elbow a scrap of paper with the whole thing correctly worked out. What a landlady!

In the light of what my more discerning friends have told me during the years intervening, I incline to their view that my mathematical incompetence was due to faulty teaching at Watson's, right from the outset of my six sessions there. Faulty where *I* was concerned, though eminently suitable where almost everybody else was concerned. I had arrived at my *pons asinorum* long before I turned the page to Euclid's Fifth Proposition. Yet, as readers of *Auld Reekie: Portrait of a Lowland Boyhood* will remember, little was done to help me to cross it. No step was taken to encourage *me* to emulate those numerous Auld Reekie schoolboys who carried in a blazer pocket, as the hallmark of intellectual attainment, a tiny manual of mathematical tables—those logarithms and anti-logarithms, those natural and log sines, co-sines and tangents, co-tangents and secants, co-secants and squares, cubes and roots, circular and radian measure—Price: One Shilling. Such

119

a terrific bob's-worth, I always thought, although hardly the sort of thing I would have spent a bob on! Yet, so very fitting in Auld Reekie, as I must concede. All in the true John Napier tradition. This you will appreciate when I remind you that the radian is the angle subtended at the centre of a circle by an arc equal to the radius, nearly $57°.3$. It's as simple as that!

If any mentor or master had spotted in a pocket of mine printed matter as significant as that little manual, it would have been sensational. Indeed, in Sheridan's words, he would have been struck all of a heap.

In the quiet reflection of my Golden Lamp, I was not slow to recognise that, even had I desired it, there was now neither time nor opportunity to make up, in this noble field, a leeway greatly increased by those wasted years of war, and that the Arts and some Law, with a probable bias toward Letters, would be the sort of province most likely to claim me. So I began to give a thought to literary matters, especially to literary form, although aware that this was a matter of import to relatively few. Hoi Polloi, even then, studied form all right, but only in race-horses, whippets, and film stars. The vital statistics of the last mentioned have since become a very serious branch of figurative fact-finding.

One singular achievement of mine in Geometry I must record, however, since I went to the trouble some years ago to make a special trip to the new George Watson's College, in Colinton Road, in order to certify whether there existed documentary proof of it, or whether I had carried for thirty years and more the delusion that on one solitary occasion my mathematical mind was so lucid for the space of one hour as to have earned me One Hundred Percentum.

Was this accidental? Yes, I think it must have been!

Had I been lucky enough to guess, in time for preparation, the questions on that examination paper? Yes, I think I must have!

I hardly need say that my father was so startled by the entry of 100% in Geometry in that term's school report as to have wondered what his blockhead of a son had been up to. He was convinced either of collusion or of some grave error. Someone had blundered. Otherwise it was a clear case of favouritism on the part of Bunny Philip.[1] That eminent Doctor of Science, you must understand, was a Gaelic-speak-

---

[1] Dr. George Philip, a brilliant Mathematician and Natural Philosopher, died in 1937, at the age of 59. He joined the staff of George Watson's in 1906, and remained on it until 1919, the year he was appointed Director of Education for Ross & Cromarty, at Dingwall, in the county of which he was a native.

ing Highlander. His mother-in-law was a Lewiswoman whom my father knew well. In fact, she was a connection of ours. My classmates, aware of all this, were convinced, therefore, that my One Hundred Percentum was attributable solely to a bit of Highland nepotism. It was generally agreed that I, a certified dunderhead, could never repeat this feat under another master. This was, assuredly, the unkindest cut of all!

Just as every cloud is said to have a silver lining, every silver lining would appear—certainly to me in the present context—to have its cloud. My achievement that term in Geometry was suitably counterbalanced by an achievement in Algebra of ₅%. This was actually in the nature of an *ex gratia* award. After all, I had written my name clearly on the outside of my exam. paper, and had at least been gracious enough to register an appearance on this formidable occasion. That was worth something. Furthermore, I had patiently put in a vacant hour whilst others around me were confidently recording their quadratics and the like.

In recalling this Algebraic performance of mine, I quail at the thought of Dr. John Wallis, whom one supposes to have been among the most distinguished mathematicians since Newton. Do you realise that, as a boy of fourteen, already proficient in Hebrew and the Classics, already versed in Logic, already an accomplished Musician, this seventeenth-century mathematician spent his holidays in poring over arithmetic, not as a formal study, but as a pleasing diversion during his spare hours? Small wonder he was able one evening to extract the square-root of a number expressed by 53 figures, and accurately dictate the result to 27 places the following morning! A brain such as his was well able to discover the principle of the differential calculus, and to invent the symbol for infinity.[1]

While reading late one night at Miss Aitken's I reached the ungenerous conclusion that Charles Darwin's arithmetic, like my own, wasn't too reliable. Dipping into his stupendous *Origin of Species* in the quietude of my Golden Lamp, I came upon the passage where he remarks, on the authority of Linnaeus, that, if an annual plant produced no more than two seeds (and there exists no plant quite so unproductive), and their seedlings produced two the following year, and so on, there would be a million plants at the end of twenty years.

Now, one does not require to be much of a dab at maths. to discover

[1] One of the founders of the Royal Society, he was, for over half a century, Savilian Professor of Geometry at Oxford. His *Arithmetica Infinitorum*, published in 1655, when he was forty, contains the germs of the differential calculus.

this, *plus* half as many seeds again. Even *I* can make an attempt at a calculation of this sort, and without my having to rely on somebody of the stature of Linnaeus. What Auld Reekie boy, educated in a city revering the name of John Napier of Merchiston, that distinguished citizen of old, has not derived *something* helpful in arriving at the sort of conclusion Darwin ought to have worked out for himself in the matter of plant increase? Certainly, during my own schoolhood there, father reminded me often enough that at Merchiston, but a few minutes' walk from our home, Napier, in 1614, delivered himself of his immense and amazing *Mirifici Logarithorum Canonis Descriptio*. The following year his *Rabdologia* explained the use of those numerating rods popularly known as 'Napier's bones', and the metal plates for effecting multiplications and divisions. In this, he invented the earliest form of the calculating machine, now so universally in use. Four years later, and therefore two years posthumously, his *Constructio* was published. So you appreciate the extent to which he simplified for a rather important section of mankind all manner of calculations. It cannot but be regretted that his achievements, like countless others in the realm of Science, do not appear to have helped mankind toward much in the way of *moral* attainment.

The problem of estimating (as I still was able to do in the inspiring glow of my Golden Lamp) the increase in the number of seeds is merely one of raising 2 to the 20th power. That is to say, calculating what 2^{20} amounts to.

Now, the logarithm of 2 is .3010. Multiply that by 20, and you get 6.0200.

Look up the anti-logarithm of 6.0200, and you will find that it works out at 1,470,000. It's as easy as that!

So you see that Darwin, in accepting Linnaeus's conservative estimate, was nearly half a million seeds short. Just in case some reader might think I write a little disrespectfully of him, however, let me correct any such impression.

The year, 1958, was the centenary of the occasion upon which were read before the Linnaean Society of London those profound communications from Charles Darwin and Alfred Russel Wallace. The year, 1962, was the centenary of the two lectures on Evolution which Huxley delivered in Edinburgh. They prompt the question as to whether, in the realm of scientific inquiry, there has ever existed, contemporaneously, and in the same country, such brilliance. One need read no more than half a page of the stupendous 'Origin' to realise what that titanic trio—Darwin, Wallace, and Huxley—achieved. We are, to so large an extent, the unworthy inheritors of their incalculable knowledge and application, of the fruits of their epic devotion, since most of us are better informed on trivial matters of radio and football pools.

In seeking to assess the achievements of this trio, one instantly sees what pious nonsense is the declaration that all men are equal, other than conventionally "in the eyes of God"—whatever that may mean in these days when, in face of the insane recrudescence of nationalism the world over, largely encouraged by ourselves, Our Christ is slowly dying again in our midst.

I have never perceived anything irreligious in the findings and pronouncements of these three very great men. I see nothing heretical in the concept of agnosticism. On the contrary, I see in their findings a sober and profound basis for a decent Humanism.

Of the fantastic field of figures, there is little I have ever been able to master, and as little I seem to have remembered of the little I once thought I had. However, I do recall the mnemonic for π to thirteen decimal places. Together with the corresponding figure which the number of letters in each word signifies, it runs like this:

How I wish I could recollect of circle round
3 1 4 1 5 9 2 6 5

The exact relation Arch'medes found!
3 5 8 9 5

Thus we have fourteen words denoting thirteen places after the decimal:

3.1415926535895.

Is it not to be deplored that to some this is simplicity itself, whereas to others it should be unmitigated torment?

There was one particular type of dream I longed for, both at school and at college, but with which alas! I was never favoured. I refer to that which would have disclosed beforehand questions set in an impending examination paper. That such dreams have been dreamt, I have no doubt. Indeed, I recall an established instance. It occurred when a clergyman named Morris, at one time chaplain of Walton Gaol, Liverpool, was sitting a series of exams. at Cheltenham for a school-master's certificate.

The distracted entrant spent the evening before his Geometry ordeal in trying to spot the questions he might be asked. That night he dreamt he was sitting in the examination hall with the pertinent paper lying on the desk in front of him. When he woke, he remembered so clearly the questions that he immediately applied himself to their solution. When the examiners distributed the appropriate question-paper among the candidates at the appointed hour that day, lo! he found to his astonishment that the questions set were precisely those he had seen in his dream. He obtained full marks.

How singularly helpful it must have been to be able to dream like that! Had *I* been as fortuitously endowed, I would have achieved with the greatest ease my father's prime ambition for me, namely, that I should pass with distinction into the Indian Civil.

On such dreaming, Mr. Brian Wicks, of Malmesbury Road, Chippenham, believing that every worried examinee must at least have dreamed of the opportunity of having a pre-view of his examination papers, wrote to *The Times* in the autumn of 1960, mentioning that, prior to his finals, he requested copies of old exam. papers. The university authorities obligingly posted him those of the impending examination. Unfortunately for Mr. Wicks, they discovered their mistake before *he* did!

In the matter of the exam. papers that confronted me throughout three or four of my Golden Lamp years, there is no saying to what heights a little prevision in dreams might have carried me!

CHAPTER THIRTEEN

William Roughead, W. S.

MR. MOSS AND HIS WEEK'S GOOD DEED

IF IT had occurred to me during those Golden Lamp years at Miss Aitken's that one day I might have felt encouraged to set down all these ongoings, I would have kept a diary, or at least made notes at the time on people and incidents likely to be of use when putting together pages such as these. A few written observations on the persons with whom one came in contact would assuredly be helpful now. They would at all events confirm, or otherwise, matters of chronology where memory may be faulty and fanciful.

Even without this aid, I recall fairly clearly certain fellow bathers at Warrender, particularly those elderly ones who crowded selfishly round the hot sprays with an air of imperturbable priority, compelling such of us as were young to wait until they had finished reminding one another of this and of that when *they* were young. Their big talk, designed to impress the feebler specimens of mankind meantime shivering around them, was but a pretext for their gerontocratic exchanges.

"Mind the day, Wullie, when we used tae dive frae the Chain Pier?"

"Ay, my, Rab! Ah dae *that!*"

This was an indication that they were about to embark on reminiscences certain to delay indefinitely their moving away from the sprays so that others might enjoy them. They must needs impress us once again—and in these very words—with their aquatic heroics in the years before most of us were born.

The Chain Pier at Trinity, forsooth! It was swept away by a storm in 1898, roughly a quarter of a century before the period with which this volume is mainly concerned. Listening to those vain old fellows, however, as they monopolised the sprays, one would have thought they were recalling their experiences in antediluvian times. In the end, patience was rewarded: sheer ennui eventually carried them tottering from the sprayroom to their towels.

One of the less selfish of that generation was an Episcopalian clergyman whom I remember very clearly, for he and I were to become good

125

friends—so good, indeed, that, when he moved to a living in one of our woollen towns in the Borders, he promptly invited me to spend a week's holiday with him there. But by now the Borders were less accessible: I already had moved to London.

Our Pisky's ritual at the baths never varied. After half-an-hour's soak in the sprayroom, he toddled forth to make his usually uncouth dive—knees improperly bent, with resounding result! He did not surface immediately. Oh dear no! Rather than be seen at the spot where he had crashed, he swam a complete length underwater, to emerge at the shallow end, blowing and bloated. This he did, as he once told me, in the hope of arousing apprehension for his survival in Mac, the most lovable and capable of our curators in those days. But Mac paid no heed. The water then was far too clear and transparent to allow of this swimmer's deceiving anybody as to his whereabouts when he remained rather long below.

When feigning death on one occasion, he lay at the foot of the pond like a drowned lobster. The youngest of our attendants did get alarmed at this. He thought our Pisky visitor had really carried his pretence too far—had perhaps struck the bottom with his head, and been rendered unconscious. Rushing for the long-handled scoop with which the pond's sides were washed down at intervals, he thrust it under our Pisky's centre of gravity, and proceeded to fish him out. This infuriated him. Thomas Bunyan (since that was the name of this frequent scooper of bathers in difficulties) got a hearty dressing-down! He unwittingly had unfrocked the elderly cleric, obliging him, in full view of a score or more of spectators now assembled at the scene of operations, to step ashore without his pants, blushing from head to toe at this indecent exposure of his person.

The Pilgrim's Progress of our twentieth-century Thomas Bunyan was everything the most ambitious could have desired. When last I heard from him, he had graduated from scoop to superintendent-in-chief of Edinburgh's several swimming-baths.

Some quite eminent people dipped their frames at Warrender, among them one whom I got to know well, having rescued him from drowning there, as he was going down for the last time. Not for some days afterwards, however, did I learn who he was.

The incident occurred at an hour when the baths are usually deserted, except for an occasional visitor whose time is his own, and who can therefore bathe when the place is at its quietest, and even the attendant need hardly be within call. In any case, at the moment concerned, the attendant was downstairs at his gas-ring, brewing a pot of tea for his late lunch. The pond lay still, as a comely, courteous, and distinguished-looking bather, roughly thirty years my senior, emerged from the sprayroom to descend, rather slowly, the marble steps at the deep end. There was nobody present to witness this but myself. The mild disturbance his entering the water occasioned had scarcely reached the shallow end when I heard a gentle plop—just a little noise such as one associates with a silent pool at eventide when a leaping trout falls back to send forth a series of concentric and ever-widening rings.

I didn't pay any notice to this until I heard it a second time. Now scanning the surface of the water, I observed something not so much afloat as awash. Dashing along the bank, I plunged in to retrieve that sinking something. Whoever he was, he showed his profound gratitude when sufficiently recovered. I escorted him quietly to his box. Twenty minutes later we were both leaving the baths in our respective directions.

The incident was one to which I had no occasion to give further thought until a week or so later, when I was reminded of it in a casual way.

"Yon man ye saved—he was askin' me for yer address," said Mac. "Ah telt 'im it. He's wantin' tae write ye a word o' thanks."

"But I don't think he even knows who I am!" I replied.

"He kens noo," Mac answered. "There wasna a soul he could ask, he telt me. When he mentioned a collie-dog waitin' for ye, Ah kent fine. That would be Ruairi. The three o' ye left thegither."

"And who is he anyway?" I enquired. Mac was astonished that I didn't already know.

"Yon's Wullie Rougheid ye saved! Wullie Rougheid, Writer tae His Majesty's Signet. My! ye'll be famous all ower the Court o' Session by this time." (Mac, you see, was pawky like Miss Aitken.)

To be sure, a letter of thanks did arrive a day or two later. It came from a posh Edinburgh address—12, Belgrave Crescent. Through this incident began my acquaintanceship with a man whom I corresponded with in a desultory way up to the year of his death in 1952, but whom the reader may not yet have identified. He was William Roughead, W.S., that popular doyen of criminologists, author or editor of some twenty substantial volumes on crime and criminals. He was responsible for several in the *Notable British Trials* Series, published over the years by William Hodge & Company, the well-known law publishers. These carefully documented volumes by Roughead occupy an important place in the literature of crime.

William Roughead was born in 1870, and admitted a member of the Society of Writers to the Signet in 1893. While still an apprentice, he happened to attend the trial of Jessie King, the baby farmer. With this began his lifelong interest in criminology which found expression in the steady succession of volumes resulting from his patient and meticulous examination of old court records, newspaper files, and many an obscure source of information. These volumes gained considerable popularity in the United States, as well as in this country. The first of them, published in 1906, dealt with the trial of Dr. Pritchard, whose execution in 1865, for the murder of wife and mother-in-law, was the last to take place publicly in Glasgow. Subsequent volumes were devoted to the trials of Deacon Brodie, Captain Porteous, Burke and Hare, Oscar Slater, and so on.

Throughout nearly two decades of doubts and misgivings arising from the trial in 1909 of the German Jew, Oscar Slater, on the charge of having murdered Miss Marion Gilchrist the previous year, Roughead remained closely associated with Arthur Conan Doyle in the contention that there had been a shocking miscarriage of justice, and that, upon such evidence as was led, Slater should never have been convicted. He had been sentenced to death. Less than three weeks later, this capital sentence was commuted to penal servitude for life.

In 1927 he was released. In 1928, nineteen years after a jury, by a majority of nine to six, had found the panel guilty as libelled, and Lord Guthrie had assumed the black cap and pronounced sentence of death in the usual form, Oscar Slater's conviction was quashed on Appeal. He regained his freedom through the untiring efforts of Conan Doyle and others, whose agitation at last resulted in the reopening of his case. At this, Roughead gave additional evidence showing that on legal grounds the conviction could not be upheld.

At that hearing I myself was present. It took place within the High Court of Justiciary, at Edinburgh, on July, 9th, 1928, before the Lord Justice-General (Lord Clyde), the Lord Justice-Clerk (Lord Alness), and Lords Sands, Blackburn, and Fleming. I well remember it. Years before this, I had entertained my first doubts about Capital Punishment. Since listening to that Appeal, I have been rigorously opposed to it, particularly when one realises how easily the innocent can be 'framed' by politicians, police, and crown authorities.

Nowhere can one find a more glaring and discreditable example than the Oscar Slater Case of the persistence with which The Establishment, whether in Parliament, in Local Government, in the Church, or elsewhere in executive authority, uses public resources to perpetuate injustices to individuals, to conceal wrongs committed—often vindictively—by public officials, and to persecute those who would have such wrongs put right. Power certainly corrupts; and in reviewing the published evidence available on this case, one cannot but recall the

The late George Denholm, miller at Preston Mill

The old pack-bridge spanning the Gala Water at Stow

Allan Cameron
MacDougall on his
Graduation Day at
Glasgow in 1915

Gwoa as I knew him

terrifying reality of Lord Acton's dictum.

Four Secretaries for Scotland (Lord Pentland, McKinnon Wood, Lord Alness, who, as Robert Munro, occupied that office from 1916 until 1922, and Sir John Gilmour) refused to do anything about this shocking state of affairs, even though the inaccuracies of the Lord Advocate's speech, Lord Guthrie's misdirection to the jury, and the highly dubious conduct of the Glasgow City Police in regard to the case, were common knowledge among those who are disturbed by injustice.

The only politician who showed any conscience in the matter was Ramsay MacDonald. Not until 1927, when Ramsay was Leader of the Opposition, and it had been rumoured that he meant to raise it in the Commons, was anything done. This splendid Scot, so universally hated and abused by foe, so traduced by erstwhile friend, had allowed himself to be fully informed on the wilful injustice of retaining Slater in prison. In September, 1927, he wrote: " . . . I have been going into the case, and am quite convinced that this man has received a most horrible injustice, and that the matter must be wound up, not only by releasing him, but by clearing him. What further steps can be taken to indemnify him and to carry the charge into other channels, is another matter."

I believe Ramsay MacDonald to be the greatest public figure of our time. I see him as a man of deep conviction and unswerving integrity who, one day, in contradistinction to the Baldwins and the Winston Churchills of public life, must be vindicated. In his moral stature he is immensely greater than any of his public and political contemporaries.

Roughead's zest for the grim and macabre was infectious. The manner in which he was wont to relate the more complicated aspects of criminological situations made me a little envious at times that I, too, had not entered this field, then by no means over-written. But I would have stood little chance of success during the lifetime of so formidable an expert.

Those friends who have survived him recount many a story, many an anecdote, about him. Some of these are true: some are apocryphal. But which fall into the one category, and which into the other, it is often impossible to tell. He had had so many curious experiences during his active years of criminal investigation that any one of them could have been true: the truest were the most unbelievable, the most fantastic.

Apart from our Warrender Baths, the setting in which I clearly visualise him is the High Court of Justiciary, which I used to know particularly well, having sat through several trials there, usually when

E

my friend, the Lord Justice-Clerk (Lord Alness), presided.

Some of the best stories told of Roughead relate to this favourite haunt of his. When the courts were in recess, he used to visit this scene of famous trials and tribulations to derive literary inspiration from it. Seated there, he absorbed its atmosphere until he felt he had envisaged to his satisfaction the circumstances in which some notorious criminal had stood in its dock.

When Roughead and I were alone in our Warrender sprayroom one afternoon, he described to me how his enthusiasm for criminology began when he was a young man, eager to visit the scene of such trials as he could. Together with H. B. Irving, son of the actor, and Harry Hodge,[1] general editor of the *Notable British Trials* Series I have mentioned, he slipped into the empty High Court at Edinburgh on more than one occasion, in order to re-enact certain passages from famous trials that had taken place there.

Among the regrets I had when leaving Edinburgh to take up residence in London in the late nineteen-twenties was the interruption of a friendship with William Roughead which would certainly have deepened, had I not come South, but which was now to be sustained rather sketchily by occasional exchanges of letters. He died in 1952, at the age of 82, while I was on my walkabout in the vast deserts of Australia.

I sometimes wonder whether I shouldn't just drop Messrs. Hodge and Messrs. Cassell, his publishers, a wee line, quietly apprising them of their indebtedness to *me* for at least some of Roughead's later volumes. You see how much poorer the literature of crime would be but for my having heard at our Warrender Baths that trout-like plop!

Among the oddest of the 'odd bods' patronising our swimming-baths in the early nineteen-twenties was a quaint, dapper, little fellow, completely bald, and rotund of proportions. He waddled along duck-wise, or perhaps penguin-wise, carrying his greatly prized walking-stick which he was apt to swing a little dangerously as though, in an

[1] Harry Hodge, Managing Director of William Hodge & Co., Printers, Publishers, and Shorthand Writers, was born in Edinburgh in 1872, and educated at Glasgow and Leipzig Universities. The son and grandson of a printer, he followed his father as one of the most expert shorthand writers in Scotland, and for half a century was a kenspeckle figure in the Scottish Courts, both in that capacity and as a publisher of legal works. In 1905, he founded *The Notable British Trials* Series, which now extends to some 80 volumes, commencing with that *cause célèbre,* the Trial of Madeleine Smith. Hodge was steeped in criminology all his life. He held the view that a trial must be at least twenty years old before it can prove itself to be notable, although this view had to be modified under modern conditions. Outside his business life his main interest was music. He died in 1947.

impulsive moment, he meant to lambast at random some unoffending passer-by. This walking-stick was made to look the more expensive by reason of a broad, metal band designed to catch the envious eye. We believed it to be of gold, of *pure* gold, or at any rate of gold to the maximum carat fineness the goldsmith's ingenuity could achieve. And what could have been more indicative of his great riches than that gold band?

He was in his middle sixties, one would have said. He dressed in a light grey suit, wore brown, shining shoes, and exhibited a flashing tie-pin. His trilby's backward tilt exposed to the fullest inspection a countenance as beaming as it was devoid of intelligence. The gold watch-chain, measuring with distinction the more substantial sector of his perimeter, lent to him an air of opulence and amplitude. His button-hole bore either a pink rose to match his complexion, or a marigold calculated to tone in with his footwear. We even knew the florist from whom, each morning, he purchased, personally, his floral embellishment.

His name was Mr. Moss. To his more intimate friends, as he was pleased to confide, he was Sonny Moss, or just plain Sonny. In his case, Sonny rhymed with Bonny, not with Bunny.

Sonny had some connection with Moss's Empires; but precisely what this amounted to, we never discovered. We knew, however, that any lawful day he might be seen in or about the Empire Theatre, in Nicolson Street—scene of The Great Lafayette's disaster in May, 1911. As youthful swimmers convinced that Mr. Moss had an important financial stake in this concern, each of us, in turn, aspired to being 'chief' with him, trusting that one day he might take notice, and possibly show us some favouritism. We were all agreed, of course, that the most acceptable form in which he could extend any charity was by letting us have, if only occasionally, a free pass for the Empire. Yet, for all our years of expectation and of feigned deference, we never once heard of his having given anyone a pass, even for the cheapest seats. Nevertheless, the spirit of hope was ever alive in us; and we continued to show him marked courtesy up to the end.

Mr. Moss was very, very deaf, though not stone-deaf like Miss Aitken. We had a suspicion that he found it advantageous to affect a degree of deafness greater than actually assailed him. Like many a deaf person, he hated one's knowing that at times he heard quite distinctly, since this would have rendered us more careful about our utterances in his presence, and he enjoyed hearing, as precisely as possible, what was being said about him and around him.

"Pretty lassie I saw ye wi' last night! Hey, hey, hey!" he might remark in cackling tones to one of us who, perhaps, had caught his eye as he waddled past. "Who was she? Hey, hey, hey! A bonnie lass! Eh! a bonnie lass!"

"That's a grand show at the Empire this week, Mr. Moss," a self-reliant by-stander might now venture.

"Eh!" he would reply with a nod of his head, "it's a nice day, a braw day. Hope it keeps fine. Eh—."

"Had a nice swim, Mr. Moss?"

"Eh, A'm brawly, thank ye! A'm brawly! Never felt better!"

With a repetition of such trite observations he would move on, resolved to avoid unnecessary converse. In face of such consummate tact, we could make no headway where free passes were concerned.

Once a year, however, we were emboldened to make more definite contact with Mr. Moss. The occasion was our annual Gala. A week or two before this event, an official of the club was deputed to approach him for a donation toward the purchase of prizes, but not before his attention had been drawn rather pointedly to the large posters displayed on the premises. This admirable object he always supported—*after he had obtained his solicitor's consent,* as he informed us in whispered gravity.

It was known among us that he hadn't the power to do as he liked with his money. Such benefactions were therefore disbursed on his behalf by a firm of solicitors, through whom we received his cheque each year, and also a much coveted prize in the form of a silver cigarette-case. His contribution was greatly appreciated. "He's no' a baad spud!" was the unanimous verdict when, in due course, the figure his cheque bore was disclosed at the business meeting.

Mr. Moss, with astonishing regularity, put in an appearance at our baths once a week. This was on a Saturday afternoon, at three precisely, when a full attendance of members often made it difficult for one to swim more than a foot or two at a stretch without banging into another swimmer, or being banged into. Diving in such congestion was quite impracticable.

We regarded Mr. Moss's half-hour in our midst as the week's *pièce de résistance.* The entertainment it afforded us was his week's good deed. Having struggled into his pants behind the screen provided, he waddled along to the sprayroom for a few seconds, in order to give at least the semblance of his having complied with the municipal regulation requiring bathers to wash before entering the swimming-pond. On Saturday afternoons, this steamy apartment was so packed that he could do no more than wet his feet, and splash a little water over face and forehead.

He then emerged, making for the bank amid the swarm of

spectators who looked forward each week to his pretty performance. Quietly and unostentatiously, the pond was vacated. Bathers and staff now lined its sides as our doughty visitor turned his steps toward the high-dive. Up this lofty structure he clambered, emitting a grunt or two in his slow ascent, as if sorely troubled with 'the rheumatics' of which he complained each Saturday when pausing halfway up to take a breath. The top step he would never have reached but for Mac, whose invariable practice it was to arrive on the scene whenever our tubby entertainer was seen to approach the high-dive. Mac climbed up one side of it so that Mr. Moss, on the other, might steady himself by placing his hands on Mac's shoulders when aspiring to the topmost platform. (We all hoped that he would have remembered Mac in his will for the public service he thus rendered every Saturday afternoon, over a number of years; but poor Mac pre-deceased him.)

Waddling to within a few inches of the edge, and depressing his heels firmly, lest he inadvertently *fell* off, instead of *dropping* off, as was his custom, our daring visitor, preparatory to his great plunge, swung his arms violently in a backward motion, and smacked his lips. The swinging of the arms—purely a nervous gesture—often overbalanced him, putting him dangerously off his mark, and necessitating a fresh start with all those recognised preliminaries which, by long practice, intervened between the moment at which he reached the top and that at which he sustained the full, resounding impact of H_2O. Vigorously feeling the matting with his toes, he stood firm, taking stock of his surroundings. He couldn't see his feet, you must understand, since his middle quarters hung round him like a shortened crinoline, and a forward bend to the required angle would have put him off his balance, and carried him headlong into the pond before all was set for this supreme adventure.

Silence now reigned, silence such as our baths knew only when closed. Every bather held his breath. Below Mr. Moss the waters lay tranquil, waiting to receive him in their ample embrace. He smiled. He snorted. He smiled again. Soon the full significance of what confronted him—the entire pool to himself, lying a dozen feet below, and eight feet of wholesome, Pentland water below that, right under his very nose—transformed a countenance of bland optimism into one of grave resolve. No, he would have to go through with it . . . He had never funked it yet . . . He simply couldn't disappoint us.

As if delaying for a moment or two so as to ensure that all eyes were upon him, he would give an impatient tug at his misfitting pants. These, by the way, scarcely covered as much of his person as was required by the by-laws our civic guardians had enacted in the interests of decency. His last-minute adjustment of this scanty garment always made matters plainer.

After a little more backward swinging of the arms, followed by a deep and audible inhalation, he closed his eyes, as if in supplication to his Maker. A grunt, and he was off! In a fraction of a second he had 'come a gutser', as we used to say in Auld Reekie. The waters parted, sending a substantial wave to right and to left. Surrounded by a fringe of bubbles and fizzing foam, our hero now lay afloat like a huge, dead, pink frog, his chubby legs a-sprawl. He was waiting until he could be quite certain that his buoyant self had risen to the surface. Meanwhile the rafters rang with the cheer we gave him every time he braved this dizzy height to smack the water. On resuming active consciousness, he set out in breast-stroke fashion for the shallow end, bubbling and spluttering as he went.

Slowly he climbed out by the marble staircase, tired but triumphant. The great event of the week was over; and he knew full well that we would all be present the following Saturday to witness a repetition. He waddled to his dressing-box, stood dripping by the door of it for a moment, wiped the water from his eyes with his knuckles, shook the drops from his ears as though they were wasps about to sting, entered his box like a war-worn warrior, closed the door with a bang such as might have convinced us that he was still very deaf, and proceeded to dress, never speaking a word to anybody.

Ten minutes later he emerged, fully clad, confident as a cock-sparrow. Having given Mac his customary see-you-again-next-Saturday nod, he pushed himself sideways through the swing-door and waddled away. His good deed for the week he had performed with as great a measure of satisfaction to himself as to an ever increasing array of spectators. Finally, and for the express benefit of the lassie in the ticket-office, he delivered himself of an appreciative squeak while squeezing through the turnstile to waddle out into what remained of the afternoon.

And that was all we ever saw or knew of Mr. Moss.

CHAPTER FOURTEEN

Cases in Court

✦✦

MY MENTIONING in Chapter Thirteen the Oscar Slater Appeal recalls a number of criminal trials through which I sat as a young and intensely interested spectator in the High Court of Justiciary. I would like to refer to three of these. Two belong to my Golden Lamp years. The third and earliest took place in Edinburgh in 1915, shortly before I went to the war. It had some considerable bearing upon the Oscar Slater Case, heard six years previously, and also upon Slater's Appeal, heard thirteen years later.

You must understand that, although I was still an Edinburgh school-boy in 1915, I already had notions of going to the Bar, and that, consequently, I frequented a good deal the Court of Session, the High Justiciary Court, the Burgh Police Court, and in fact any court to which I could gain admittance, anxious to familiarise myself with legal procedure and, of course, with the seamy side of human nature!

In response to a written request from my father, I was actually allowed off from school to attend two particular High Court Trials, about which a Court of Session official had notified me in good time. I should explain that, young as I was, I did have a 'friend at court' in the literal sense. This accrued from my family's connections with the Lord Advocate at the time. Once seen in the Parliament House of Edinburgh in company with anybody as elevated as the Lord Advocate, one was assured of an open-sesame in that city for the rest of one's life. If any further passport were required there, it had merely to be bruited that one was a person of such standing as to be admitted to a judge's robing-room after a trial, and had been observed walking home with him to tea. Such are our superficial values.

No aspect of Scottish public life betrays more patently its provinciality and cosseted respectability than the obsequiousness shown in Edinburgh to its bar-and-bench fraternity, which has dominated that city for a century and more, and not necessarily advantageously except as regards snobbery and the personal gain and aggrandisement of its members. Even its Lesser Legal Luminaries are accredited with

135

being in direct communication only with The Almighty. They are of a Celestial Purple quite of their own.

This lamentable, dead-hand state of affairs is not entirely un-recognised in Edinburgh itself, as is seen in that city's own parodied versions of Bossidy's theme.[1] The variant I like best is that in which Edinburgh's super-elite are substituted for the Lowells and the Cabots of Boston:

> *Here's to dear Auld Reekie,*
> *City of soot and fog,*
> *Where the Blackburns speak to the Pitmans,*
> *And the Pitmans speak only to God.*

The Pitmans were three brothers, all of them partners in a leading firm of Edinburgh lawyers. In the Edinburgh of which I write, the Pitman coterie, like that of the Haldane, almost took precedence of the Blood Royal.

My kinsman, Sheriff John MacGregor, in reminding me of his early associations with Lord Blackburn, before whom he frequently pleaded, hopes that my quoting here what he refers to as "this scurrilous piece of doggerel" won't detract from the reputation of a kindly disposed man, who was really quite a good Judge.

The Faculty of Advocates, whether in matters of Church or of State, whether in relation to social grading or propriety, has always considered itself the king-pin of Scottish society and of Scottish opinion and behaviour. It has also maintained, and without serious challenge, its place as a hotbed of gossip. Indeed, it enjoys a virtual monopoly in this uncharitable field. I know it is commonly supposed that women are the best and the worst gossips. I have questioned this ever since I first became acquainted with the canards that emanate from the Parliament House of the Scottish Capital. The pride with which, over so many years, I frequented it quickly ebbed away as I began to adjust my values and priorities. This worship of legal people, as though they were always omniscient and upright, does us a lot of harm. Their crashing legal blunders are seen in our Appeal Courts all the time. The misdemeanours, usually of a fraudulent nature – well, only a few ever come to light. How right was Sir Walter Scott when, a century earlier, he described Parliament House as 'a sand-cart of a place'! Similar sand-carts have multiplied enormously since then.

[1] *And this is good old Boston,*
>   *The home of the bean and the cod,*
>   *Where the Lowells talk to the Cabots,*
>   *And the Cabots talk only to God.*
> John Collins Bossidy (1860-1928), *On the Aristocracy of Harvard.*

Placed in chronological order, then, the three trials I adumbrated are:

(1) That held in 1915 of David Cook, a Glasgow solicitor, and Detective Lieutenant John Thomson Trench, of the Glasgow City Police, before Charles Scott Dickson, the Lord Justice-Clerk. They were jointly charged with resetting jewellery in the former's house. Resetting is the receiving of stolen goods, knowing them to have been stolen.

(2) The trial, late in 1921, or early in 1922, in Glasgow, of a street-gangster, whose name I now forget, It may have been Doyle. I was present on this occasion, not as a mere onlooker, but as His Majesty's Guest, in the best sense, for I was the person who prevented the prisoner from committing murder, who detained him for the police, and was the Crown's principal witness in the High Court of Justiciary in Glasgow. Though I actually forget the date of the trial, I am able to supply the date of the offence by referring to a letter I turned up the other day, written to me by the Chief Constable of Glasgow at the time. The date was the 5th of November, 1921.

(3) The trial in the High Court at Edinburgh of John Donald Merrett before my friend, the late Lord Alness, Lord Justice-Clerk, and a jury. Merrett, at the instance of His Majesty's Advocate, was indicted and accused of murder and uttering. The trial began on February, 1st, 1927. It lasted seven days.

In March, 1914, when Oscar Slater already had served five years in prison, Sir Arthur Conan Doyle received from a Glasgow solicitor named David Cook a very remarkable letter, the purport of which was to show that his friend, Detective Lieutenant Trench, who, with so many others, had been engaged in the police investigations regarding Miss Gilchrist's death in 1908, and had made in the witness-box some truly startling comments on the identification parade which brought Slater to trial, was not satisfied with certain aspects of police conduct in connection with the prosecution of Slater, whom he believed to have been innocent of the crime of which he had been found Guilty. These aspects Cook's letter set out in full. I need not trouble you with them here except so far as to say that they showed Slater to have been wrongly and collusively convicted.[1]

On July, 14th, 1914, Trench, a most admirable police officer, a man who, in the opinion of a major under whom he served in the Great

[1] The letter appears *in extenso* at page 155 of Peter Hunt's *Oscar Slater: The Great Suspect*, published by Carroll & Nicholson in 1951.

War, was "loved by his comrades, scorned to do a mean action, desiring justice for everyone," was suspended from duty by the chief constable, and his conduct reported to the Glasgow magistrates. On September, 14th, the said magistrates dismissed him from the police force. They had found him guilty of having communicated to persons outside the police force information acquired in the course of his duty, without the express sanction of the chief officer of his force. The persons were David Cook and McKinnon Wood, then Secretary for Scotland. To the letter he addressed to Wood, stating that he had deemed "your invitation to send the information, and your acceptance thereof, as ample protection against any breach of discipline," he received no reply.

Penniless, and with a wife and several children to support, he enlisted in the Royal Scots Fusiliers in November, 1914. On May, 15th, of the following year—the day before he and his regiment were due to sail for the Dardanelles—he and Cook were arrested and charged with having resetted, in the latter's house, jewellery to the value of £503. 16s. 3d.

Now I come to that trial I attended three months later. There, in the dock, stood Trench and Cook. This was the very dock in which Trench had seen Oscar Slater face his accusers six years previously. My boyhood hands were among those which greeted with applause—soon to be suppressed—the jury's unanimous verdict of *Not Guilty*. Scott Dickson, who preceded Lord Alness as Lord Justice-Clerk, stated that on the facts it would have been exceedingly difficult to convict these two men. "If a man received stolen goods for the purpose of handing them back to their owner," he added, "accepted a fee, and carried out that purpose, you could not call that man a resetter."

The really important point was that everything Trench had done in regard to the jewellery concerned had been done after consultation with the chief constable and procurator-fiscal of Glasgow. This was a case trumped up by the Glasgow Police against two men who had shown that the Police had trumped up the case against Slater.

Neither Trench nor Cook took any further part in the Slater Case. The former, after his acquittal, returned to his regiment, and was promoted to quartermaster-sergeant. His colonel considered his acquittal "a mighty triumph". He died in 1919, at the age of 50. David Cook died in 1921. Several years were now to elapse ere Oscar Slater was to benefit from their courageous actions and sacrifice.

Did these two men find themselves in the dock because they had shown how the Glasgow Police had succeeded, wrongfully, in securing the conviction of Slater? Was this a malicious prosecution by the chief

constable and procurator-fiscal of Glasgow and those other police
officers who had denied this and that? I think it was.

Anyway, as I listened to the verdict in that grim courtroom in 1915,
something very fundamental happened to *me*, though I was too young
then to assess its quite terrifying implications. As John Thomson
Trench and David Cook left that dock to resume the freedom they
never should have been compelled to forfeit, the former smiled to me,
the only young person present on that dramatic occasion. I now knew,
and for the first time in my hitherto innocent life, the significance of
the Commandment, *Thou shalt not bear false witness against thy
neighbour,* and how easy it is for people in power and authority to do
so, not only with impunity where condign punishment is deserved,
but also at no cost whatever to themselves. Taxpayers and ratepayers,
quite unconcernedly, meet the bills arising from such calculated
delinquencies. The amount of public money used every year in covering up official irregularities is very considerable. But few really mind.
That's what democracy has come to, which is one reason why I don't
believe any longer in democracy as generally acclaimed.

Ever since that day in the High Court of Justiciary at Edinburgh,
I have realised that those proceedings were essentially identical with
those in which Christ has been involved. Trench and Cook got off—
in a sense. Christ got Himself Crucified. Ever since that day, moreover,
I have been opposed in principle to Judicial Trials, Tribunals, and Inquiries held in secret, even such as are conduted thus on some
puerile pretext of national security. Secrecy cloaks official incompetence
and criminal wrongdoing, alike.

I cannot but repeat Acton's aphorism: *Power corrupts; and absolute
power corrupts absolutely.* Official secrecy and the protection it affords
official scamps must therefore corrupt, whether in military, in judicial,
on in police circles, whether in cabinets, parliaments, or local borough
councils. One remembers in this context that extract from the speech
John Curran delivered in Dublin as long ago as 1790: "The condition upon which God hath given liberty to man is eternal vigilance,
which condition, if he break, servitude is at once the consequence of
his crime, and the punishment of his guilt." Liberty cannot be
guaranteed by the uncritical worship of authority, and fear of such
consequences as may follow—and usually do follow—one's challeng-
ing it. In these days of football-pools without football and epidemic
bingo, who cares?

We now come to the second case.

Having already related (and not too immodestly, I trust) two
instances of my having rescued someone from drowning, I must per-

mit myself a page or two about the occasion when I saved a man from being MURDERED!! I shall be brief, and as little boastful as possible.

Throughout my Golden Lamp years, my father and I paid two or three visits to Glasgow together every year. These were usually in connection with some Highland function or other. My father was an office-bearer of this and of that, which meant that he regarded at least some of these visits as being in the nature of statutory jaunts, as it were. With unfailing regularity, for instance, we travelled from Edinburgh to Glasgow to attend the annual concert and dance in the St. Andrew's Halls of the Lewis and Harris Association. This function is always held on the evening of the first Friday in November. Attendance was to some degree incumbent upon us, since my father was one of the foundation members, and I had been enrolled as a life-member when but a few weeks old. I should add that the Association publicly disowned me in 1949, and invited me to resign my life-membership, following upon the appearance of my book, *The Western Isles*. It didn't like what I wrote about drunkenness and laziness and the like in Lewis and elsewhere. I refused to withdraw any statement that book contains; and, indeed, were I re-writing it, I would amplify the passages objected to.

Anyhow, these periodic visits to Glasgow meant quite a lot to my father, since they afforded him the additional pleasure of walking leisurely the streets of a city he had known intimately in his college days there, during the late eighteen-sixties. He was, by the way, a distinguished graduate of Glasgow University.

The first Friday in November, 1921, then, found us in Glasgow for the reason stated. We devoted the following day to looking up college cronies and Gaelic associates of his. That evening—a Saturday evening—as was our custom on these occasions—I saw him to his train at the Central Station, whence he travelled home to Edinburgh by himself, while I spent the weekend with friends in Glasgow, returning to Edinburgh on Monday in time for such university classes as I had to attend that day.

When his train left, I made for the station exit bringing one down into Glasgow's celebrated Argyle Street. There I came upon a seething mob, under the Highlandman's Umbrella, that being the popular name of the part of Argyle Street sheltered by the railway-lines overhead, terminating in the Central Station. Glasgow at this time was notorious for its gang warfare. The shrieks of women encouraged me to dash in and investigate matters where even angels would have been hesitant. With some difficulty I reached the heart of the mob which, every moment, was becoming denser and more menacing. There, in the centre of it, I found a man cutting another man's throat with a razor. The mob, as I soon realised, was very hostile, particularly toward the one-legged victim, who lay on his back, gasping beneath a slashing razor, and weltering in gore. I closed with his assailant, struggled with him in an ever-menacing ring of gangsters, fighting desperately to prevent my own throat from being slit open with the razor he still brandished, or to avoid having my head bashed in by hostile members of the mob around me.

The mob, in the main, consisted of two rival gangs. Its sympathies were largely with the assailant. Apparently, he belonged to one of Glasgow's more popular gangs at that time. I knocked the razor out of his hand. It fell to the ground. A shawl-clad woman rushed forward, picked it up, and disappeared with it among the dense crowd. With one mighty lunge, I sent the gangster reeling against the crowd. He dropped to the ground. I thought I had killed him. I, too, dropped to the ground, in order to examine the victim of his aggression who, meantime, was bleeding profusely on the roadway among surging feet, while his assailant lay, knocked out, a few yards away.

With my handkerchief I bandaged the wounded man as best I could. The mob, as is customary with mobs, was now about to set upon *me*. However, I believe that by this time I had intimidated it sufficiently with my bravado to make it cautious. Actually, I could have done little against anyone bent on bludgeoning me from behind.

By now, an immense crowd had gathered under 'The Umbrella'. For a mile on either side of it, the Argyle Street tramcars were packed immovably. While victim and assailant both lay senseless on the road, and I by this time was pretty exhausted, and deplorably dishevelled, three bulky policemen forced their way into the heart of things. I asked them why they had been so long in intervening. I had seen their helmets on the fringe of the crowd while I was fighting desperately. They were now on the point of arresting *me!* But they soon noticed that I was lifting off the road, by the back of his pants, a fellow who looked more deserving of their attention.

With the preliminary proceedings at the Central Police Station, and the details of how we all arrived there eventually, I need not trouble you here.

My father, already safely back in Edinburgh, knew nothing of this until the Monday afternoon, when a friend whom he met accidentally in the High Street of Portobello remarked, facetiously, apropos a newspaper placard displayed a few feet away, "I see Alasdair's been in the hands of the police in Glasgow!"

"My God!" exclaimed a startled father. "Why in the name of Heaven did I not bring him back with me on Saturday evening? I ought to have known he would get himself in trouble sooner or later! What has he done?"

His attention was now drawn to the placard:

EDINBURGH
STUDENT'S
GALLANTRY
IN GLASGOW

When shown in the newspaper the item to which this referred, he was immensely relieved.

Of this incident in Portobello I knew nothing until several weeks later, for, although I visited my father late that same Monday evening, I never mentioned this Glasgow episode to him, and he never mentioned it to me. I had no reason to suppose that he knew anything about it. As he had said nothing, I concluded that he had neither read about it, nor heard about it. Such was our mutual reticence.

Soon afterwards I received instructions to attend a precognition in the Sheriff Court House in Edinburgh, with a view to my being called as the chief Crown witness in the prosecution then pending. Owing to the victim's condition, however, the trial had to be postponed until he had recovered sufficiently to be able to leave hospital and give evidence.

In due course I found myself at the High Court of Justiciary in Glasgow, the object of more public deference than I had ever been shown in my life hitherto. Lord Ormidale, the presiding judge, in his summing up, said a lot of quite nice things about me. Addressing the prisoner, whom he sentenced to a year's imprisonment, he told him that he had to thank *me* for the fact that he had not been charged with murder. The prisoner, a hard case, who had tried to slash me for interfering, gave me a malevolent nod by way of acknowledgement; and I, unhampered by precedent, nodded back. We smiled agreeably to one another, however, as he was being conducted below.

It took the Chief Constable of Glasgow six years to write me officially, commending me "for the services rendered by you to the public and the police of this City in seizing hold of, and in securing the apprehension of, a man who, with a razor, had attacked and seriously assaulted another man to the effusion of blood in Argyle Street, near the Central Railway Station, and also for subsequently having given valuable evidence at the High Court of Justiciary, Glasgow, at the trial of the man, who was convicted of the crime".

This letter (it lies by my elbow as I write these words) concludes with an apology for undue delay on the part of the police authorities in thanking me. The excuse proffered was that the papers relating to the case had been mislaid in the divisional office! I suppose that, when I received that letter, so many years ago now, I thought it very wonderful and gratifying. Today it seems very trivial when I think of the dangers and hazards the few really brave people of life voluntarily face. Nevertheless, when at the same time one considers the scalliwags to whom civic authorities so often give the Freedom of the Burgh (usually the pretext for a binge at the ratepayers' expense), I cannot help thinking that Glasgow might have done something along these lines! A civic luncheon, for instance! I'm still open to such a suggestion, although it's more than forty years since the incident which might have warranted something along these lines!

Lastly, we come to the trial, in February, 1927, in the High Court of Justiciary at Edinburgh, before Lord Alness, the Lord Justice-Clerk, and a jury of fifteen, of John Donald Merrett, charged with having, by shooting, murdered his mother, Mrs. Bertha Milner or Merrett, and also with having uttered forged cheques upon her bank account.

This case interested me enormously throughout its seven days' hearing. I learnt a lot through my having attended it. Undoubtedly, it ranks with the most famous of our Scottish murder trials of the present century. I recall certain aspects of it as clearly as if I had witnessed it yesterday. It is frequently brought to mind by the trivet standing on the sittingroom hearth of my home at Odiham, in Hampshire.

When Mrs. Merrett and her son came to England from New Zealand in 1924, with a view to the latter's completing his education in this country, she rented at Mortimer, near Reading, from my father-in-law, a cottage on his property there. She had found her tenancy of this cottage so agreeable, and my father-in-law so pleasant to deal with, that, when she left it in 1926, having by this time arranged to move with her son to Edinburgh in order that he might attend the University there, she presented my father-in-law with a souvenir in the shape of this trivet—a large, handsome thing upon which Patricia and I frequently place our buttered toast and the like.

When Mrs. Merrett arrived in Edinburgh, she was a woman of fifty-seven. Donald, upon whom she doted, was eighteen. Mother and son had been in the Scottish Capital but a couple of months when, in the flat she had taken at 31, Buckingham Terrace, Mrs. Merrett was shot by a pistol. That was on the 17th of March, 1926. Hurried off by ambulance to the Edinburgh Royal Infirmary, she was detained there, in Number 3 Ward—a place with barred windows and locked doors—as a prisoner to be charged with attempted suicide. There she remained, incommunicably. Her consignment to this ward resulted in her becoming the subject of silence. Neither those attending her, nor those visiting her, would tell her what had happened. In that ward she died on April, 1st, without ever knowing what had befallen her, although she was conscious and clear-headed up to within a few days of the end.

That same day a post-mortem examination was made in the Royal Infirmary's mortuary by Harvey Littlejohn, Professor of Forensic Medicine in the University of Edinburgh, and that city's police surgeon. Littlejohn, whom I knew through my father, stated in his report that, so far as the position of the wound was concerned, the case was consistent with suicide. To anybody who sat through that trial, or who has read the published evidence, this was clearly one of those important cases where the experts were—as they usually are—WRONG!

Anyhow, two days later—on April, 3rd—the unfortunate Bertha Milner or Merrett was buried at Piershill Cemetery "with such maimed rites as the Church accords to those who have laid violent hands upon themselves," as William Roughead put it. "If she were in fact guiltless of her own blood, that suicide's grave was indeed the ultimate irony of Fate."

Six months later, a warrant was granted for the arrest of Donald Merrett. Early in December he was brought in custody to Edinburgh from Hughenden, in Buckinghamshire, and committed to prison for further examination by another old friend of mine, the late Sheriff Gordon Jameson. The following week he was committed for trial. On February, 1st, 1927, as you know, his trial opened. At the first day's hearing Mrs. Merrett's housekeeper described how she had left her mistress writing at a table in the livingroom at Buckingham Terrace, and her son reading there. No sooner had she reached the kitchen than she heard a shot, followed by a scream and the thud of a body falling to the floor. Donald rushed into the kitchen and said: "Rita, my mother has shot herself".

Rita described Mrs. Merrett as a healthy and active woman. On the morning of the tragedy she appeared to be her ordinary self. When Dr. R. S. Holcombe saw her later, she was quite conscious, and mentally normal. To his asking her what had occurred, she answered: "I was sitting down writing letters, and my son, Donald, was standing beside me. I said, 'Go away, Donald, and don't annoy me'; and the next I heard was an explosion. I do not remember any more."

With further details of this long and extremely painful trial, I will not detain you here, though I recall many of them. They may be found in the late William Roughead's exhaustive account, published in 1929.

The jury's verdict on the first charge—that of having murdered his mother—was, by a majority of 10 to 5, *Not Proven*. The verdict on the second charge—that of uttering, that of forgery—was *Guilty*, unanimously. In respect of this second verdict, the Lord Justice-Clerk, taking into account Merrett's youth, restricted the sentence to a year's imprisonment.

The court then rose. A few seconds afterwards, a legal acquaintance of mine said to me in the lobby outside this courtroom: "When you see your friend, Lord Alness, you can tell him from *me* that yon b—— shot his mother all right, and that he should have been given three years anyway for uttering. Yon lad will give more trouble before he's done."

Everybody who, like myself, had been present at this trial, was convinced that John Donald Merrett had intentionally shot his mother, and that she had died in the Royal Infirmary as the result of his having done so.

Seated in that court, and likewise following the proceedings with avidity, was another young person. I often wondered who he was. Not until the spring of 1963 did I discover. I happened to have occasion to write William Hodge & Company, the Edinburgh publishers, on some matter connected with the late William Roughead, with whom the late Harry Hodge, as we have seen, had had such close associations, and for whom he had published, in his *Notable British Trials* Series, so many volumes. The letter was answered by Harry's son, James, one of the two directors of this house which has made available, during the last half century, such a splendid corpus of criminological literature. James Hodge was the other young person. He was at that time an apprentice with an Edinburgh firm of chartered accountants, and as such took law classes, including criminal law. He attended this trial partly because of his legal studies, partly because he eventually would be going into the family business, and partly because William Hodge & Company were, as they still are, the official shorthand writers to the High Court of Justiciary in Scotland.

"Merrett's was the first murder trial I ever attended," James wrote me recently. "I knew him before he killed his mother. He was a most unpopular and highly unpleasant person even then. I met him both at the University here [Edinburgh], and on a boat when sailing on the Clyde. I also saw him frequently at the Dunedin Palais de Danse, where a large number of young people at that time used to waste their Saturday evenings. I doubt whether our parents knew much about this!"

*   *   *

The years pass, and the wicked Donald slips out of mind. A little over a quarter of a century later, something happens to replace him there.

In February, 1953, a man identified by the German Police as Ronald John Chesney, whom Scotland Yard had been anxious to interview in connection with a double murder at an Old Folks' Home in Ealing, was found shot dead in a secluded wood near Cologne. Most of his face was blown away: only the lower part, together with traces of a brown-grey beard, were recognisable. Identification was assisted by scars on his hands.

Chesney was the husband of Mrs. Isobel Veronica Chesney, aged 43, who, along with her mother, the self-styled "Lady" Mary Menzies, aged 72, was found dead some days earlier in an old and gloomy Victorian mansion in Ealing's Montpelier Road. The daughter had been drowned in her bath: the mother had had her head battered, and had been strangled.

When found in that German wood, Chesney was wearing a blue suit, grey overcoat, and brown hat. He clutched in a hand a Colt revolver. His pockets were stuffed with newspapers carrying reports of the murders at Ealing. A British passport found on him bore the name of John Donald Milner.

Investigations showed that Mrs. Chesney was strangled in her bedroom. Her killer, in order to make it appear as though she had been drowned accidentally, then deposited her body in the bath, and left it there. According to the police's re-construction of the crime, he then went downstairs, trapped "Lady" Mary Menzies in her room, strangled her, bashed her head in with a pewter mug, and left the scene in a car he had parked outside. Scotland Yard had no doubt that the murderer had fled the country immediately. A description of the man it wanted to interview was flashed to the police in France and Spain, in Germany and Switzerland, and even in Australia and New Zealand. Interpol was soon on the lookout for him.

Police inquires showed that he had entered Germany by way of Holland on the day of his crimes. One wonders what the late Sir Bernard Spilsbury would have said about all this, had he lived to learn of it! I remember well his forensic evidence on the sixth day of the trial. It was largely due to this eminent pathologist's evidence for the defence that in 1927 the prosecution failed to secure Merrett's conviction for murder. One wonders, also, what Lord Alness thought about it! Had I not been in Australia at the time, I would have asked him. He died at Bournemouth in October, 1955, at the age of 87.

Apart from emotional considerations, it was that element of doubt Spilsbury raised in the jurors' minds, especially in the minds of the

six women jurors, which resulted in the jury's returning the verdict it
did. Not one of the fifteen composing it found the accused *NOT
GUILTY*.

Able at this distance of time to study this case coolly and in per-
spective, one asks oneself, as did my friend, Roughead, how the
accused would have dealt with the situation his forgeries had created.
By fraudulence he had so depleted his mother's bank acount as to have
deprived her, certainly for a time, of her income and livelihood.
Detection and apprehension appeared inevitable, if not, indeed,
imminent. That some physical accident should have occurred, resulting
in his mother's death, was highly improbable. Her suicide was even
more so. What would her son's position have been, had she survived?
As Roughead puts it, "How was the plot to end?"

That handsome trivet at Odiham, which at tea-time there has kept
warm so much buttered toast and so many crumpets since I married
Patricia, is a constant reminder of that memorable and dramatic week
during my Golden Lamp years. A little disturbing and unsettling, I
do admit, since it diverted me for a while from pursuing what, for a
few years now, had been the professional purpose of my pen.

CHAPTER FIFTEEN

Celtic Madness

THE OCCASION mentioned in the preceding chapter when my father and I travelled together from Edinburgh to Glasgow to attend that annual gathering was one of the many during my Golden Lamp years. Such visits, until their primary purpose had been served, were always, for me, a time of fear and apprehension, since they were invariably distinguished by some embarrassing, if not terrifying, 'incident'. In fact, they had been so ever since the very first visit I paid to this city in boyhood, some years before the First World War. Life with father was at all times replete with 'incidents'. One couldn't avoid them. They were the inescapable corollary of being with him as his son. Certainly, they seemed inseparable from those kilted occasions, for which Glasgow has long been famous—those occasions when the Highlanders living there give themselves over to what the Lowlanders humorously describe as 'tearing the tartan'.

Somewhere about 1910 my father took my brother and me to Glasgow to the first annual gathering of the Lewis & Harris Association I ever attended. It was held, as always, in the vast St. Andrew's Halls. Our father was presiding on this occasion. Throughout the hour's railway journey from Edinburgh, he talked aloud to himself in a foreign tongue, to the alarm of the other passengers in the compartment. There were no corridor trains on this line in those days, which meant that those who believed themselves closeted with a madman had no means of escape. To the embarrassment of his young sons, as also to the apprehension of his fellow passengers, he was rehearsing his speech in what he affirmed was the language of the Garden of Eden.

As the train began to slow up at journey's end, my father turned to Iain and me and said, with a withering seriousness: "It is just possible that, in the course of my speech tonight, I may refer to my having brought you both with me from Edinburgh. I may mention in passing, Alasdair, that *you* have a particular right to be present on the platform with your father, since you are one of the Association's oldest life-members. I enrolled you when you were about six weeks old. If my

148

reference to you both should appear to meet with the audience's acceptance, I shall turn round to draw its attention to you both. You will then rise and bow politely. Do you understand, Iain?"

From that moment any anticipation of pleasure in Glasgow was blasted. We duly alighted from the train, and drove off to a hotel in a cab. So preöccupied was our father with thinking out his Gaelic peroration that, as far as I remember, he never addressed another word to either of us until, before this vast audience of some thousands, he reached the appointed juncture in his speech. By this time he was in complete control of the gathering, standing there in his kilt, girt about with the usual accessories, and holding forth in the Gaelic with remarkable eloquence and fervour. Iain and I meantime formed part of the platform party of roughly three hundred Gaels. Similarly attired in our kilts, we were seated a row or two immediately behind our father, quaking in every limb, lest he should remember to carry out that part of the performance about which he had warned us in the train, some hours previously. His speech was punctuated with loud bursts of applause. He then began to interpolate a song or two of his own composition, rendered lustily by himself, unaccompanied. The reception accorded this quite unusual behaviour on the part of a chairman was truly deafening. "Ah!" whispered Iain with relief. "*He's forgotten us!*"

Just then arrived the dreaded moment, as though our father had received a telepathic communication. ". . . and I have brought my two young sons with me from Edinburgh this evening. [Loud applause as he turned round with dramatic gesture to point us out.] Alasdair has been a life-member of the Association since infancy, and—."

"*A Thighearna! A Thighearna!*" [O, Lord! O, Lord!], he now began in the Gaelic, followed by more oaths and blastings that, although hardly printable, were well understood by the Gaels forming the bulk of this quite appreciative platform party.

Picture our wrathful father, now roaming up and down this large platform, threatening fire and brimstone, while his offspring, covered with embarrassment, lay out of sight under the chairs! The proceedings were suspended until Iain and I could be located, and publicly exhibited. Knowing well our father's determination, and realising that, sooner or later, we would be obliged to emerge from our hiding, we held brief and decisive counsel under those chairs, amid the din of a hilarious but sympathetic audience. Then, grasping one another by the hand, we shot up simultaneously into the air for a split second, and collapsed out of sight again.

The reception the audience now gave us was stupendous. Not in all my experience of public platforms have I ever been the recipient of such an ovation as on this, my first, public appearance, lasting for that fraction of a second. This packed assembly clapped and yelled and whistled so uproariously that for some minutes our father found it quite impossible to proceed with his duties as chairman. These seemed to consist in the main of his supplying as much of the entertainment as he thought his indulgent and quite uncritical audience would tolerate. The maxim that a good chairman should get up, speak up, and shut up never made any appeal to *him*. Such a maxim he considered the antithesis of good chairmanship.

No less memorable was the occasion when he was asked to preside at a similar function specially arranged for him in the town hall of his native Stornoway—memorable not through my having been present, but because he nearly lost the only boat that would have enabled him to reach Stornoway in time. The fault wasn't entirely his, however.

With ample time in hand, I escorted him to Princes Street Station, proud to see him off on such a happy venture. He duly presented himself at the appropriate window of the booking-office to purchase a ticket for Kyle of Lochalsh. What with audible ruminations, what with humming the Gaelic songs with which, as chairman, he intended entertaining his Stornoway audience, he was slow to realise that a man standing in front of him was engaged in a long conversation with the booking-clerk, and that the wide margin of time he had allowed himself was being dissipated. For several minutes he had been standing there, without exhibiting the least impatience—a rare occurrence for my notoriously impatient father, and one that could only be explained by his having been caught up in a whirl of Celtic Reverie, murmuring to himself in the Gaelic at one moment, humming to himself at another. At length he felt an urge to interrupt the conversation of the man in front of him, who by this time had his head, arms, and shoulders well inside the booking-window, as though he and the clerk were exchanging confidences.

Now afforded an opportunity of asking for his ticket, he learnt that the train for which he had arrived in such good time had just left. The scene that followed this announcement beggars description, to use a phrase so dear to nineteenth-century writers. All the higher officials of the Caledonian Railway Company within reach were summoned. All the gold braid on the premises now assembled in the stationmaster's office in an endeavour to placate the raging Colonel MacGregor. At a vital conference held therein, it transpired that the wretched booking-clerk, pressed for an explanation, had been conducting a long and garrulous conversation with a friend of his, and that, consequently this regal Gael had missed the only connection shown in the time-table that would have enabled him to reach Kyle in time for the Stornoway mailboat.

What was to be done? There existed no alternative air service in *those* days. While my father raved, the officials, admitting liability in the matter (a most unusual occurrence nowadays in any sphere of public activity!), were studiously engaged in devising ways and means.

A small train consisting of a light engine and a single carriage, complete with guard, was seen and heard as it steamed demonstratively to within a few yards of him. By way of announcing its readiness to depart with him, it emitted a long and piercing whistle that drowned his non-stop protestations. Visualise the change of scene, the miraculous resipiscence, when he found he was being provided with a train all to himself! Royalty, for all its full-time and obsequious entourage arranging this and that, could not have been more amply catered for.[1]

Off they sent him aboard this little train into the heart of the Highlands, perhaps to Crianlarich or to Callander, to overtake by a different route the connection he had missed. In the meantime a crowd of at least a hundred had gathered to witness his departure, to see him well and truly off. They raised a hearty cheer when a hilarious guard blew his whistle and vigorously waved his flag, and the little train puff-puffed out of sight, its sole passenger, now mollified, waving regally to us all from his carriage window. He caught the mailboat, and reached his destination as originally planned.

Relatives in Stornoway told me some years later that it was midnight before the evening's artistes were given an opportunity of appearing on the platform at all, since the first few hours of the proceedings were occupied by the remarks of a chairman who insisted on singing a dozen or more of his own Gaelic songs, interspersed with extempore commentaries. Nevertheless, they used to say that he was

[1] On March, 26th, 1963, the very day Dr. Beeching announced his drastic plans for reshaping our railway system, British Railways showed themselves still capable of rectifying matters in this way when at fault. According to *The Times*, a Rochdale businessman had a whole two-coach diesel unit to himself, when British Railways ran a one-man special from Rochdale to Manchester for him. The man had arrived at Rochdale station in the morning to catch a train to Manchester; but the platform indicators were out of order because of repainting. As no announcement was made over the address system, the train arrived and left, while the passenger waited on the wrong platform. Not only did he complain. He insisted that it was essential that he should get to Manchester to catch an aircraft. So the duty station inspector arranged for this diesel unit to run non-stop to Manchester Victoria, whence its sole passenger, with the compliments of British Railways, took a taxi to the airport bus in St. Ann's Square.

the most entertaining chairman they had ever known, and that everybody was quite sorry when, at last, he gave way for that evening's programme as advertised.

At times my father exhibited a primitive vanity where rank and title were concerned. I know it is popularly held that the Scots treat with democratic indifference such expressions of the superficial and temporal. *"A man's a man for a' that!"* is sung by them every January the world over. For the rest of the year the type of man Robert Burns proclaimed as "the gowd for a' that" is shown no more consideration north of the Border than anybody else. The Scots, and especially the Highlanders, despite their bardic lays, are the most insufferable snobs, the most unctuous climbers. They thrive in an atmosphere reeking of Balmoralism and 'the gentry'. Even the newest of the *nouveaux riches* in their midst, so long as they are thought to possess in abundance the status symbol of money, are fawned upon, and accredited with exceptional virtues.

On the other hand, when, by the studious application to mythical hereditary claims, and not infrequently aided and abetted in this nonsense by the Court of the Lord Lyon and its fatuous pronouncements, they conduct their campaigns for social status and recognition with an assiduity and assertiveness unknown in any other country in the world, they are usually rewarded with success in the form they seek. The extent to which the office of the Lord Lyon King of Arms has intensified in Scotland in recent decades all this feudal flummery is unbelievable. Just look at some of the clan chiefships it has recognised during the present century! The Word as revealed to Moses on Sinai never carried half the authority attached to the humbug upon which the Lord Lyon has set his seal during the last century and a half. If you should wish to delude yourself into believing that you really *are* somebody, somebody with something elevating to impart, don't tell it to the Marines, for it's just possible that they might not believe you. Reserve it for the Lord Lyon.[1] He will help you all he

[1] The Court of the Lord Lyon, at Her Majesty's Register House, Edinburgh, is the Scottish Court of Chivalry. It includes the genealogical jurisdiction of the *Ri-Sennachie* of Scotland's Celtic Kings, adjudication of rights to arms and administration of *The Scottish Public Register of All Arms & Bearings* (under 1672, cap. 47) and *Public Register of All Genealogies*. The Lord Lyon presides and judicially establishes rights to existing arms, or succession to chiefships, and a lot more nonsense based largely on the flimsiest of claims and a good deal of hereditary assumption. The snob value of all this has increased greatly in recent years. We know in the Highlands that in countries like Australia there are persons much closer in hereditary descent than those who have managed to get themselves acknowledged as the chiefs of this clan or of that.

can. Take any ancestral bee out of your bonnet, lay it firmly enough (being careful not to squash it) on the Lord Lyon's desk, and there's no saying how exalted you may find yourself!

For years my father was friendly with the Lord Lyon, the late Sir Francis Grant. I feel sure that, had he not realised, deep down, how meaningless it all is, he could have convinced Francis that he was entitled to be proclaimed anything he might have cared to suggest. After all, he had convinced himself that Gaelic was the language spoken by Adam and Eve!

I can't think why it never occurred to him to put forward a claim to the chiefship of the MacGregors! You see, anybody carrying the surname of MacGregor ought to be able to establish a better claim than the present *soi-disant* MacGregor of MacGregor family, who are MacGregors merely by adoption. In other words, they are not MacGregors at all! They are actually Murrays, as I shall show in our next chapter but one, if only to satisfy those who regarded as unfair my observations in *Skye and the Inner Hebrides* on the Clan MacLeod chiefship, without even a whisper that the Clan Gregor chiefship is a bit farcical too.

Let me repeat here what I did say about the MacLeod chiefship, so that you may be a little conversant with things by the time you reach that part of the next chapter dealing with MacGregor chiefship:

"Of course, there is perpetuated about the Highland chiefs an enormous amount of nonsense. Take the position of the MacLeods of Dunvegan, for instance. The present chief is a Mrs. Walter, who lives at Dunvegan Castle, which she inherited from her father, the late Sir Reginald MacLeod. Her contribution to the controversy over our companion volume, *The Western Isles,* in 1949, was an endeavour to throw doubt upon statements made in that book of mine because, in her view, I had wrongly numbered the MacLeod chiefs! It would appear that the MacLeods have re-enumerated their chiefs recently. They now seek to include additional chiefs, two of whom were "young boys, accepted by the Clan as successors to their fathers, though they died young and never actually led or administered the Clan". The quotation I give you is from a letter written me by Flora herself, in answer to my request for some guidance in the matter. I had not heard, at that time, that the Mac-Leods had discovered two or three additional chiefs!

"But was the chiefship hereditary? Or did each clan select for its chief the clansman most likely to lead its armed men victoriously in battle? The numbering of these Highland chiefs is, of course, quite arbitrary and fanciful. It would not bear historical scrutiny.

According to this new enumeration, Flora now describes herself as the 28th Chief of the MacLeods.

"It would seem as though we were going to have a surfeit of Mac-Leods during the next few generations, for only a few years ago we read a family announcement from Dunvegan that Flora's elder daughter, Mrs. Alice Macnabb, and her husband had assumed with Flora's consent, under the authority of the Lord Lyon King of Arms, the additional name of MacLeod, and were now to be known as Archibald Corrie Macnabb MacLeod and Alice Macnabb MacLeod of MacLeod. And, as though this were not enough to establish the survival of this clan nonsense, in May, 1951, John Wolrige Gordon, elder son of the late Captain Wolrige Gordon and of Joan, Flora MacLeod's younger daughter, had "by the wish of his grandmother", assumed the name of John MacLeod of MacLeod. We are given to understand that the Lyon King has also assented to *this* change. So you see how easy it is nowadays to perpetuate these arbitrary chief-ships! But the important question is whether there is any serious historical basis at all for a woman being a chief."

But were matters to be allowed to remain thus, in what to all intents and purposes looked as though they were agreeably settled for life? O dear no! Archibald Corrie Macnabb MacLeod was soon to find something better in the way of feudal affiliation. He was to renounce his bit of MacLeod nonsense in 1954 (we can hardly suppose "by the wish of his mother-in-law"), when Sir Thomas Innes of Learney, the Lord Lyon King of Arms, gave judgment in his claim to another chiefship! The Lord Lyon was now to recognise him as Macnab of Macnab, the 22nd Chief of the Clan since Gilbert Macnab of Bovain, 1336. His elevation from being a minor MacLeod at Dunvegan to a major Macnab in his own house at Kinnell, surrounded by the 6,000 acres he bought with it when he retired from the Indian Civil Service in 1949, necessitated just one small adjustment, namely, the loss of a 'b'. He's no longer just plain Archie Macnabb. He's now *The* Macnab He's quite a good chap, and all that, though he's got caught up in all this clan flummery, as I called it earlier.[1]

[1] I wonder whether it would simplify matters if one were to quote what Archie (born in 1886) has to say about himself in *Who's Who!* He is listed there as Macnab of Macnab, Archibald Corrie, and tells us that he "assumed in addition the name of MacLeod, 1943 (relinquished it and re-verted to surname of Macnabb, 1949; recognised as 22nd chief of clan, as A. C. Macnab of Macnab, 1954); his wife assumed the name of Alice Macnabb MacLeod of MacLeod, 1943 (changed to Alice MacLeod Mac-nabb, 1949, to Alice MacLeod Macnab of Macnab, 1954)."

It's all a matter of assuming, you see. Assuming by adoption and assumption.

So you see that you may call yourself anything you like, especially in Scotland, where such feudal fiction fosters much fawning and subservience.

So far as the MacGregors are involved in this airy-fairy business, I cannot but believe that my father knew what a lot of humbug all this sort of thing is, but accepted it as one is apt to do with cherished beliefs, even after they have been exploded. At times he showed himself very much one of those who, on attaining rank or position, resented any little omission, even on the part of lifelong acquaintances, to extend to them a deference often to be deplored. Thus he went white with passion, and literally quaked with indignation, when anybody, either through ignorance or inadvertence, addressed him as *Mister* MacGregor, instead of *Colonel* MacGregor. A spate of royal rhetoric, carrying everything before it, torrential as a Highland burn after a cloudburst, was certain to follow any such indiscretion or inadvertence. Colonels weren't quite ten-a-penny then!

On the other hand, one can go to the opposite extreme. Take the case of the commoner—the father-in-law of a fairly recent Marquis of Bristol, I think he was—who, proud to remind visitors to his home of his lowly origin, albeit he had got on in the world, and had managed to marry his daughter off to a peer of the realm, installed on the drawing-room piano an old wheelbarrow, the humble vehicle with which, early in life, he had set out to conquer!

The Highlanders residing in centres like Edinburgh and Glasgow have altered little since I came south to London in the late 1920s. This I see from the occasional perusal of such northern newspapers as record their doings. They hold the same functions in studious competition with one another. They sit down at the same dinners year after year. At these they deliver themselves of the same obsequious speeches. They stage exactly the same type of concert as they did in bygone ages. The songs sung at the last mentioned are just those they listened to in my boyhood, half a century ago. Innovations are highly unpopular. Everything is done to maintain a completely uncritical attitude.

One of the first concerts of this kind I ever attended was held in Edinburgh's Synod Hall, the venue on such occasions, before the erection of the Usher Hall. This, of course, was during my boyhood. It was incumbent upon my father, as one of the Scottish Capital's more prominent Gaels, to be present. The male Gaelic soloist on this occasion was a certain Murdo MacLeod, a native of Elphin, a township of Wester Sutherland, set among those primordial mountains that have a fascination weirder than any I know. Murdo had a little joinery business in Dalry Road, where from time to time my father dropped in for a few minutes' Gaelic conversation.

Murdo was the brother of the much better known Gaelic singer, Rory MacLeod. Rory owed his career in this sphere to my father, who, on his return from India in the 1890s, happened to hear him, as a lad employed at the Palace Hotel, Inverness, singing Gaelic songs as he went about his duties there. Greatly impressed by his Gaelic fluency, and by the ease with which he sang Gaelic songs, he took him south to introduce him to the Gaelic Society of London, of which he was a prominent member at that time. So that was how Rory MacLeod's career as a Gaelic singer and Mòd Medallist began. I am writing, you understand, of happenings roughly a decade before I was born.

My father and Rory, some years later, fell out, in the usual Celtic manner. It was over something as trivial as this: Should Rory, at some Mòd or other, have sung with the Inverness Gaelic Choir, or with the Stornoway? My father thought he should have done so with the latter. But just why, I never understood, particularly as Rory had been resident several years in Inverness, where he had a tailoring business.

But we must return to the Synod Hall and Rory's brother, Murdo, who had by far the finer voice, a voice with a lyrical quality wholly lacking in Rory's. But Rory could turn on the nasal bellowing, and at a volume the more modest Murdo had the good sense—and taste— never to attempt.

Knowing that my father was bound to be present at this Synod Hall concert, Murdo included in that evening's repertoire a couple of his Gaelic songs. This thoughtful gesture ought to have gratified my father. There was his name, emblazoned in the programme opposite two of the items to be rendered.

As he was a little deaf (Need I remind you of the cannon that burst by his ear during the Burmese War?), he had taken two front seats, one for himself, the other for me. This he had done in order that he might hear the more critically how Murdo dealt with his songs.

Murdo's performance with the first of these pleased everybody except its composer, who considered that he had made a hash of it, and who, throughout the rendering, did not fail to let both singer and audience know that he thought so. Though Murdo, looking so spruce in his concert togs, bowed deferentially to my father as he took up his position on the platform, the latter sat there, in the front of the hall, writhing with rage, unaware that, although *he* was too dull of hearing to appreciate just how much disturbance he was creating, his more than audible comments were annoying to everybody around him, and embarrassing as much to his young son as to the unfortunate singer. "The conceit of the fellow!' my father was heard to interject between his cherished verses.

If poor Murdo's performance up to that point in the proceedings had not pleased Colonel MacGregor, it was unlikely that, after remarks such as this, what was still to come would be any better, if indeed as good.

Anyhow, the conclusion of the song brought vociferous demands for an encore. And didn't the good-natured Murdo respond with another of my father's songs? Far from being flattered at such a reception, this infuriated my father still more. What should he do? Should he make some protest from the front of the hall, or should he go behind the scenes afterwards and box Murdo's ears? Father and son sat on, the former fulminating, the latter too nervous to move or utter.

When we got home after this trying experience, my father, seizing pen and paper, commanded me to stand by. A letter must be posted that night. Murdo must be made to realise just where he stood with Colonel MacGregor, Honorary Bard of the Clan Gregor:

Dear Sir,
  I must ask you never again to sing any of my Gaelic songs in public, after the horrible mess you made of them tonight.
                              Yours faithfully,
                                  John MacGregor.

Such a letter to a friend who had done his best was scarcely calculated to improve matters among Edinburgh's Gaels, who like Gaels everywhere, are always quarrelling over their vanities. Charged with the responsibility of dropping it, there and then, in the nearest pillar-box, and of 'reporting' to my father immediately afterwards that I had done so, about midnight I left his august presence with this brief but pungent epistle, returning a few minutes later to tell him that I had carried out his mandate when, in fact, I hadn't.

The following day, in desperation, I hurried off to find the session-clerk of our Gaelic church, taking this uncharitable document with me. I quoted to him, from memory, its terms, having heard my father read the letter over, aloud, just to make sure, as it were, that it carried adequately what he wanted to say. I suggested to the good Mr. MacKinnon that he might be able to soften the blow by taking the letter to Murdo personally, and telling him, in sorrow, the nature of its content, without necessarily handing it over to him. Later that day, Mr. MacKinnon visited Murdo at his joinery, and was happy to be able to tell me that very evening that, in everybody's interest, he and Murdo had agreed the letter should be destroyed, unopened.

Years later, the quiet and modest Murdo MacLeod stopped me in the street to tell me how he had appreciated my effort to soften the blow. "Och, your father's not a bad old chap, you know! A bit autocratic at times, though. Perhaps, his long period of service in the East explains his unpredictable temper. A good Highlander for all that. I believe he knows the Gaelic better than anyone living or dead, though maybe he hasn't much idea about music. But—Man Alive!— doesn't he carry the kilt to perfection? He has 'the leg for the kilt' all right! We can forgive him *anything,* after seeing him sailing along Princes Street like some Celtic King of olden times!"

Wasn't that generous of a little Edinburgh joiner from distant Sutherland? Generous of a man whose performance had been marred by my father's distracting behaviour, and who knew, furthermore, that my father had written him an impulsive letter—a letter he was charitable enough not to read?

In recalling Colonel MacGregor's royal rages and public explosions, which were quite a feature of the Edinburgh scene, even as late as my Golden Lamp years, it was fortunate for those of us who had to deal with him that he never took any of his pleasures in liquid form. In less than the twinkling of an eye, and wholly without benefit of drink, he could stage the most fantastic fury. This is a species of madness to which I believe the Celt to be particularly prone. I cite a truly historical example in our next chapter.

CHAPTER SIXTEEN

Glasgow Memories

THE TRAGEDY OF THE TROUSERS

IN THE preface to a book I published a few years ago, and as a solacement for those Glaswegian readers and correspondents who had expressed their regret at my having written so little about their city, with which, as they knew, I had had many associations, particularly during my Golden Lamp years, I promised that one day, to some extent at least, I would make good my omission. I seek to do so now. If a little belatedly, my recounting even the trousers incident related in this chapter would seem to provide an adequate pretext.

When my father and I travelled to Glasgow together for some function or other, we usually arrived sufficiently early to enable us to linger through the haunts and howffs he had known so well in his student days there, to wander among the ships berthed at the Broomielaw or moving in and out of the great docks on the Clyde, farther downstream, and perhaps to visit one or two of his college contemporaries. Occasionally he would insist on making an unostentatious pilgrimage to Gilmorehill, his *Alma Mater*. Had he not been one of her more distinguished graduates half a century earlier? Had he not carved his name deep in one of the lecture-room forms in an idle moment, just as thoughtless people do on the trunks of unoffending trees?

The first of these pilgrimages to his University I remember well, because it provided me with the first tangible proof I ever had that monstrous animals roamed the face of the earth in time pre-historic—creatures, oh! so much bigger than those elephants about which my father used to tell his offspring when dilating on India and Burma and Cambodia, or describing his adventures in the Land of the White Elephant. On this particular visit to Gilmorehill, he had taken me into the Bute Hall, where he had been capped so many, many years before. This provided him with an opportunity for reminding me of how notable a student he had been in his day, and how lamentable, therefore, was the persistent backwardness of his elder son. He then conducted me through the Hunterian Museum, where I saw many

159

strange things I still recall—dug-out canoes, such as were used by ancient man; relics from Roman forts in Scotland, including the wheel found in a refuse pit somewhere or other, and believed to have belonged to a Caledonian war-chariot captured by the Romans; Eskimo Kayak paddles; exquisitely small examples of Bronze Age pottery from Jericho, the city about which we had read so often during family-worship; and—and—and an almost complete specimen of an adult ichthyosaur. That, to be sure, was too wonderful! In memory's ear, I can hear my father announcing with measured particularity the Greek derivatives of this pre-historic monster, the better to impress its principal characteristics upon my all too vacant mind.

Just as he had been in the habit of doing in regard to Old Edinburgh, he sometimes insisted on conducting me on an educational tour of Old Glasgow. This usually meant a visit to St. Mungo's, and also to Provand's Lordship, claimed to be the oldest house in the city. It would have delighted him to see how commendably the National Trust for Scotland restored this ancient building in 1936.

His interest in these, however, was mild as compared with that he exhibited in those historic parts of Glasgow rendered the more famous and romantic because of their Clan Gregor associations, as set forth by Sir Walter Scott in *Rob Roy*. Thus a casual stroll to the Glasgow Cross became a necessary feature of our excursions to this city. Glasgow, of course, is preëminently a place of crosses—Charing Cross, St. George's Cross, Anniesland Cross, Gorbals Cross, Bridgeton Cross, Govan Cross, to mention a few of the better known. But not one of these is so historic as the Glasgow Cross, where the Saltmarket, the High Street, the Trongate, and the Gallowgate converge. The ghost of Prince Charlie, and he at the height of his gaiety, surely flits along the Gallowgate. And, although the ancient, crow-stepped buildings of the Saltmarket are no more, this thoroughfare still breathes of the Tobacco Lords and of the lesser, though no less pawky, merchants of olden times—aye, even of the Bailie Nicol Jarvie himself! Was not the Bailie's father—'Rest and bless him!'—a weaver in the Saltmarket?

Near at hand stood the Old Tolbooth, the only surviving part of which is the Steeple—a tall, square tower nearly 120 feet in height, containing a four-dialled clock and a chime of forty-eight bells. As youngsters we all had a great reverence for anything associated with the Old Tolbooth. It was the place where our ancestor, Rob Roy MacGregor, held tryst with the Bailie Nicol Jarvie, with Mr. Owen, with Francis Osbaldistone, and the faithful Dougal Cratur!

A little to the west stands another structure upon which we gazed for a moment or two in passing along the Trongate. I refer to the

Willie Morrison at 47, on his becoming Postmaster-General in 1940

Willie at 66, as Speaker of the House of Commons

Lowood Cottage, rehabilitated

A hazy morning by the Tweed at Lowood

Tron Steeple, which was attached to St Mary's Church until fire destroyed the latter in 1793. No one the least knowledgeable about eighteenth-century Glasgow, or about Scotland in general at that period, comes this way without recalling the exploits of the Tobacco Lords and, perhaps, also those of the hapless MacGregors, put to the horn at the Mercat Cross,[1] and hanged in the Gallowgate, nearby.

Though in my schooldays architectural elegance and the like mattered little to me, I must admit that my father did manage to provoke some interest in this direction when he drew my attention to the plaque in the Trongate, facing Tron St. Mary's, marking the site of the house in which Sir John Moore was born in 1761. How often had I laboured in vain, after school hours, to commit to memory his *Burial!* And there, before my very eyes, was the site of the house in which I so often wished he had never been born!

Of course, in recent years the face of Glasgow has altered enormously. Vast demolitions and vaster re-constructions have been its lot, in common with every other big city, The Glasgow of my Golden Lamp years has virtually vanished. Most of the shops and warehouses one knew then, most of the city's venerable landmarks of one's youth, have been modernised out of all recognition. Only the river seems to have retained anything of an abiding quality.

Yet, there is much about its citizens which has altered little. They are still as uninhibited as when I first had dealings with them. I was reminded of this while fingering my war through a notebook of anecdotes and observations entered three or four years ago, when I was approaching sixty. Let me give you an example of the sort of conversation in which even the grandest may find themselves involved with a waitress in Glasgow.

After a lapse of some years, I had gone to a hotel in Sauchiehall Street one evening. At breakfast the following morning, I had to explain to the waitress that I was a vegetarian. I see from my notebook that I recorded therein, at the time, our duologue:

"Parritch or prunes, sir?"

"Parritch," says I. "But I've an awkward piece of information for you: *I'm a vegetarian.*" After I had made it clear to her what this meant, she affably suggested scrambled eggs. I concurred. She returned with a plate of porridge, and a wee dish containing three rather sorry-looking prunes.

"Am I being allowed both?" I asked.

[1] *To put to the horn* is to denounce as an outlaw or rebel for failure to answer to a summons. In Old Scots Law a man was outlawed by three blasts of the horn at the Cross of Edinburgh.

F

"Och, ay. Ye better hae somethin' sustainin'. Ye ken whit folk say aboot a growing boy?"

"Growing boy!" I repeated. "Do you realise that I'll soon be sixty?"

"Gude's sake! Yer mair like a laddie o' twenty! A'm ower seeventy masel."

Some minutes later she returned without the scrambled eggs. Leaning down confidentially to explain without being overheard, she added: "There's a new chef on duty the day; and he's a wee bittie strange tae the job; and the lassie wha helps in the kitchen hasnae turned up, and—"

"And it would be simpler," I interposed, "if the eggs were boiled instead of scrambled."

"That's jist the position! Ye must hae 'the second-sicht'!"

A few minutes later she returned with a couple of boiled eggs. Her eye wandered to the little piece of porcelain reserved for sugar. It contained no more than a few grains.

"How's the sugar situation? It looks a bittie strained. Ah'll get ye a wee thimblefu' mair"—which she promptly did.

As I was leaving the diningroom after a good breakfast, I approached to tell her when I hoped to be in for my next meal. She leant an elbow on a sideboard, and crossed her ankles. She was obviously thinking over things that required a little lateral support. As I left the room, she waved a napkin at me, and announced in tones loud enough for everybody present to hear: "Ay, my! Ah thocht ye were a laddie o' twenty! Ah think Ah'll be a vegetarian masel!"

At this the entire diningroom broke out into hilarious laughter. This sort of thing is happening in Glasgow all the time. One could scarcely imagine it in staid Edinburgh.

It was my father's function as Bard of the Clan Gregor to write odes, laments, salutes, and all that sort of nonsensical composition, for all sorts of nonsensical occasions connected in one way or another with the MacGregors. Matters relating to the chief and his family and his somewhat diminished patrimony were always regarded as eminently suitable for such muse as the Bard could muster. Anything to do with the ancient and proscribed MacGregors, with the triumphs and misfortunes of 'The Old Name', was almost as much a religion with him as were the precepts of the New Testament, upon which he had been nurtured, and on which he dutifully had reared his children. Little wonder that, in recognition of his services to the Clan Gregor, and of his being its first Bard for some hundreds of years, the heritors granted him a lair beside Rob Roy and his kith and kin, in the old graveyard on the Braes of Balquhidder, in the heart of the MacGregor Country!

There, in 1932, during a snowstorm, his ashes were buried; and there a slab of grey granite, somewhat inadequately inscribed, marks the spot:

> *On it spread no flimsy roses,*
> *Fresh and fragrant though they bloom,*
> *Since they're not the tribal emblems*
> *That should grace my Highland tomb:*
> *Place instead some purple heather!*
> *Plant a sprig of stately pine!*
> *For they're both supremely loyal,*
> *And, by birthright, both are mine.*

Often for days at a time he would shut himself up in his study, in true bardic gloom, composing, or ferreting out some obscure genealogy, of maybe arranging his material as a disputant in one of those interminable controversies in which the Celts specialise.

Prior to 1914, bardic matters took him occasionally to Perth, where lived his nonagenarian clanswoman, Miss Murray-MacGregor of Mac-Gregor, aunt of the late chief, Sir Malcolm MacGregor of MacGregor. This very old lady had written some books, and had devoted much of her life to the affairs of clan tradition and genealogy. It was held that she and my father, between them, knew everything worth knowing about the MacGregors. In many a fierce newspaper controversy they loyally supported one another. With solemn regularity, week by week, they exchanged clannish correspondence. Not even the letter my father had received from Queen Victoria's secretary, commanding him to attend at Buckingham Palace, nor yet that from the Prime Minister, annoucing some monetary award or other for his services to the Gaelic language, gave him as much pleasure as did the receipt of a letter from this remarkable and venerable clanswoman. A trip to Heaven with all expenses paid could not have occasioned more delight than did those comparatively short train journeys to Perth, where he conferred with her on matters in which both of them were so absorbed.

Like himself, she was a prominent office-bearer of the Clan Gregor Society. Up to the time of her death, at the age of nearly a hundred, she occupied the position of Sennachie, or Clan Historian. It was only natural, then, that there should have been a good deal upon which Bard and Sennachie conferred. The former sang the praises of the clan in poetry and song: the latter recorded its deeds and lineage.

Shall I ever forget the afternoon I found my father seated pensively in his study, affectionately fingering a piece of official notepaper artist-ically headed with the crest of the MacGregors, the names of the clan's principal office-bearers embossed in Gaelic thereunder? The inclusion of his own on that impressive stationery was a source of infinite pride to him. There he appeared, in very truth, as Honorary Bard, in company with the Chief, the Sennachie, the Standard-bearer, and the Honorary Piper.

The death of Miss Amelia Murray-MacGregor of MacGregor was a sad blow for my father. No one ever could take her place in his MacGregor world, the world in which he now lived almost exclusively. He mourned her passing as he never mourned the passing of anyone else in his life. It was as though 'The Old Name' had received a setback from which it might never recover.

In December, 1922, there was held in Glasgow the centenary dinner of the Clan Gregor Society, an occasion I am not likely to forget because of an incident that preceded it. My father's attendance was, of course, essential. In his capacity as Bard, he had written a special pipe-tune—*Clan Gregor's Salute*—for the opening ceremony. An advance copy of this he had forwarded some months beforehand to his old and loyal friend, the late John MacGregor Murray, the Honorary Piper, together with instructions as to how it should be treated, and mentioning that he hoped to arrive from Edinburgh in sufficient time to allow Bard and Piper, privately, to rehearse the *Salute* before they tried it out on the centenary gathering.

For months my father had been counting the intervening days. "I hardly suppose that I shall live to see another Clan Gregor centenary," he would remark in mournful accents, when I mentioned that I thought this forthcoming function was getting a little on his brain.

"Do you realise I am now well into my seventy-fifth year, and that in the ordinary course of events I cannot expect to have much more to look forward to on this planet?"

Daily—nay, hourly—the centenary dinner of the Clan Gregor Society crept nearer and nearer, until at length it assumed an importance that could not have been exceeded had the Day of Judgment been imminent. Fear that some calamity might overwhelm mankind, ere we reached that appointed day in December, was ever present with him. If only the great, big world could be persuaded to go on turning until after this event, it mattered little what catastrophe befell the human race thereafter. Life on this planet might become extinct, if God so willed. But it was hoped that He would not ordain any serious alteration in the solar system until the Clan Piper, followed by the Bard, had piped the procession into the banqueting-hall to the strains of *Clan Gregor's Salute*. All the dynasties in creation might collapse after that. The very oceans might engulf our civilisation, but not before the Universe had heard the martial strains of this little masterpiece in pipe-music, played lustily by the Clan Piper, under the Bard's critical direction!

In order to facilitate the packing of such clothes as were necessary for this supremely important event, it was agreed that I should take my father's evening dress home to Miss Aitken a day or two beforehand, so that she might examine it carefully, and give it any attention it required. It would have to be pressed, and so on. It was also agreed that this evening dress of his, as well as my own, should be packed in the same suitcase, which I would have with me when I met him at the Waverley Station in good time for the train by which we had decided to travel to Glasgow. As that train carried us westward on the appointed day, he broke the silence of the railway compartment several times to enquire of me whether I had remembered to pack this and pack that.

"Are you certain you have my cuff-links? My necktie? The proper studs?" The more he asked, the more impatient I became.

"You know perfectly well," I added finally, "that I've never once let you down about such things all the years we've been attending these blessed functions together!"

Ah! These were, indeed, Famous Last Words, as you shall see! Scarcely had they left my lips than I became vaguely conscious that, perhaps, after all, Miss Aitken, to whom I always entrusted any packing, might not have been as efficient as I had fancied. By the time we reached Queen Street, I was distracted by so frightening a thought. I tried to appease my uneasiness by remembering how meticulously careful old Miss Aitken had been in matters of this kind—how she insisted that this sort of packing was *her* province, rather than mine, and that, if *I* undertook it, something was certain to be left behind.

In due course father and I found ourselves at the Grand Hotel, by Glasgow's Charing Cross. We had selected this place for our night's sojourn because the centenary function was being held in its spacious banqueting-hall. As crowds of MacGregors and their followers had arrived there before us, we were obliged to occupy bedrooms some little distance apart. This we thought a little awkward at the outset. But I had reason to be truly thankful some minutes later for this protective separation.

Since the Bard had arranged to meet the Piper somewhere in the basement of the hotel, in order to rehearse with him the very especial pipe-tune he had composed for the occasion, he was desirous of dressing without delay. I therefore opened the suitcase, and laid out upon his bed what purported to be his half of its contents. There appeared to be two of everything. In fact, there *were* two of everything. But I was too much of a coward to examine them, having an almost paralysing premonition. I hurried to my own room at the other end of a long corridor to dress immediately and—wait developments.

For several minutes matters seemed to be proceeding smoothly enough. Yet, I felt that the sooner I was properly attired, the better I would be able to cope with any untoward situation which might arise. Suddenly, the orderliness of the hotel was disturbed by a plethora of shouting and cursing. I rushed to my bedroom door and peeped out. There, in the distance, stood Colonel John MacGregor, Honorary Bard of the Clan Gregor, in his bedroom doorway, in his shirt-tails, leaning heavily on his walking-stick, hobbled, shackled, scarcely able to move, and calling for me by all the naughty words he could summon in two languages. Miss Aitken had packed two pairs of trousers all right; but neither of them fitted by a foot my father's girth. Both belonged to Alasdair, then a lithe and graceful creature! The pair I had left for him on his bed he had succeeded in getting over his ankles. But he now found himself able neither to pull them on, nor to pull them off.

"Why in the name of God have I been cursed with a son who is a congenital idiot? Whatever possessed me to marry that—, your mother?"

Such were the rhetorical posers which he addressed to himself, and in a volume that sent them echoing through the Grand Hotel.

"Do you remember what you said in the train an hour or two ago? You told your old father that you had never let him down! *A Thighearna! A Thighearna!* This is what comes of having married that—, your mother!"

He now struck out at me with his stick. Had his hobbled circumstance not curtailed his movements, he would have succeeded in striking me; and I might well have been no more. (Bards on bardic occasions can be gey fearsome, ye ken!)

By this time my father was quite definitely in a state of temporary insanity. Had it been possible for him to have laid hands on me, he would assuredly have strangled me. For a man of seventy-five, he was enormously powerful. Unable either to retreat to his bedroom, or to get out into the corridor to apprehend me, he remained in the doorway, in his shirt-tails, moving just the few tottering inches his fetters would allow, thundering away whenever he caught sight of me, breathing brimstone in my direction and fumes of Tartarean sulphur, and swearing heavily in the Gaelic. In other circumstances his bad language in that tongue would have been understood by nobody except myself, for whom it was designed. But on this occasion the Grand Hotel was crowded with Gaels who, like our mad selves, had arrived for this centenary celebration.

Que faire? What was one to do? My predicament was truly awful. Apoplexy threatened.

Hotel porters, page-boys, chambermaids, and laundresses had now assembled within what they deemed a safe distance of the roaring Bard, which was a good deal nearer than *I* dared venture, not merely because I feared he might break his fetters and make a wild dash at me, but also because his rage appeared to diminish as I receded. Conversely, the closer I came, the more it increased.

I now threw myself on the mercy of the head-porter, to whom I had no need to explain my plight. Putting our heads together, we decided to despatch an impish page-boy to a secondhand clothes shop of which he knew, in the hope of borrowing a suitable pair of trousers. Upstairs I rushed again, followed by the page, who carried a measuring-tape. From a distance of about ten yards I yelled to my father to retreat to his bedroom as best he could, assuring him that all would *still* be well, if only he reverted to a modicum of sanity.

"You told me that you had never let me down:" he went on repeating.

"*I won't let you down even yet!*" I screamed at him, confident that my resourcefulness in situations of this kind would solve our dilemma if only I could have his coöperation. I reminded him that although, to all outward appearances, I had played him a dirty trick, never in our long and strenuous dealings with one another had we been confronted with a situation from which one or other of us had not succeeded in extricating us both.

Coöperation, forsooth! Would he hearken to anything as reasonable? Not he! But how, otherwise, was it going to be possible to get his waist measurement? I dared not approach within arm's-length of him without risking instant strangulation. The page, on the other hand, was too tiny to take the height and girth of a man as rotund and demented.

"I shall never live to see another centenary!" he now began; "and I've been looking forward to this one for years. And this is the sort of trick you play on your old father!"

With commendable presence of mind, the page dangled the measuring-tape before his wild eyes, into which a touch of softness now crept. This at last enabled me to persuade him to retreat with his shirt-tails from the gaze of an ever-increasing number of spectators. But the problem of his dimensions still had to be overcome. It was as obvious that the page could not get his little arms round my father's girth as it was that any endeavour on my part to do so would have robbed our tactics of all value. So the head-porter underwent the necessary peril. After coaxing my father to retire into his bedroom—

an act in which he rendered him the necessary balancing assistance—
he speedily took the more important measurements in rough approx-
imation, turned to the page standing by, and ordered him to flee, as
never before in his life, to a secondhand clothes shop in Buchanan
Street, which might still be open. Down the long staircase, in a series
of dizzy circles, dashed the fugacious page, holding in one hand the
tape, firmly fixed between finger and thumb at the correct place for
the waist measurement, and in the other a pound note, his well-oiled
hair like a porcupine's bristles. Judging by the speed at which he
quitted, we calculated that he would be back in less than twenty
minutes, when the Grand March was due to begin. Would it be possible
to have the Bard on his feet in that time, clothed in trousers of *some*
sort, as well as in his senses? Titanic as such an undertaking appeared,
it had to be attempted.

As the page sped through the city, the Bard resumed his jeremiad
behind the bedroom door. He could be very trying and embarrassing
when he thought his inmost thoughts aloud, and particularly dangerous
when he thought them with a sturdy walking-stick in his hand! I
tried to explain to him that, since a suitable pair of trousers might be
available at any moment, time could be saved if we now proceeded
to remove from his ankles those he could neither pull on nor pull off.
But, for him, the day was lost, the position irretrievable. Indeed, he
now seemed to wish it to be so. After all, he had expended a good
deal on rage; and it would be a pity were the cause for all this uproar
heartlessly removed. The moment had arrived, however, when I felt
that if any solution were to be achieved, it was incumbent on me to
take the offensive. So I quietly transferred his bedroom door-key to
the outside, and manoeuvred him to a position sufficiently close to his
bed to make possible my pushing him backwards over it. This I did.
Seizing the ends of my trousers, while he kicked to the rhythm of
more Gaelic swearings, I ripped them off his ankles with a vehemence
rendering them permanently unserviceable. Leaving my father more
on the floor than on the bed, I rushed from the room and locked the
door behind me, trusting that a spell of solitude might help him to
regain his feet with a minimum of embarrassment, and such equi-
librium as so dramatic an unfettering might have inspired. Listening
intently at the door, I soon realised that a touch of Celtic Gloom had
settled upon him. Walking-stick in hand, and no longer entrammelled,
he began to wander round the room like a caged animal, trying the
door handle every now and then. No one must venture near him, I
realised, unless armed with a pair of suitable trousers. Otherwise, one
ran the risk of inducing a fit of apoplexy, an end which he sometimes
felt might have been his.

While I stood outside his door, determined not to permit of another display in shirt-tails, the page came tearing upstairs with the necessary garment. When I imagined my father to be farthest from the door, I opened it and threw it sharply across the room toward the bed, just as one throws a scrap to a mordacious carnivore. "Try them on!" I yelled.

But what if they don't fit? Such a prospect brought me out in beads of perspiration. And, if they do fit, will it be possible to produce the living, mobile body of the Bard within the next few minutes, and as that of a tolerably sane person?

In the matter of girth, the trousers turned out to be ample. In the matter of length, however, they were nearly a foot too long. When he moved in them, they flopped in front of his toes like a sea-lion's flippers. He was still as certain as he could be that all was lost. He afforded me no opportunity of telling him that I had arranged for a little postponement of the opening proceedings.

"Take them off for a moment," I advised. "We can rectify the length in a few seconds."

With the assistance of chambermaid and laundress, we turned them in at the foot, pressed them with a hot iron, and tacked them in position. They now looked admirable.

"One day you will have reason to laugh over this episode," I assured my father as he sought the hotel staircase.

"Laugh?" he replied with sarcasm. "This is no laughing matter! Nothing has gone right with me since the day I met your mother!"

Poor Mabel, meantime four hundred miles away, in Fleet Street, was even held responsible for Miss Aitken's having packed the wrong pair of trousers, for how otherwise could he have been cursed with such a son? That at so critical a moment in his career Fate should have found the Bard to the Clan Gregor hobbled on the landing of a Glasgow hotel, with nothing on but a shirt and a pair of sock-suspenders, was all her doing. What a judgment upon him! Mabel's evil and scheming influences were still dogging his footsteps!

For all this, the Bard a minute or two later was moving freely and proudly among the throng awaiting him downstairs, while he looked earnestly for MacGregor Murray, the Clan Piper. When at long last the function was about to begin with the traditional Grand March, neither Bard nor Piper could be found. Were it not that my father had now been a teetotaller for many years (part of his sacrifice to ensure that his children should be educated), one would have suspected that he and MacGregor Murray had slipped out together to the nearest pub. The master of ceremonies was nearly frantic with this further delay. A search-party was organised. Someone reported that every now and then a note or two of pipe-music could be heard, as if emanating from some remote apartment of the hotel, a door of which was being opened and closed at infrequent intervals.

We all listened intently, anxious to trace to their source these elusive strains. Eventually, Bard and Piper were located in the staff lavatory somewhere in the basement, where they were trying over *Clan Gregor's Salute,* prior to their inflicting it on the already exasperated assembly. For the time being, all was serene where my father was concerned. The Tragedy of the Trousers, as the incident was referred to ever after, was forgotten.

What a relief it was to be able to sit back and watch the Grand March in a completely detached way! Off it went at last, led by the Piper gaily playing the *Salute* composed for the occasion, and immediately behind him the Bard now so dignified and quiescent, in hired trousers!

When, later in the evening's proceedings, it devolved upon my father to deliver his bardic rhapsody—his catalogue of all the noble things MacGregors had done since the dawn of history—he prefaced it with a lurid account of his son's delinquency in connection with those trousers. This immediately had the company in convulsions of hilarity. Aware that earlier in the evening several clansmen and their women-folk had seen him fettered in the bedroom doorway, in his shirt-tails, he felt that some official explanation from the Bard himself would not be altogether inappropriate.

I was by no means unconscious that, while we were facing that frightful situation in Glasgow, dear Miss Aitken would be seized by distraction in Edinburgh. I knew that by now she would have found, unpacked, my father's trousers, and that she was facing a sleepless night.

Never was I more thankful to return to the restful atmosphere of my Golden Lamp than after that experience in Glasgow. When I got back to Miss Aitken next day, I found her sobbing in her chair by the kitchen fire. She had been sobbing all night, and since dawn. "Cheer up!" I said. "We managed fine without them!" As I described to her how, in the end, I had succeeded in rendering the Bard presentable the previous evening, her sobs were increased to laughter and streaming tears—the tears that flow when some great anxiety is past.

"You're a bad, bad girl!" exclaimed my father when he called on Miss Aitken a few days later. "You sent the Bard of the Clan Gregor off to Glasgow without his pants!"

CHAPTER SEVENTEEN

The Murray Baronetcy

DOUBTLESS, you will have noted that the year of that Clan Gregor
Society Centenary function in Glasgow was 1922. This would seem
to warrant a brief examination of Clan Gregor's position at least a
hundred years earlier, if merely to satisfy those who wonder why I
should have questioned the validity of certain clan chiefships, without
examining that of the MacGregors. You may well feel entitled to know
what justification there is for my having said in a previous chapter
that the correct surname of the present MacGregor of MacGregor
family is Murray, and not MacGregor.

My task has been simplified enormously by the care and diligence
with which my lifelong friend, Sheriff John MacGregor, Q.C., has
studied the relevant papers in the John MacGregor Collection at the
Register House, in Edinburgh, as well as those at the Scottish Record
Office. The result lies before me now, in a form carefully set out and
as carefully documented. I have known for years of the Sheriff's
sharing my view that the claim to the Clan Gregor chiefship would
bear as much or as little scrutiny as most. His retirement from the
Bench a year or two ago provided him with the time and opportunity
to ascertain *the facts* of the case, without necessarily expressing an
opinion on them. Briefly, the facts are as follows:

In 1774, the year that the proscription of the name of MacGregor
was removed, the MacGregors owned not an acre of land in Scotland.
Their patrimony had been taken over by their betrayers and traducers.
Furthermore, all the clan's leading families had either been exter-
minated or dispersed. Ever since the lifting of the ban on the name,
however, the clan has increased in numbers, in prosperity, in fame,
in prestige. Its survival and ultimate recognition, after some centuries
of persecution and oppression, have bequeathed to it an enviable history
and romance. For this, those of us legitimately bearing 'The Old
Name' owe our greatest debt to Sir Walter Scott. It was *he* who,
more than anybody else, put us, the Children of the Mist, on the map,
to use a current cliché. It was *he* who restored us to public favour,

171

who resuscitated us, and recorded, for all the world to see, those enact-
ments against the "Lawless Limmers," designed to exterminate us:

> *Though they rob us of name,*
> *And pursue us with beagles,*
> *Give their roofs to the flame,*
> *And their flesh to the eagles!*

In virtue of all this, one can appreciate the resentment felt by those
genuinely and legitimately bearing the surname of MacGregor against
those who so complacently usurp it.

In the centuries of clan warfare and civil strife inseparable from
the activities of various claimants to the throne, the reason for a clan's
having a chief or a leader is easily understood. It required that the
man chosen was the one who, on his personal merits, seemed best
fitted to occupy such a position. He might or he might not be the eldest
son of the previously acknowledged leader, or even a younger son.
He might be—as, indeed, he often was—a member of another family
of the same clan. In other words, *this leadership was not hereditary.*

Sheriff MacGregor cites Alasdair MacGregor of Glen Strae as a
good example of a leader selected entirely on account of his personal
record and qualities, in order to deal with an exceptional set of
circumstances in which the clan found itself. That the government of
the day regarded Alasdair as the clan's leader is shown by his arrest,
trial, and execution at Edinburgh in 1604, the year after the Mac-
Gregors' defeat of the Colquhouns at the Battle of Glen Fruin. "There
is no evidence," as the Sheriff rightly maintains, "that he was called
chief before the battle, nor that he was heir-apparent, because it is
known that his elder brother, John MacGregor, was killed in
the battle."

Quite clearly, a study of the papers and documents in the Mac-
Gregor Collection and in the Record Office supports the conclusion
that the Clan Gregor never had a hereditary chief, and that, while
there may have been leading MacGregor families, no such family had
—nor ever assumed—the right to nominate a chief.

There is evidence that MacGregor of Balhaldie was elected Captain
and Chief of the clan in July, 1714. There is also evidence that in
1746 MacGregor of Glen Gyle led a band of MacGregors into battle
at Falkirk. He held the rank of colonel in the Young Chevalier's army.
With the collapse of the clan system after the Jacobites' final defeat
at Culloden in 1746, there was no longer any necessity to elect a clan
chief. Such heritable jurisdiction as had survived up till then certainly
went then. The MacGregors, like many another clan, remained with-

out a chief thereafter, until somebody of the name of Murray thought he would like to have himself regarded as such. Historically, this is what happened:

A man named John Murray, born in 1745, was employed as a clerk in the London office of the East India Company. After a time he was posted to the Auditor-General's department in India. Capable and industrious, he soon amassed a considerable fortune. During one or other of two visits he paid to Scotland, he purchased from the Campbells the Perthshire estate of Edinchip, situated near Lochearnhead, now owned by the family calling itself MacGregor of MacGregor. The Campbells had been in possession of Edinchip from 1730 until 1778. This John Murray also bought Balquhidder. There he erected the mausoleum one sees on the left side of the road leading westward from Kingshouse in the direction of the church and burial-place of Balquhidder, where Rob Roy and his kindred lie buried, and where, as already related, my father also lies—his ashes, anyhow. On his retiral from the East India Company, Murray took up residence at Lanrick Castle, situated by the River Teith, a few miles west of Doune. This he also had bought. I have seen in the John MacGregor Collection a copy of a fulsome treatise of his, purporting to trace his ancestry back to Achaius, who reigned in Scotland toward the close of the eighth century!

In 1787 this same John Murray instructed a notary in Killin to prepare a deed declaring him to be Chief of the Clan Gregor. (Such cheek! if I may permit myself a parenthetical observation.) A copy of this was posted at four Perthshire centres of population, including Killin; and persons of the surname of MacGregor were invited to sign it. Some hundreds appear to have done so. My father's old friend, the late John MacGregor, Writer to the Signet, made notes and comments on these signatures. These are to be found in the John MacGregor Collection, for which John was entirely responsible, and which, at his death in 1937, he bequeathed to the historical department of the Register House—of the Scottish Record Office—at Edinburgh.[1]

Murray's bold assumption was challenged by several MacGregors, notably by MacGregor of Glen Gyle, but without upsetting this quite fictitious claim to the Clan Gregor chiefship by somebody of another clan and surname. There is in existence the correspondence between Murray and Lieutenant MacGregor of Innerhadden, in which the latter takes Murray to task for having failed to implement certain

[1] John MacGregor, W.S., his associations with my father, and his inestimable Collection form the subject-matter of Chapter V. of my book, *The Turbulent Years*, first published by Methuen in 1945.

promises, and mentions that his behaviour had occasioned much adverse comment and dissatisfaction among several of the MacGregors who had signed the deed ostensibly recognising him as their chief. The Lieutenant reminds him, moreover, that he was merely *elected* Chief of the Clan Gregor, and that he had no claim on the title, hereditary or otherwise. To this Murray wrote an evasive reply. In fairness to him, it should be noted that at no time did he assume the surname of MacGregor. He left it to his Murray descendants to do that! The nearest *he* ever got to doing so is probably the occasion when he affixed to a letter his signature as John M. Murray of MacGregor. This letter is in the John MacGregor Collection.

When the said John M. Murray retired from the East India Company, he was known to his colleagues as Colonel Murray. This is clearly shown by the address with which they presented him at a farewell dinner. In 1793 he was created a baronet in the name of Murray. He died at Portobello in 1822, and was buried at Balquhidder, in the mausoleum he had erected there.

This Sir John Murray was succeeded in the baronetcy by his son, Sir Evan Murray, who, under the name of Murray, had served in a cavalry regiment in India, whence he had retired some little time before his father's death. Evan signed a letter relating to his father's funeral arrangements as Evan J. Murray. But before long Sir Evan J. Murray was to adopt the surname of MacGregor. And this is the point at which the real bluff and mischief begin.

In 1822, the year of his father's death, the Clan Gregor Society was formed—which explains, of course, how, a hundred years later, Colonel John MacGregor, Bard of the Clan Gregor, and father of the unworthy Alasdair Alpin MacGregor, was to find himself in Glasgow without his trousers!

In a statement dated Lanrick Castle, September, 25th, 1822, signed E. J. Murray MacGregor of MacGregor, and lodged in the office of the Lyon King of Arms, he sets out his claim to be MacGregor of MacGregor, founding it on his alleged descent from the Glencarnoch family. It is a little odd that the Registers of Sasines[1] record no entry whatsoever relating to any MacGregor of Glencarnoch. But Sheriff MacGregor did discover during his recent researches an entry pertaining to Robert Murray, Younger of Glencarnoch, anent his having taken sasine of half of the town and lands of Craigruie, in the Lordship of Balquhidder.

When Sir Evan Murray, now styling himself MacGregor, died in the Barbadoes in 1844, he was succeeded in the baronetcy by his son,

[1] Sasine in Scots Law is the act of giving legal possession of feudal property. It means simply infeftment. (*cf.* seisin.)

Sir John Murray MacGregor, just as the late Sir Malcolm MacGregor of MacGregor, in 1879, when a mere boy, succeeded his own father, Sir Malcolm MacGregor, and was himself succeeded in 1958 by *his* son, the present Sir Gregor MacGregor. Gregor, like his predecessors, and therefore through no fault of his own, calls himself MacGregor of MacGregor. By the same token he regards himself as the Chief of the Clan Gregor, although he is actually the 6th Murray baronet.

So this quite arbitrary claim to the MacGregor chiefship really dates from the Lord Lyon's endorsement of Sir Evan Murray's claim to be MacGregor of MacGregor. Can there exist more flimsy genealogical grounds?

Documentary evidence, far from establishing the claim that the MacGregors had a hereditary chief, clearly refutes it. Anybody spoiling to challenge me on this should first consult the Historical Papers relating to the Jacobite Period, 1699-1750, edited by Colonel James Allardyce of Culquoich, and printed in Aberdeen in 1895 for the New Spalding Club. Let me quote a relevant passage:

> "CLAN GREGORE . . . They have no freehold or Barron Amongst them are few or None that have any heritage they have no present Chieften the Said Dignitie being Just Now Elective and Continues no longer than the Current Expedition and is *Detur Digniori* they can raise amongst them 500 Men and Are rarely Absent from any Great Convocation whatever the Quarrell may be, Since plunder and Booty is their Business."

You will agree that this disposes of all the hereditary chiefship nonsense, popularly perpetuated in regard to the Clan Gregor.

This evidence is cited by Colonel David Stewart in his *Sketches of the Character, Manners, and Present State of the Highlanders of Scotland*, published in Edinburgh in 1822 by Archibald Constable, in two volumes. Both John Murray and his son, Evan Murray, were alive when Stewart was writing his *Sketches*. The former died at Portobello the year of their publication: the latter died in the Barbadoes twenty-two years later.

I trust you are now satisfied that those who have been describing themselves as MacGregor of MacGregor for the last century and a half are not MacGregors at all, but are Murrays in disguise! Nobody —not even a Murray—can claim direct lineal descent from the Mac-Gregors of old merely by choosing to adopt their surname, and then putting himself forward as the chief of their clan! Surely, that is clear to anybody!

Having accepted this ludicrous position, just consider what happened in 1913. In May of that year, when I was still an Edinburgh schoolboy, there was held in the Royal Hotel, in that city's celebrated Princes Street, a Special Meeting of the Clan Gregor Society's Council which, as I well remember, my father attended. What it was convened to discuss, I never knew until quite recently, and as the result of a little serendipity while fingering my way through papers in the John MacGregor Collection. In any case, I would hardly have been interested at my age in 1913.

This meeting, as I now know, was called to consider an application by the Clan Gregor Society of America for affiliation with the Clan Gregor Society in Scotland. When in the course of discussion on this application it transpired that the American Society included members with surnames other than MacGregor, the application was triumphantly rejected by a large majority! The Clan Gregor Society, although prepared to condone a succession of Murrays as chiefs of the MacGregors, mustn't run the risk of dilution, mustn't allow its rank and file to be contaminated by admitting to affiliation a clan organisation which, two thousand miles away, actually confessed—and without a blush—to having among its members some whose surname wasn't MacGregor!

But let us look for a moment at a somewhat altered picture in 1962, nearly half a century later, when dissatisfaction was expressed at a neligible membership of 221, more than half of which had been recruited the previous year. In the spring of 1962, the Council's report to the Annual General Meeting of the Society complained that members of the clan had not been joining the Society in sufficient numbers. It was therefore proposed, seconded, and duly carried that—

(1) Persons of the surnames of Grier, Greer, Grierson, and Magruder should be admitted as full members.

(2) All MacGregors of the first generation on the maternal side should likewise be eligible for full membership.

The terms of this motion are now embodied in the Rules of the Clan Gregor Society. I am not quite certain, however, whether applications for membership under the second heading must be accompanied by a birth certificate!

I would have you notice that the first three surnames from which the ban has been lifted are of Lowland Scottish origin. They are in no way related to the MacGregors, not even on the pretext that their ancestors may have adopted these surnames when the name of Mac-Gregor was suppressed. Grierson is, of course, a Dumfriesshire name.

The only Magruders I have ever heard of have been Americans, who got it into their romantic heads that they were in some way connected with the MacGregors. My father once conducted a long and tedious correspondence with a Magruder living in New York. He was anxious to have the Bard to the Clan Gregor confirm that his family's name was a misspelling of MacGregor! My father, resolved to defend 'The Old Name' against such fashionable presumption, could not persuade himself to do so, although the Magruder claim to recognition as MacGregors was being aired, and indeed heavily canvassed, at that time in the correspondence columns of certain Scottish newspapers.

It must not be forgotten that those oppressive Acts of Parliament, ultimately finding expression in the proscription—in the outlawry of the very name of MacGregor—did not apply to Murrays, Griers, Greers, Griersons, and Magruders. They were directed solely against people bearing the name of MacGregor.

Apropos these Murray chiefs of the MacGregors, I can only add by way of conclusion that, if time and space allowed, I would deal with a few more baseless claims to clan chiefships and the like. Scotland has never been more replete with humbug of this nature than she is today.

CHAPTER EIGHTEEN

A Visit from Catriona

I CANNOT quite recall the year of this visit, this veritable visitation; and my youngest sister, Catriona Mairi MacGregor, and I are so agreeably estranged as to leave family matters quietly undisturbed. So I have no alternative but to hazard a guess. If I could remember Catriona's age, I believe I could make an accurate deduction. As she and her mother had been at pains to prevent anyone's knowing they had, respectively, in me, a son and a brother whom they regarded as too odd and shamefully inept to be exhibited, I am hardly in a position now to enquire of Catriona either her age or the year in which occurred the visit from her now to be described. Besides, if I did make any enquiry of her, she would suspect—and rightly—some ulterior motive on my part. The motive now lies unmasked before you: this chapter of this book. I think the year may have been 1927. It was shortly before I came to London.

In order to clarify family relationships a little for readers unfamiliar with my earlier Trilogy, I had better begin by explaining that my mother had left my father many years before, and was living in London, gainfully and not altogether unimportantly employed at journalism in Fleet Street, and much admired and respected in her profession. Catriona was educated, not in Scotland under our father's auspices, but in England, under our mother's, primarily in accordance with the latter's snob values. She was about to complete two years at a finishing school in Paris when there arose a situation about which I must now tell you.

Five days before Catriona was due in London, I received from my mother, in the form of a registered letter, a sort of ultimatum. Posted in London on the Monday, it reached me in Edinburgh the following day. Its terms were pretty much as follows:

Catriona arrives at Victoria from Paris on Saturday afternoon. I have spent on her and her education over the years a great deal, and can spend no more. When I told her that her old headmistress at Clewer had agreed to engage her immediately she returned to England (chiefly because of her fluency in French and English), and that six months' teaching there would give her time to consider what she wants to do with her life, and at the same time relieve me, if only temporarily, of the financial burden which she has been for so long, she writes me that she has no intention of going to Clewer, nor anywhere else for that matter. She has studied so hard in Paris, she says, that, when she returns, she is going to have, for at least a year, what she describes as 'a good time'.

When I ask who is expected to maintain her while she is having her 'good time,' I can get no answer. I have written her that I shall meet her at Victoria on Saturday, and that I shall ask her immediately whether she means to respect my wish with regard to Clewer, or whether she would prefer to give you and your father an indefinite spell of her company. If she decline Clewer, it must be Edinburgh. This would mean my taking her straight from Victoria to King's Cross, and putting her on the night train. She would arrive next Sunday morning at the Waverley Station. In any event, it would not do you and your father any harm to have to cope with Catriona for a bit.

I am sorry to give you such short notice of Catriona's highly probable arrival.

Quite so! Five days' notice of something rather perplexing, and fraught with all manner of uncertainties.

"Yer gey worried-like, laddie!" Miss Aitken remarked, enquiringly, later in the day. "I recognised an envelope in yer mither's handwriting among yer letters. Ye certainly ha'enae been yer auld self since it arrived. What's she up tae noo?"

We looked at one another in silence for some seconds. "Ah ken fine there's something in yon letter that's upset ye."

Miss Aitken knew all right; and it wasn't long before the dogs were made aware that a crisis was upon us.

"Can ye no' trust me enough tae let me *see* the letter?"

Reluctantly, I handed it to her. "I think I'll just—". She interrupted me.

"Nae need tae 'think', laddie. Nae need tae answer. Meet the lassie at the Waverley on Sunday morning; an' nae mair aboot it. That's if yer mither implements her threat. Jist bring the lassie straucht hame here. We'll dae oor best for her. Ma certie! aifter a' thae graund cairry-ons in Paris, she'll hae tae mak' dae wi' the best we can provide her wi'. Ah've never met yet mither; an' Ah dinnae want tae. But—ma certie!—if ever she comes *ma* way, she'll get the shairp end o' ma tongue. Ay, my! Yer puir, auld faither!' "

As it happened, we had accommodation available for Catriona, since one of Miss Aitken's lodgers—a theological student—had just completed his classes for the session, and was on the point of returning home on long summer vacation.

The next few days passed agreeably enough. Miss Aitken had got Catriona's room ready for her, just in case mother's ultimatum expired otherwise than in my favour. Saturday evening saw her place a wee bowl of flowers on the bedside table. We had had no news that Catriona wasn't coming after all, and were correct in assuming that she was. Indeed, Miss Aitken now seemed to be looking forward a little to her coming, partly out of curiosity, but mainly because she wanted our mother to realise that we were quite capable of handling complacently the situation she had threatened to impose upon us.

Miss Aitken, you must understand, was too proud, and too jealous for *my* reputation, even where my own mother was concerned, to allow me even to acknowledge my receipt of her letter. I must just ignore this ultimatum. Together we must face with dignity and equanimity whatever it might entail. We agreed, by the way, that I should not mention the prospect of Catriona's visit to my old father until she actually had reached Edinburgh—just in case she didn't!

At tea-time on Saturday afternoon, I returned from my usual pranks at the swimming-baths. A twinkle in Miss Aitken's eye carried my own to that famous spot on the kitchen mantelpiece, between the base of the gas-bracket and the tea-caddy. Everything of importance in our joint lives was inserted there, either for immediate attention, or for due consideration when circumstances seemed propitious. Telegrams and the like went up there the moment they were opened and read. This proved an admirable plan, since it provided a notice-board, as it were, confined to important matters about which, owing to Miss Aitken's stone-deafness, there might otherwise have been oversight or confusion when coöperation and understanding were essential. It was just there, between that gas-bracket and tea-caddy, that she had placed that first letter from Messrs. W. & R. Chambers, announcing their acceptance of my first book. Now its place was occupied by something significantly orange—a TELEGRAM!!

"Dinnae mind, laddie!" said Miss Aitken as I put forth a hand to take it down. "We're a' prepared—me an' the dogs, onyway. Ah've telt them a' aboot Catriona, and that they'll hae tae be on their best behaviour. It's no' ev'ry day we hae a veesitor a' the way frae Paris! 'Deed no!' "

Turning to the dogs for confirmation, she addressed herself to Ruairi. "Noo, sodger," she began. "wi' an author for a maister, ye ken fine yer weel edicated. Whiles ye'll be hearin' bits o' The Doric. Whiles, bits o' the King's English. Whiles, a moothfu' o' the Gaelic. That's like *three* languages ye ken already. Afore lang, ye'll be acquirin' a smatterin' o' French. So that'll be anither for ye!"

The not too welcome telegram was brief and to the point. It announced the time of Catriona's arrival at the Waverley early the following morning. Fearful lest we should sleep in (the Scots equivalent of oversleep), Miss Aitken set the alarm clock. At an hour on a Sunday morning when Auld Reekie was scarcely awake, Ruairi and I, but for a porter or two, stood alone on that great platform at which East Coast trains from London to Glasgow draw up. With one notable exception, all its passengers were still a-bed, or in the process of rising languorously. As the train slowed up, a window went down with a terrific bang, and that notable exception leaned out, waving frantically to brother and collie. When the train stopped, Catriona promptly alighted, not knowing in the least the sort of reception that awaited her.

"I must say you *do* look pleased to see me!" she said.

"Pleased?" I answered, all too unsympathetically. "Pleased at this hour on a Sunday morning?"

"Is Miss Aitken expecting me?"

"My God! She is!"

"I do hope you're not going to make things too beastly difficult for me. Does father know I'm arriving?"

I replied that things would not be too difficult if she could adapt herself to our humble ways at Gladstone Terrace. She must endeavour to fit in. Miss Aitken, I explained, was both elderly and deaf—stone-deaf, in fact. She was, nevertheless, amazingly aware, and competent. "No vanities, Catriona!" I added. "You may as well drop any bluff and gaiters now, for she will assess you—see through you, I mean—in a jiffy."

"Is that all the luggage you have?" I continued, observing how little she carried from the compartment she had been occupying.

"Oh dear no! You don't seem to understand that I've come straight to you from Paris, except for a few acrimonious hours with our mother in London yesterday, between my arrival at Victoria and the time of the first train leaving King's Cross for Edinburgh. Do you realise that she guarded me as though she were a policewoman, and I were someone escaped from a reformatory, captured in France, and brought back to England to be handed over? She never allowed me out of her sight. Escorted me very closely over to Zeeta's, and gave me the longest and most boring tea I've ever had. This was her idea of putting in time. We didn't even kiss one another at the station. 'Well, Catriona,' she said, 'which is it to be? Clewer or Scotland?' I said 'Scotland', without a moment's hesitation. And here I am!"

By now, the long, sleeping, Glasgow-bound train had unburdened itself not only of Catriona, but of three enormous trunks. These, as I noticed, had been deposited on the platform from the Guard's van, away down at the back-end of this long train, where they awaited a claimant.

"Good God! Catriona! What's in these?" I asked as I proceeded to handle them.

"Everything I possess," she replied. "All my Paris clothes and— Could you, please, tip the porter for me? I'll pay you back sometime, possibly when I've raised a little ready cash by a plan I have in mind. You see, I haven't a bean! Not a soo! My God! That b——, our mother! *She* saw to *that!* Had I managed to escape from her in London yesterday, I would have dashed down to Jessie's, at Wimbledon. But I didn't even have a bus fare. Mother gave me a single ticket, and then put me in charge of the guard at King's Cross in case I should alight at York or somewhere, and return to London. But I'd nothing to return on. I will admit she gave me a good supper before I left. So here you see me. I'm awfully sorry, Old Thing; but I really couldn't help it. Clewer! My God! What a prospect!"

So enormous and ponderous were those three trunks that we were obliged to hire *two* taxis. Catriona, Ruairi, and I travelled in one, together with the smallest of them. The others had a taxi to themselves. Each required two men to move them.

From the large window at Liberty Hall, Miss Aitken and Torquil witnessed our arrival. They also witnessed the coöperative efforts of myself and the two taxi-drivers to transfer the trunks to the foot of our common stair at Number 12. There they lay while Catriona ascended to be formally introduced to Miss Aitken and to what would be her quarters for—well, nobody quite knew for how long. In the words of *Kathleen Mavourneen*, it might be for years; and it might be for ever!

Catriona seemed delighted with her new, though humble, surroundings. "Such freedom!" she exclaimed.

"All meals in the kitchen with Miss Aitken and me," I began, believing that at the outset one should be informed of all the snags as well as of all the advantages. "You will make your own bed each morning, and all that sort of thing, and be helpful in any little way you can."

Catriona agreed that she would. "But, Alasdair! Such freedom! Such *FREEDOM!* I might have been beginning an incarceration at Clewer like some of the nuns I've just left. They were dears, of course;

but, oh! so frustrated! I was very happy with them, of course; and I think they've probably 'finished' me all right. But the idea of going back to Clewer after two years at a finishing-school, with no certainty of ever getting away—NO!—NEVER! Death itself would be preferable. I've always dreaded the danger of being frowsy and frustrated."

Miss Aitken, meanwhile, was lip-reading as best she could. "Ay," she interposed in her pawky way. "A finishing-school! We ken a' aboot that. But see ye dinnae finish US wi' ony graund ideas ye may hae brocht hame wi' ye frae France! We're no' anti-French or onything like that; but we dinnae want ony o' their queer capers here. Yer brither an' masel are simple folk, ye must understand. Nae frills here! Nane o' yer French cairry-on in Gladstone Terrace, mind ye!"

"What is she saying?" asked Catriona, turning to me in bewilderment. I interpreted, adding that in no time she herself would have acquired a smattering of 'The Doric'.

"Can she speak English as well?" asked the bewildered Catriona. I answered that she could.

"Why doesn't she do so, then?"

"The language she uses has suited me for years, and has been understood by quite a number of famous people with whom she and I have dealt, many of them in this very house. Famous authors and even Court of Session judges have sat with us here, at this very kitchen-table of ours, and have valued, and indeed enjoyed, her every utterance."

I fished out and handed to Catriona a particularly fine letter Miss Aitken had written me years before, and which I had retained as a specimen of her *English* at its best. "Read *that!*" I said. Catriona was astonished.

"If she can *write* like that, I cannot understand why she doesn't *speak* like that."

My reply was laconic enough: "*I* can, Catriona!"[1]

Within an hour or two my sister, to all appearances, had settled in, and was anxious to start to her unpacking. Never can travelling trunks have been so meticulously crammed. Catriona, already in the genus of Parisian *déshabillé* in which she was to waft through the house for several hours each day during her sojourn with us, descended the stair with the keys appropriate to her trunks, dumped there, as I have explained, because the taximen had found them too weighty to carry up two flights of narrow, spiral, stone steps on a Sunday morning. Their contents therefore had to be borne aloft in innumerable relays.

---

[1] I do trust no reader will be ungenerous enough to suggest that I should have furnished, in respect of passages quoted in Scots throughout this volume, a translation, or, at least, a glossary!

I myself was fair exhausted with the ups and downs this transportation entailed. Every spare coat-hanger in the house was pressed into service. Every expression of human inventiveness was encouraged to cope with clothing so fine and abundant that, as Miss Aitken shrewdly remarked, it would have enabled one to open a high-class dress shop. The quality of the stuff, apart from its quantity, quite overwhelmed her. Not in all her experience (and I remind you that she had been a court-dressmaker in her younger days) had she handled more beautiful material. "Yer mither must hae been fair daft. A' that extravagance on a mere lassie still at the schule. Wicked! Wicked! That's what it is!"

While the sorting out of Catriona's wardrobe proceeded, Miss Aitken reminded me that it was time I set off for Portobello. Otherwise, I would be late. My father, as you already know, had retired there with his books and manuscripts. Every Sunday, accompanied by one or other of the dogs, I cycled down by the King's Park and Duddingston to lunch with him. One dog usually had to remain behind with Miss Aitken on Sundays just in case she went out visiting in the afternoon. "Ah like tae hae yin o' them wi' me, ye ken, tae show him aff. Sae ye mustna' deprive me o' baith!"

The journey from the Newington district of Edinburgh, on the fringe of which we lived, was about three miles by way of Duddingston. Idyllic in summer, with the waterfowl cruising complacently on Duddingston Loch: exhilarating in winter, when icicles clung to Samson's Ribs, and the bulrushes by the loch's edge stood tufted and frosted like things in Japanese prints.

"Well, Boss, any news?" was invariably my father's opening gambit when I arrived.

"How would you review the prospect of Catriona's coming to stay for a bit?" I asked, not too subtly.

"I thought she was in Paris."

"Well, she *was*, father, until the boat-train brought her to Victoria yesterday."

"And where is she now?"

"Don't be unduly alarmed when I tell you she's actually at—Miss Aitken's. Ruairi and I met her at the Waverley early this morning."

"Great God in Heaven!" my father exclaimed. "Am I now to be saddled with *her* at my time of life?"

Pacifying him as best I could, I explained the position fully—just how Catriona's dramatic arrival in the North had been precipitated, and adding that Miss Aitken had volunteered to do what she could for the lassie in the meantime. My father was exceedingly worried. He anticipated that "she might be on our hands indefinitely. Ah! that b——, your mother! That *I* should have married such a woman! And that *she,* the w——, should have dragged the ancient and honourable name of MacGregor in the mire!"

To my fanatical father, as readers of my earlier books will remember, the slightest reflection upon this *clarum et venerabile nomen*—this illustrious and venerable name—was more serious than anything which might befall the unfortunate offspring of his marriage!

Miss Aitken and I tried to see Catriona's arrival in a more reasonable light. It was just one of those things, as we say nowadays. The kind of situation enforced by what W. E. Henley described as the bludgeonings of chance—bludgeonings Miss Aitken already had mitigated immeasurably, and which she felt we would all survive. Unfortunate for us, no doubt; but even more so for the wretched Catriona, as she was soon to realise.

By the time I got back to Gladstone Terrace, Catriona's dress establishment was already in some order. Two lengths of old clothes-pulley rope now stretched between large hooks screwed into the woodwork of the window-frame and the jamb at the back of her bedroom door. These would do just nicely, if only she could borrow a little cash wherewith to purchase a few dozen cheap coat-hangers at Woolworth's.

Our father had mentioned an hour or two earlier that he would contribute a pound a week by way of pocket-money for Catriona during her stay; while I guaranteed her half that amount. On the strength of this, I cautiously gave her a little in advance. Those lengths of rope sagged more and more each day with the ever increasing weight placed upon them. The door-jamb seemed resistant enough; but the window-frame was beginning to show signs of the strain. So the ropes had to be supported about their centre by a couple of shortened clothes-poles from the communal back-green.

The extent to which all this flounce and flummery occupied Catriona's apartment to the exclusion of its ordinary daylight was seen in the reduction of light hitherto reaching our lobby by means of the fanlight above its door. From this inner temple, Catriona's prying and disapproving brother was rigorously kept out. So likewise was Miss Aitken, though she had been promised an invitation to the private view, once the exhibits were arranged and hung, No temple, no shrine, was more jealously and zealously guarded, more strictly retained under lock and key. Never did the patron-saint of the rag trade officiate more competently. Determined that no unauthorised person should enter and discover what sort of ritual was being observed within, Catriona locked herself in when within, and locked herself out when without. No door-key since Gladstone Terrace was built had ever functioned more continuously and punctiliously.

Only once did *I* get a glimpse of the dark forest within, throughout the weeks of its existence, though its looming shadow made it impossible to see what letters, pushed through the slit in the front door, lay behind it. In order to ascertain this, one was now obliged to open the front door to admit the necessary light.

That glimpse I mentioned was quite accidental. I had slipped my latch-key into the front door, which stood adjacent to Catriona's, before she had had time to extricate herself from its dense and entangling undergrowth in order to close it.

However, I must confess to the occasion on which I contrived to look down on this forest from a height. On the pretext that the fanlight above her door now required more than ever the application of a little soap and warm water, I mounted the household steps one day while she was out. But all I could see were serried ranks of multi-coloured finery, the like of which our staid, Presbyterian terrace can never have housed before. To much of Edinburgh, even as late as this, anything Parisian savoured of the truly wicked. Bad enough if it had all come from Jenner's or Darling's; but *from Paris!!*

Such a thing was hardly mentionable.

Day by day matters went on in this manner. To Miss Aitken and me, it all seemed meaningless and pathetic. Ere long, however, we had reason to suspect that something was afoot, that Catriona had some wily scheme up her sleeve. A Dress Show, perhaps. Or a Private View. Or, maybe, a Sale.

Carefully locking her door behind her one afternoon, she entered the kitchen to make to Miss Aitken a truly ominous announcement. She didn't really want all this Parisian splendour and extravagance, she said. "What I require is a few simple frocks."

"Ay, my!" Miss Aitken remarked as soon as Catriona had retreated to her forest. "I kent fine she had some scheme on hand."

When Catriona informed us later that a gentleman of the very greatest importance was coming to see her the following day, she begged that I wouldn't embarrass things for her by being present. It didn't matter so much about Miss Aitken for, being deaf, she wouldn't hear any conversation. Catriona was convinced that her interview would be a success, if only I promised to absent myself. "Perhaps, you could be out somewhere. At the swimming-baths—or—out with the dogs somewhere."

I respectfully absented myself as requested. I am quite certain that I did so without realising in the least what was pending. I rather thought Catriona had arranged for somebody to call on her with regard to some sort of temporary employment for her.

It transpired later that Catriona had interviewed the buyer of a well-known dressmaking firm in George Street, who had made an appointment with her to come to inspect her wardrobe, and possibly make an offer for it. While I was out a-swimming, he duly arrived, complete with van. I returned to find all Catriona's flounce and flummery had been removed, and Miss Aitken sobbing in her kitchen chair, too upset to relate what had occurred.

But I found out, bit by bit. In conformity with true business acumen, it took the buyer no time to convince Catriona that her wardrobe was worthless. Rather than that she should be too terribly disappointed by this pronoucement of his, he had a suggestion to make. He would like her to accept a little something—an honorarium, as it were. After all, valueless clothes were no asset to anyone, least of all to a young lady so recently returned from the best of what Paris could offer. As it just happened that he had an empty van standing outside, he proposed that he should relieve her, there and then, of all this rubbish for—£4. This he was good enough to do forthwith.

It would be ungenerous of me were I to omit to mention that he increased his munificence by 30/- in respect of a dozen pairs of shoes Catriona thought might well be disposed of at the same time!

The injustice of this transaction literally paralysed poor Miss Aitken. For days she scarcely spoke. The materials alone, she declared, were worth a hundred pounds, which, as I afterwards learnt, was the sum Catriona had envisaged for the finished goods.

So now we had Catriona on our hands with virtually no clothes except those she was wearing. The few simple frocks we had heard of—well, what prospect was there now of these? Five pounds might just have purchased one good frock in those days. Instead, Catriona's newly acquired earnings went in buying some red material out of which she hoped Miss Aitken's coöperation would enable her to fashion a dress.

Catriona brought this material home with high expectations. In no time, under Miss Aitken's skilled hands, the dress was cut out and tacked together. Soon the sewing-machine was a-clattering in our kitchen. Yet again, dear Jane Aitken was performing one of those good deeds which theologians describe as works of supererogation.

It was now about 9 p.m. To me, occupied with my papers in my own room, everything in the kitchen appeared to be running smoothly until I overheard an ominous "Dae it yersel!" Miss Aitken, unable to thole any longer Catriona's interference, lost her temper, pulled the immature dress away from the machine, and flung it at her. It lodged in a corner, under a shelf of kitchen utensils.

"What has happened, Catriona?" I asked loudly. Miss Aitken, of course, could not hear me. Catriona came to explain.

"Do you know, Catriona, that Miss Aitken was once a very celebrated court dressmaker? She is still one of the finest needlewomen in Edinburgh. Since I came to her, years ago, she has knitted every pair of socks and stockings I've ever worn. She has made, in her spare time, every shirt I possess."

"Oh! Why didn't you tell me?" sobbed Catriona. "Mother has always said you got your shirts from a shirtmaker in Jermyn Street."

"*Has* she?" I answered. "You see, Catriona, for a variety of reasons, our mother knows virtually nothing about *me*, though she may know quite a lot about *you*."

Undisturbed in that corner, day after day, week after week, lay that contentious material, getting dustier and dirtier. Twice weekly, Mrs. Ormiston, our charwoman, came. Twice weekly Mrs. Ormiston washed the kitchen floor, studiously avoiding that red heap in the corner. She was far too wise to comment on it, or to disturb it. She knew better than to pick it up, for she knew her place to a nicety.

For all Miss Aitken cared, it might have been lying there yet but for the welcome intervention of another telegram.

When Catriona and I returned about ten from the house of some friends one Saturday evening, we found a telegram awaiting her. It had come from our married sister, Margaret, then living near Andover. Margaret, it appeared, had just learnt of Catriona's whereabouts—and plight. The telegram directed Catriona to get the first train she could. Margaret would meet her at Andover.

Miss Aitken and I received this news with relief. Catriona, on the other hand, wasn't so sure of its import. She viewed it as a mixed blessing. She would require a few days to think matters over.

"Catriona," I began with firmness, *coûte que coûte,* to resort to a language in which you are now so fluent, you're going—TOMORROW MORNING!"

"I can't! I simply can't! You don't understand! I can't arrive at Margaret's with no clothes!" she pleaded. "You know what snobs Margaret and her husband are!"

"Yes, you can!" I heartlessly replied, longing to be restored to the calm of my Golden Lamp, and Miss Aitken longing no less to get going peacefully on a serial Annie S. Swan was then contributing to that family stand-by in Scotland, *The People's Friend.* (You will recall the words she addressed to Ruairi each Thursday morning when he brought in the weekly papers.)

"You *arrived* on a Sunday morning," I continued. "What could be more appropriate than that you should *depart* on a Sunday morning?

The 10 a.m. tomorrow will suit very nicely, clothes or no clothes. You no longer have any luggage to worry about unless, of course, you'd like to take your empty trunks as a souvenir of your visit to us. The smallest of suitcases will hold all you now have, and certainly all you'll need until you reach Margaret's."

Miss Aitken lip-read this conversation; and I could see she was relieved at the firm attitude I had adopted. It worked on her like magic. In my presence, though I pretended not to notice, both she and Catriona advanced toward Sinister Corner. Without uttering a syllable, both bent down simultaneously to pick up its dusty occupant. Each caught hold of an end of it, and proceeded carefully with it to the coal-cellar, there to shake from it several weeks' dust.

As Ruairi and I left for the Waverley Station to book Catriona's seat and purchase her ticket, the sewing-machine was a-clattering once again, with the result that at least one of those simple frocks Catriona had mentioned had taken shape by the time we returned. "No alternative now, Catriona! There's your ticket! I've telephoned Margaret the time of your arrival at Andover!"

There was little sleep that Saturday night for any of us. Dressmaking absorbed the best of it. The fear that any hitch might have prevented Catriona's catching that 10 a.m. kept Miss Aitken and myself more than usually wakeful. The thing worrying Miss Aitken most was that anybody should quit her threshold so ill-clad. Catriona's travelling from Gladstone Terrace in a flimsy frock to a stylish sister, some hundreds of miles away, she regarded as a reflection on herself. Yet, in the most discouraging circumstances, she had put into this effort all her knowledge and skill. In being summoned to the kitchen to be asked what I thought of the finished product, I could not but appreciate Victor Hugo's allusion to the elegant impertinence of hands which never work.

In ample time next morning, Ruairi and I were down at the Waverley to make sure that our visitor got off all right.

"You look as glad to see me go as you looked depressed that Sunday morning you met me," she said. "I know you're relieved I'm going; and I can scarcely blame you."

Soon the figure that had leaned so demonstratively from a carriage window was leaning from another such, now moving in the opposite direction. It waved a violent adieu to that same brother and that same dog, until the smokiness of our Calton Tunnel obscured it.

With a sense of relief, slightly tinged with sadness, Ruairi and I watched that famous train move away and away, until its rear coach was gone from sight. Now we were as alone on that great platform as we had been that Sunday morning we met, at so early an hour, that same Catriona. Now she was gone, and without her mighty impedimenta, pretty certain to feel a little chilly in that flimsy frock ere she alighted at Andover quite late that evening. She had some money in her pocket this time, since the likelihood of her wanting to return was remote. She was now on her way to fresh woods and pastures new. Margaret's indulging her, as seemed likely from that inviting telegram, would soon habilitate Catriona.

Ruairi and I turned a glance toward one another. "Well, Ruairi," I said, "it'll be a whilie before we see her again; and we may well be surprised if she even drops us a line of thanks, for she believes we have hustled her away with indecent haste."

"I think we'd better just be getting back," Ruairi seemed to say. "It's past my breakfast-time."

Home we hurried, then, up Cockburn Street, along George IV. Bridge and Bristo Street and Buccleuch Street, and across the East Meadows, where we had a brief scamper together. And then over the Melville Drive into Gladstone Terrace, where Miss Aitken, at that same window, awaited us. In silence a minute or two later, Miss Aitken and I sat in our usual chairs—old leather things they were—gave one another a quick glance, and simultaneously broke down in tears. Ruairi and Torquil barked at our silliness. "O dry those tears!" they seemed to say. "We haven't had our breakfast yet!"

Miss Aitken's concern was now for my father. At lunch-time he would be expecting me as usual at Portobello; and Ruairi would be expecting his Sunday swim in the sea there. "A lunch wasted wi'oot Catriona," she added in her pawky and canny way; "but, ma certie! yer auld faither winnae mind that. He'll be ower relieved. The sooner he kens the guid news, the better."

Off we set, dogs and myself, by our usual route.

"Haven't you brought Catriona with you?" my father asked when no daughter entered.

"In an hour's time, father, Catriona ought to be as far away as York. She's off to Margaret's, at Andover."

"Good God in Heaven!" he exclaimed, "I'm more relieved than I can say!"

But he wasn't prepared to leave it like that. It did not suffice that Catriona was now off our hands. Oh dear no! Father must needs rehearse, as if once more for my special benefit, all the uncharitable things he maintained his wife had done to him during their long and bitter dissociation. Catriona's having been dumped upon us in this spiteful way provided him with the opportunity of repeatedly muttering in gruff undertones Cassius's famous words about the unkindest cut of all. *Of course,* he had sustained many an unkinder cut. But these he meant to overlook for the time being. Just as every setback, however trivial, led Uncle Toby to recapitulate his experiences at the Siege of Namur, so every domestic unpleasantness led my father straight to the tragedy of his marriage. No roads ever led as inexorably to Rome. He fervently approved the ultra-Calvinist belief in the existence of Hell, solely because it seemed the only place in any way suitable for his wife. Indeed, Hell, if anything, might be too good for her, too disappointingly inadequate. Anyhow, God, in His Omniscience, in His Infinite Justice, can hardly have overlooked the provision of some such roasting institution for the likes o' her!

This insane attitude of his reminds one of the young Frenchman whose father had left all his wealth to provide churches in uninhabited districts of France. "I wish I were as certain as you are that Hell exists," he remarked to a staunch believer in those everlasting flames. When asked why he should want to feel so, he replied: "Because I could then be certain my father was there!"

To revert to our bottles, as Montaigne might have put it, readers may wonder why my mother should have had no compunction about inflicting on *me,* eldest of her brood, the problem of Catriona in the manner in which she did, and at a none too affluent period of my life. There might have been some simple explanation, had she sought to do so on her husband. But why involve the innocent one who, after all, was doing for his father all these years what, in normal circumstances, she herself would have been doing as his wife. The explanation— well, it is too long and complicated for treatment here. The curious vindictiveness she was now to exhibit toward me, right up till her death in 1944, found expressions in ways worth recording in a subsequent volume.

Recalling Benjamin West's claim that a kiss from his mother had made him a painter, I cannot imagine what a kiss from *my* mother would have made *me!*

In reflecting on this sorry situation, one cannot but recall the words of that hag, Meg Murdockson, when Frank Levitt of footpad notoriety suggested to her how she might dispose of at least one of her afflictions. "Na! na!" replied Meg. "He was the first bairn I ever nurst . . . but man can never ken what a woman feels for the bairn she has held first tae her bosom."

I have been assured by many women in my time that this is so. Yet, I must say that Mabel MacGregor's first-born never saw in her a shadow of evidence in support of it. In her vindictive closing years she hated me with a fanatical fervour. It has been suggested that this was due, in some measure at least, to passages in my books alluding to family matters. She and the rest of the family, I rather suspect, had been giving themselves, in England, airs and graces which my uninhibited narratives tended to dispel. There is no doubt that she and my brother, Iain, and my sisters, in their snobbish way, had been giving out, like Simon, the Sorcerer, that they were some great ones.

"But who was *she* before I married her?" my father used to ask himself, very audibly, in the solitude of his study, recapitulating yet again the social nonsense his wife had arrogated to herself.

The authors of medical treatises are apt to identify the literary urge with mental unbalance, if not actually with a dangerous species of insanity. Even today, one hears the remark that this person or that *writes poetry,* indicating thereby that he or she cannot be regarded as normal, and that due allowance should therefore be made. Anybody devoted to the pursuit of poetry is looked upon by most people as being incurably lunatic.

My mother thought like this of her husband. Only a lunatic would declare to the world (as in fact he had done through the medium of *Who's Who*) that he numbered among his recreations "scribbling in prose and verse". Nothing in her view showed so unmistakably in him the streak of insanity as did this self-confession.

You may think this deduction a strange one when I tell you that the woman who made it, though so much younger than my father, spent the last thirty years of her life in Fleet Street, and was in large measure responsible for the success of one of the most popular magazines published in this country and in the United States.

Melrose Abbey

Dryburgh Abbey—the North Transept, where Sir Walter Scott and
the Haigs of Bemersyde lie buried

Edinburgh: 8, Howard Place, where Robert Louis Stevenson was born in 1850

Edinburgh: 17, Heriot Row, home of the Stevenson family from 1857 till 1887

CHAPTER NINETEEN

Miss Aitken and her Epigrams

To REVERT for a moment to Catriona's linguistic dilemma while at Miss Aitken's, she was incapable of appreciating that in a city like Edinburgh, certainly as recently as the 1930s, even 'the gentry' were still able to speak Scots fluently, very much as Miss Aitken did, and as her forbears had done in Haddington for centuries before her. No gentlewoman born and brought up in Edinburgh or in the Lothians prior to the First World War would have experienced any difficulty whatsoever in understanding every word she uttered, or in replying in like manner—in 'The Doric', as it is called. Indeed, such women retained a certain pride of race in being able to do so. As for the squire and the squire's sons, in the years of which I write, it would not have been easy to have found one of them in the Lothians who, though not necessarily using Scots as his everyday speech, could not do so, and who, on all appropriate occasions, certainly did so.

That it was by no means a foreign tongue to the educated is plainly seen in much of the best Scottish literature of the nineteenth century and the early decades of the twentieth. The gentle-folk of the Edinburgh I first knew could be every bit as pawky in their native dialect as was Miss Aitken. Indeed, they frequently reverted to it when a situation called for words or phrases carrying some precise connotation. The epigrammatical qualities of the Scots tongue as still spoken in these parts are unsurpassed. I was soon to discover this for myself when listening to Miss Aitken. She had at the tip of her tongue a Scots quotation or epigram for every circumstance, for every situation.

"Dinnae droon the miller!" she shrieked at Catriona one day when she observed her filling up the teapot with more hot water than the amount of tea could stand.

"What ever does she mean?" Catriona asked me, promptly desisting until she had been given an interpretation. "And what's that saying I heard her use about a kirk?"

Of course, I knew precisely to what Catriona was alluding: '*The nearer the kirk, the farther frae grace.*' This was a favourite utterance of hers when some clergyman or kirk-elder of our acquaintance had been found out in any way, or when one of her succession of theological students was guilty of some misdemeanour or impropriety.

There occurred an occasion when she used this epigram with singular appropriateness. I remember it vividly. In the Greenbank district of Edinburgh at that time there was an incumbent named Ratcliffe Barnett—the Rev. T. Ratcliffe Barnett. His name was pleasantly familiar to us through his frequent and acceptable articles in *The Scotsman,* rather than through his pulpit performances. He already had endeared himself to my father on account of his felicitous references in these articles from time to time to the Clan Gregor and to the MacGregor Country.

In 1924 there was published in Edinburgh, by Robert Grant & Son, at 126, Princes Street, the first of a deservedly successful series of Scottish books by Ratcliffe Barnett. It was titled *The Road to Rannoch & The Summer Isles.* I believe this title to be one of the very few things which I have envied anybody in my life. Of all the book-titles I know, this is the loveliest to look at and to hear spoken. A masterpiece in poetry, in imaginativeness. See how it rolls under the eye and under the tongue! Rannoch, an ancient patrimony of the Mac-Gregors, in Perthshire: The Summer Isles, a bit to the north of the Wester Ross home of my infancy at Applecross. Why—oh! why—hadn't I thought of this title myself?

The Road to Rannoch & The Summer Isles (Let the inward eye see it just once again!) was but a day or two old when I noticed that it contained not only some interesting reading matter about Neil Mac-Leod and his piratical accomplices on the remote Hebridean isle of Berisay, but also a photograph of the very isle, taken from the sea at some little distance. In the meantime Messrs. W. & R. Chambers were busy preparing for publication my first book, *Behold the Hebrides!.* The references it likewise, and quite coincidentally, contained to Berisay prompted the fond notion that, perhaps, I might have obtained from Ratcliffe Barnett permission to use this photograph of his, or another of that isle, assuming he possessed another.

At this time I was particularly friendly with an Edinburgh family named Thomson. Edward Thomson, its paterfamilias, was then Principal Extractor at the Register House. Much more to my purpose, however, was his being an office-bearer at Ratcliffe Barnett's church in Greenbank, where, in an honorary capacity, he was organist.

"You must know Ratcliffe Barnett very well," I remarked to him one day, with this Berisay photograph in covetous view. "I wish you'd introduce us to one another. He's pretty certain to know of me through my *own* contributions to *The Scotsman.* You can tell him, furthermore, that for years my father has been enjoying his writings, especially those mentioning the MacGregors."

Edward Thomson received my suggestion with anything but enthusiasm. "It's quite true that I play the organ in his church. Beyond that—well, what purpose would an introduction serve?"

I now had to admit that I was seeking an approach to the reverend gentleman such as might be pleasantly rewarded by my obtaining from him a print of Berisay, suitable for reproduction. To this he reluctantly explained that his minister wasn't the sort of chap of whom he would like me to ask a favour.

Time was getting on. Messrs. Chambers were proceeding apace with the production of *Behold the Hebrides!*. In the list of illustrations I had submitted with my typescript, I had left just one space. This I had hoped to fill with the Pirates' Isle. So I wrote to Ratcliffe Barnett direct, never mentioning my friendship with his church organist. In announcing my eagerness to obtain this photograph, I added that, if he could be persuaded to part with a print for the purpose of my forthcoming book, he would receive due acknowledgement therein, and also the usual reproduction fee.

Weeks passed. The publication date of *Behold the Hebrides!* had been announced. So it was too late in any case by the time I received from Ratcliffe Barnett a letter expressing his regret that he couldn't be of help in the matter, "for anything which is difficult to procure is equally difficult to dispose of".

I promptly handed his letter to Miss Aitken, who as promptly responded in her characteristic way: "I've telt ye mony a time, laddie: *'The nearer the kirk, the farther frae grace.'* Mebbe ye'll believe it noo!"

My disappointment over the Berisay photograph was negligible in comparison with the joy Ratcliffe Barnett's books have given me, and the thrill I get every time I see that lilting title of his—*The Road to Rannoch & The Summer Isles*. The volume so named occupies a permanent place on my bedside shelf of very special favourites.

Miss Aitken's store of such epigrams and quaint sayings was unlimited. I remember overhearing a conversation she once had with an Australian medical student who, at great length, confided to her that he was changing his sweetheart, and exactly why. She listened attentively to all he had to say, and then, in a shrill voice calculated to close that particular topic for ever where *he* was concerned, gave her verdict:

Changes are lightsome;
An' fools likes 'em!

"Whatever is she saying?" he enquired of me. "She's getting at me all right. I know *that* well enough." I interpreted. He left our presence in high dudgeon, and was off his food for a day or two. No love-sick swain was ever put so clean off his eggs!

One could not have been entirely unsympathetic with Catriona in the midst of all this. But I pointed out to her that she couldn't have been suffering any more from Miss Aitken's dialectic peculiarities than from what Catriona herself was subjecting *me* to by her frequent outbursts of very blasé French, always pretending that her arrival from Paris was too recent to allow of her realising that she had returned to the city where first she went to school.

"I'm beginning to follow a word here and there," she at last conceded. "But what was that Miss Aitken has just announced?" Catriona enquired at breakfast-time one morning. "Can she be talking about your porridge by any chance? If so, she does so in the plural. This barbarous language she speaks, and you seem to understand so easily—well, if you don't mind my saying so, it certainly has some idiosyncrasies."

I conceded that this was highly probable. Porridge—and indeed soup—are invariably referred to in the plural by the Lowland Scots. "Are ye no' comin' ben for yer parridge, ma laddie? They're gettin' cauld. It's a whilie syne they were poured oot!"

There's no denying, however, that Miss Aitken and her generation gloried in their fluency with the Lowland tongue. As Scots of the Bannockburn order, they resorted to it in a defiantly nationalistic way, especially when dealing with the English. Since Miss Aitken considered the Highland-born Catriona Mairi MacGregor as English as anybody she had ever met, she regarded a little extra emphasis on her mother-tongue in Catriona's presence as well warranted.

I cannot but recall in this context a Scots landlady of Miss Aitken's generation and calibre, with whom one of my Hebridean relatives lodged in Finchley when first he came south to London to seek the fame and fortune he eventually achieved. His landlady, an Edinburgh woman, left badly off by the sudden demise of her husband, was as suddenly confronted with the problem of finding a means of livelihood. She had no alternative but to take in lodgers, as they were called in those realistic days. (They're now paying-guests, of course.) Unfortunately, she wasn't in a position to pick and choose, which explained how, with the exception of my kinsman, all her lodgers were Englishmen, and for this reason were treated with a touch of contempt.

When she felt a little in need of sympathy in her straitened circumstances, she would rush into my kinsman's room, close the door very tightly behind her lest anyone should overhear, and then seat herself on the end of a family heirloom from Edinburgh—an old horse-hair sofa. Having observed these formalities and acquired in so doing a measure of repose, she would then give utterance: "Thae English! Thae English! Ah cannae be bothered wi' them! Ah cannae bide them! They're that stupid! Their heids are like their hooses—a brick an' a hauf thick!"

Like Catriona, who couldn't understand why Miss Aitken didn't use an English word when she thought she ought to have done so, the relative who told me of his Scots landlady in Finchley used to complain of my own literary lapses. Having himself acquired literary distinction, he insisted that, if only I would permit him to iron out all offending Scotticisms and MacGregorisms appearing in my manuscripts before they went to the printer, my books would be free of all irritants.

I could not help being reminded of this when, the other day, I turned up a letter received a few years ago from the late Frank Whitaker, during whose long editorship of *Country Life* I contributed so much to that estimable weekly. "The article you have now sent me is truly in your best style," runs the pertinent passage. "It has none of those tricks of speech that transform a peace-loving Englishman into a homicidal maniac, and I shall therefore be glad to publish it."

I confess to having benefited quite a lot from this, though I would be loth to deny that I am still tempted occasionally to insert into my writings a MacGregorism or two. When I incur criticism by so doing, I remind my critics that even Scott and Stevenson, by deliberately inserting an odd word or phrase here and there, demanded of their readers in England some little effort, just as I find is demanded of myself when reading, say, Hardy. Better far that Hardy's exquisite flashes of West Country dialect should be examined and understood, rather than that they should be translated for simplification, to the impoverishment, alike, of speech and literature.

Better far, also, that at least a few of Miss Aitken's flashes of Braid Scots should be recorded rather than forgotten.

The attitude of that Scots landlady at Finchley toward her English lodgers was very similar to her own in regard to some of her *Scots* lodgers over the years. I remember a particularly dour and stupid one who was in his second year at the Congregational Hall, within half a mile of us. "Dinnae gang near 'im" she once warned me when he was in a mood more surly and stupid than usual. "The Black Dog's on his back! It'll bite ye, mind!" Some years were to pass ere I discovered in *Lodgings for the Night* that our well-beloved R.L.S. had given this mordacious monster a place in literature. "The Black Dog was on his back, as people say, in terrifying nursery metaphor."[1]

When nursing her wrath to keep it warm, she used to ring the changes quite amusingly on this student's glaikit (senseless) behaviour:

> *There nae mair in him than the spune* [spoon] *pits in 'im.*
> *He's a gey queer fish!*
> *He hasna' the wit tae ca'* [drive] *the cat frae the milk.*

Even the dogs were treated to her Scotticisms, so many of which she had acquired as a young woman through reading Burns, Scott, and R.L.S. "Ah see ye, sodger! Ah see ye fine!" she would shriek when Ruairi or Torquil tried to wheedle her in some way. "Ah see ye a' richt! Nane o' yer wiles wi' *me!* Ye cannae hae read *The Heirt o' Midlothian,* or ye'd ken a wink's as guid as a nod tae a blind horse!"

Although everybody who came in contact with Miss Aitken appreciated how her deafness limited conversation with her, except for those whose lips she had been in the habit of reading over the years, they also knew that nothing escaped her. With suspicion not always undue, they often knew when, *sotto voce,* she was saying something a little uncomplimentary about them, even when they hadn't heard. Her deafness prevented her from knowing when her criticisms (usually meant very privately for *me*) hadn't been quite *sotto* enough! If challenged on such an occasion, she was swift to deny the charge, and to acquit herself on some quite invalid pretext or other.

One recalls in this context how the civic authorities of Edinburgh, when interrogated before the House of Lords in connection with the Porteous Mob, answered in the good, Scots tongue, designedly adopted to confuse their examiners. When the Duke of Newcastle asked a witness with what kind of shot Captain Porteous's guard had loaded its muskets, he received the answer, "Ow, jist sic as ane shoots *dukes* an' *fools* wi' ".

This infuriated the southern barons. Indeed, they regarded it as contempt of court. Provost and magistrates might well have been punished for it, had not the accommodating Duke of Argyll acted as interpreter. He explained that the words objected to, when rendered into intelligible English, signified *ducks* and *water-fowls!*

This spontaneous adaptation was worthy of Miss Jane Aitken.

---

[1] I would not deny, of course, that there were occasions when I myself carried the Black Dog. I was then at a stage in my career when the most trifling annoyance was apt to assume proportions justifying a real, thundering rage. But Miss Aitken soon neutralised my acidity by the admixture of a little of her splendid alkaline qualities.

CHAPTER TWENTY

My First Seven Guineas

EARLY LITERARY TRIALS AND TRIBULATIONS

IT WAS while convalescing at Cambridge in the autumn of 1918, shortly before the Armistice, that I first felt the desire to see myself published in the columns of some newspaper. Apart from *The Deserted Garden* (reprinted in a subsequent chapter) and a few other poems, I had never managed to get anything of my own into print, certainly anything in prose. The time had now arrived, I felt, when this undistinguished state of affairs ought to be rectified. But what topic could I select? To be acceptable, it would require to have some bearing on the war. It wouldn't matter how trivial and untruthful.

Seeking possible inspiration at Heffer's one day, I purchased two slender volumes forming part of a neat, pocket-size series then being issued by (I think) Dent at sixpence each. One of these had something to do with Turkey. Its title I forget, as also the title of the other volume. Nevertheless, in some curious way these slight volumes fostered in me a determination to write something and get it published. I skipped through the Turkish volume in no time, and then sat down to write the most superficial 300 words of which I have ever been guilty. I bestowed upon them the high-sounding title of 'Turkey in Transition'. This was at a time when the word, transition, was being applied by politicians and journalists to literally everything, which perhaps explains how I, too, thought I might use it. It looked so important, so authoritative. War correspondents were also caught up by it. I felt confident that, in exploiting this cliché, I was on a really good wicket.

Those 300 words I blush at recalling. They were nothing more or less than a very amateurish piece of plagiarism, rounded off as by a writer competent in matters of phraseology, and intimately informed on the intricate affairs of Turkey in Europe, as well as in Asia. A typewriter borrowed at Emmanuel College enabled me to submit my thesis, as it were, in readable and, as I hoped, publishable form. My name, of course, appeared impressively at the top of my typescript:

TURKEY IN TRANSITION
Decay of the Ottoman Empire
by
Alasdair Alpin MacGregor

If the editor of *The Cambridge Daily News* were ignorant of the presence within the precincts of Emmanuel of one who, though still comparatively young, could write so convincingly on matters concerning the Middle East, he must be made less so, and at once. My mission to enlighten him and his learnèd city must brook no delay. With confidence and speed, I called on him. When I was shown into his august presence, he cannot but have observed how ill I looked. I was actually recovering, and very slowly indeed, from rheumatic fever, contracted through exposure in The Trenches. He received me courteously, and invited me to tell him just how important it was that mankind, through me and the hospitality of his columns, should know all about this transition business in Turkey. As I left, he assured me of his willingness to give my proposed contribution a degree of sympathetic consideration vouchsafed to few who called on him in the manner in which I had done. I left his office with high hopes.

The following day I was handed at the porter's lodge an imposing envelope, the first I ever received in my life from a newspaper. In my innocence I believed it contained a proof. I knew such things existed, for my father had been having them over the years, but without my paying much attention to what they were or signified. The envelope, on the contrary, contained my rejected article, together with the first of those nice, little things I was to receive so very numerously in subsequent years. I think they're called Rejection Slips. I name them with capital initial letters merely to emphasise their significance to the beginner. They pile up and up as he becomes more and more industrious and persistent. I shall have something to say about them later. But meanwhile let me record just what I felt about that first one.

On my receipt of it, I could not imagine why, in addition to it, there wasn't some sort of nice letter from the editor of *The Cambridge Daily News*. I thought he at least might have thanked me for writing to him, and perhaps explained just why he had rejected my 300 words, or made some suggestion such as might have rendered them more acceptable for his purpose. I had much to learn, you see. For example, I had to learn how devastatingly impersonal is the relationship between the editor and the unknown writer. It's the most casual of all human relationships. Heart-breaking when first one realises it. Paralysing, and disappointing in a degree hard to understand by those who have never experienced it. There are reasons for it, of course, in the rat-race conditions of modern times; but these would seem to lie outwith our present purpose.

The reception of two or three rejection slips in quick succession has put off many a potential writer for ever. It might well have put *me* off, had I not convinced myself that those 300 words had a message for the world. I could not allow myself to be discouraged quite so easily, quite so casually. I would send my tidy bit of plagiarism to the only editor I could think of who might well see fit to accept it straight away. So off it went to Inverness. If it were not good enough for the learnéd of Cambridge, my father's friend, the editor of *The Northern Chronicle,* might review it in a more pleasing light. He did! So there I was, in print, in no time!

From a copy of his paper, which he sent me, I cut out my little gem, folded it neatly, and inserted it in my pocket-book, readily accessible there for anybody whom I might deem worthy of its perusal. I treasured it until it began to fall to pieces at the folds, then at the edges. Gradually it disintegrated and vanished, but not before I had landed a second contribution on this same editor. What this was about, I cannot now recall; and without the title of the other little volume purchased at Heffer's, I'm never likely to do so. It would be something quite fatuous, of course, and no more suitable for a paper like *The Northern Chronicle* than had been its forerunner. Had the editor not recognised me as my father's son, neither of these amateurish contributions would ever have appeared in his columns, and I might never have become a writer. I think that another rejection slip or two just then would have altered my career.

With great forbearance I awaited the monetary rewards for these first efforts. My speculating on such sums as might eventually reach me occupied a lot of time and thought. How long would it be before I heard anything in that connection? Were newspaper contributors paid at the beginning or at the end of each month? Or at the beginning or the end of the year? Or when? And at what rates? And what did one do if payment seemed excessively delayed? Did one write a reminder? Or did one follow the example of a penny-a-liner friend in the North who submitted her account to this very paper at regular intervals? All very confusing. I counted the lines. At a penny a line, it came to about 3/6. Even *that* would be something, I thought. A first payment at all events, plus what I imagined would be of enormous publicity value to me in the North.

"Did you mention a price?" my father asked when, months after publication, I mentioned my dilemma. "You ought to have pencilled 10/6 or some such figure at the top of your typescript."

I hadn't the confidence to do anything like that!

"Only 10/6, father?" I replied indignantly. "They're worth far more than that. I expect a guinea each, *at least!*"

I have no reason to be proud of the admission that this is as far as I ever got with journalistic remuneration in Inverness. I like to ask myself what interest even two half-guineas would have earned for me during the intervening years at compound proportional increments. An unsettling speculation!

The year, 1919, saw a further literary effort, and with an article which, in style and content, was to be the first of several hundreds I have written and published in the interim, for the most part in publications like *Country Life* and *Scotland's Magazine*. I had spent a brief holiday with friends on the Black Isle. When I returned to Miss Aitken at the beginning of my first term at Edinburgh University, I gave her, as always, a graphic account of that holiday. After I had described to her an evening I crossed the Balblair ferry from Invergordon, and walked all the way down the fringe of the Cromarty Firth toward Jemimaville, where I was staying with friends, she exclaimed with enthusiasm, 'Why dinnae ye write it a' doon, jist the way ye've telt me, an' send it tae the papers? They'll publish it for certain. Ay, my! When I see the rubbish they tak'!'"

This struck me, there and then, as something worth trying. Under the influence of my Golden Lamp, I could embellish my evening walk by the tide's edge with a few particulars about the Black Isle itself, about Hugh Miller and the Old Red Sandstone, not omitting mention of the scientific name now commemorating his contribution to palaeontology, and about this countryside as I had known it in boyhood, when I romped by the Eathie Burn, and was shown the fossil-bearing beds there, long before I could appreciate their significance. It could never have appeared the least probable then that one day Geology was to become a major preöccupation of mine; and I would be slow to deny that, in writing this early article, the foundations of this preöccupation were laid.

My Black Isle article, carefully read through by Miss Aitken, and duly amended in accord with her recommendations, was in type in no time. But where should I submit it? What editor might be interested? Here were 1,200 words of what Miss Aitken called 'The Best'.

"Try Robertson Nicoll wi' it," she urged.[1] As a Free Churchwoman (she and her family were Baptists), she knew all about the great Robertson Nicoll, who was then editing *The British Weekly,* to which she had subscribed throughout most of her life. There were always

[1] See footnote at page 44.

copies of this thoughtful periodical lying about the house, for, in addition to her own, there were those brought in by a succession of Free Church theological students who lodged with her. In homes like hers, *The British Weekly* was as essentially a part of the week's literature as, today, are publications like *The Radio Times*.

Miss Aitken fished out the current number, which we now studied together. On her advice, off to *The British Weekly* went my Black Isle article. A few days passed without its being returned, though I had enclosed with it the requisite stamped, addressed envelope. Yet, every day seemed to bring nearer to me one of those rejection slips to which *The Cambridge Daily News* had introduced me. However, there arrived instead a letter of acceptance from the great man himself, and a cheque for Three Guineas. Just fancy—Three Guineas! This was the very first payment a piece of prose ever earned me.

The weeks passed. The months passed. Miss Aitken and I were beginning to wonder whether 'Memories of the Black Isle, by Alasdair Alpin MacGregor' would ever appear. "Yon was a nice letter ye had frae Robertson Nicoll. Write him again. It'll jog his memory." I did so, only to be informed that my little masterpiece had been—MISLAID. A subsequent enquiry elicited the sorrowful news that it had now been LOST—DEFINITELY AND IRREVOCABLY L-O-S-T! !

"They should be ashamed o' themselves!" shrieked Miss Aitken when I handed her the letter announcing this final catastrophe. "If ever I get a haud o' Robertson Nicoll, he'll hear aboot it. I've a guid mind tae stop *The British Weekly* a' thegither. It'll be their ain fault if I dae. Never mind, laddie! Yon Three Guineas winnae dae ony hairm!"

Down-hearted? I must admit I was. Three Guineas were all very well; but what *I* wanted was recognition as a writer. So Miss Aitken and I now applied ourselves studiously to finding an alternative avenue for this article's publication. Our searching the pages of a borrowed copy—my father's, by the way—of *The Writers' & Artists' Year Book* suggested many possibles, but improbables. Our studying a few back numbers of *John o' London's Weekly* seemed to provide an avenue we might try. My father, who read this weekly assiduously from its inception in 1919, and not infrequently contributed to it during the first few years of its existence, always passed his copies on to Miss Aitken. Like himself, she read it thoroughly. Knowing I had a carbon copy of the lost document, she was anxious that something should be done about it.

"Mak' a nice, clean copy, laddie, and send it tae John o' London himsel'—tae Wilfred Whitten, or whatever he ca's himsel'. What

aboot yon correspondence yer faither had wi' Sidney Dark? Mak'
that yer excuse. Mind ye keep the carbon copy, though. I'll dictate
frae it while ye type. Sae it'll nae be bothersome."

Off to *John o' London's*, then, went this Black Isle article. Within
a few days arrived a smallish envelope bearing that publication's imprint. It certainly didn't contain a returned manuscript; and I could
hardly imagine it conveyed a rejection slip unaccompanied by a
manuscript. I invited Miss Aitken to open the envelope and solve our
quandary, as she did on a subsequent and very memorable occasion
about which you will hear later.

"Ma laddie!" she screamed with delight. "Yer on the road tae fame!
They've accepted! Ay, they've accepted! There's a cheque here,
forby! Anither Three Guineas! Robertson Nicoll doesna ken what
he's missed!"

"Good God!" I exclaimed. "Not *another* Three Guineas?" I was
quite overcome. Accompanying the cheque was a brief letter of
acceptance from the great Wilfred Whitten himself.

This exceptionally fine journalist, who had been acting editor of
T. P's Weekly from its inception in 1902 until 1911, founded *John
o' London's Weekly* in 1919, and edited it until 1936, contributing to
each issue its leading article, 'Letters to Gog and Magog,' under his
pseudonym, John o' London. Closely associated with him in this
enterprise, which did so much to fill in the gap left by the demise of
T. P's., was Sidney Dark, who subsequently edited *The Church Times*.
Wilfred Whitten died in 1944, and Sidney Dark three years later.

Time, as afore-time, passed. Any day now, Miss Aitken and I
supposed, my little masterpiece would be appearing under Wilfred
Whitten's benign auspices. But again the weeks passed, the months
slipped by. When I could bear the suspense no longer, I wrote
to enquire as to the fate of this twice-accepted article. Again, alas!
came the crushing reply: it was—LOST!!

"Dinnae be dooncast!" counselled Miss Aitken. "Ye've had Six
Guineas already *wi'oot* publication. An' mebbe anither guinea or twa
will be comin' yer way afore lang. Mak' a new copy frae yon carbon
copy ye ha'e, an' try *The Edinburgh Evening Dispatch* wi' it."

I did so. Accepted for publication instantly! Published three days
later!! Payment at the beginning of the following month: One
Guinea!!!

But I was still a long and arduous way from anything even faintly
resembling success, as you will see later.

Let me add a little more about *John o' London's,* and thus obviate the necessity for my having to revert to it. Wilfred Whitten was succeeded by the essayist, Robert Lynd, who carried on as John o' London until his death in 1949. Lynd in turn was succeeded in this rôle by Frank Swinnerton, under the editorship of Webster Evans. In the autumn of 1954 *John o' London's Weekly,* for economic reasons, ceased publication, after 35 years. In October, 1959, however, it was resuscitated as a weekly magazine of short stories, book reviews, and articles with a literary background, along the lines of its predecessor, with Ernest Kay as editor. In January, 1963, under Kay's editorship, appeared its first number as incorporated with *Time & Tide.*

John o' London's was a magazine with which, as an aspiring contributor, I was consistently, and perhaps singularly, unfortunate. My career with it began with its losing my first really important acceptance. Several years later I found myself at variance with the late Frank Whitaker, during whose editorship, which lasted from 1928 until 1936, it published only part of a letter of mine on the Ethics of Book Reviewing. On grounds of space, my letter was abbreviated by the omission of a salient point. To the foot of my expurgated letter was appended a long editorial note covering this very point, as though I had overlooked it. I was furious. But, curiously, this difference with Whitaker was to lead to one of the happiest and most rewarding of all my literary contacts. In 1940 he became editor of *Country Life,* to which I have now been contributing fairly frequently for nearly 35 years. One day some years later, and quite by accident, we passed one another in the passage outside his office in Tavistock Street, Covent Garden. Somebody told him who I was. He approached and introduced himself. "My God!" he exclaimed. "You're not the least like what I had imagined! I thought you were a wild, unkempt, Highland-looking chap with long tresses and wild, flashing eyes! But you appear to be quite civilised! I must confess this is a great surprise to me!"

Whitaker insisted upon taking me into his room. It was now *my* turn to say something. "My God!" I likewise began, "you gave me even better reason to imagine that you were one of those bloody awful Fleet Street chaps who—well, need I go further?"

We laughed and made friends. Our discovering subsequently a mutual interest in choral music cemented this friendship. We had a few pleasant wrangles in correspondence over the years which were to follow; but these were confined to matters of punctuation and the like. I always held that the educated English, as distinct from the educated Scots, were erratic in their punctuation, and as a rule seemed unappreciative of the extent to which thought and care in punctuating did so much more than merely decide the tempo when reading. The subtle use of commas, colons, semi-colons, and stops is an art of its

own, as essential to the construction of a word-picture as are colours
and shades of colour to a painting. Whitaker and his proof-reading
colleagues would persist in altering my punctuation by inserting
commas where there should be full-stops, by substituting semi-colons
where, for purposes of contrast and balance, I deliberately had supplied
a colon. The fact of the matter is that, to most people nowadays, punctuation means nothing. The clarity of meaning it ensures is
no longer appreciated.

I had not forgotten, of course, that Whitaker was joint editor with
Wilfred Whitten of *Good and Bad English,* published in 1939. But I
liked the idea that my very thorough grounding at Watson's entitled
me, also, to claim some knowledge of English grammar, of punctuation, syntax, and so on. In the end I was obliged to submit to what he
so often tried to impress on me, both by word of mouth and by letter.
It amounted to this:

> *Whitaker to MacGregor:* "When you write for a mag. like mine,
> and hope to continue to do so, you'll have to conform to the Rules
> of the House where punctuation is concerned, even when you think
> we're wrong. As I have told you repeatedly, you have an advantage
> over many in this regard, for you are also an author, and are there-
> fore free to punctuate, *in your books,* as you care. I'm sure you
> understand why I must sometimes be severe and make alterations in
> your contributions here and there. I know you feel my doing so as
> most people would feel toothache. But there it is . . ."

> *MacGregor to Whitaker:* "Agree to your terms, as ever. In
> Apothecary's words, 'My poverty, but not my will, consents'. Great-
> ly appreciate your reminder—your ever consoling reminder—that I
> can do as I like *when it comes to my books.* But please, oh! please!
> leave a colon and, perhaps, a semi-colon undisturbed now and again!
> How otherwise will your very estimable readers ever know of the
> *existence* of these precious symbols, apart altogether from their
> functions?"

Right up till 1958, the year of Frank Whitaker's retirement from
the editorship of *Country Life,* our relationship as editor and contributor was as splendid as any writer could have desired. He died at
his home in Beckenham in 1962, at the age of 69. I find his premature
explicit an eloquent and ever recurring reminder of my own
ephemerality.

To return to my misfortunes with *John o' London's.* In 1959, in its
resuscitated form, I suffered grievously at its hands, when I complained bitterly about the condition in which some photographs of

mine were returned to me—crushed and rendered useless by their being posted only partially protected by suitable cardboard. Everybody with experience of photography and postal risks knows that the unprotected parts of a photograph, especially of a large photograph, always get damaged in the post in a manner much less likely to occur when *none* of the photograph is so protected. In other words, protect the *entire* surface with good cardboard, or not at all. The better the quality of cardboard (the less unyielding, I mean), the worse the damage to photographs only partly protected by it. Every serious photographer transmitting his work through the post for publication is aware of this. Elementary, my dear Watson!

Anyhow, thoroughly frustrated by this incompetence, and the delay and expense the substitution of prints unfrayed and unbroken must necessarily involve—the looking out of the corresponding negatives, precise masking and printing directions, full and accurate captioning of the new prints, and the waste of valuable time—I realised I could not trust myself to write to the editor of *John o' London* the sort of angry protest the immediacy of the telephone rendered feasible. So I telephoned. And—believe it or not!—I had quite an amicable conversation with Lord Darwen, the deputy editor. Indeed, it was so amicable that I generously declined his offer to replace my damaged work. Up to this point all seemed reasonable and agreeable.

However, not long afterwards, exactly the same thing happened again. My fury was certainly in no way diminished when the pretext given me was that the photographs and typescript concerned had actually been received in a damaged condition. In other words, either the postoffice or I was to blame. If this were so, one would have thought that courtesy called for my being informed immediately the damaged material had been received.

The inadequacy of the cardboard to which this damaged material, as returned, was perfunctorily attached certainly exonerated the postoffice. Where any fault might have been attributed to *me,* I pointed out to Lord Darwen that I was no amateur in these matters, that I had been posting photographs all over the country and to many parts of the distant world for over thirty years, and that, when posted back to me, properly protected between the stiff cardboards in which I submit them, they are never damaged. I pointed out further that a busy person like me, who writes and photographs for his living, cannot find time to re-type work mutilated by incompetents; and I concluded with what I thought Darwen might have regarded as a reasonable gesture on my part, namely, that, if he would now ask the incompetent one (she had been identified by this time) to re-type my damaged typescript, so that I might submit my material elsewhere, I would solemnly undertake not to worry him with further attempts to contribute to his esteemed pages.

How do you think the blighter replied to this? He declined categorically to have the re-typing done. "We consider," he wrote, "that if we take reasonable precautions in packing manuscripts, the risk of submission must rest with the author, and probably the phrase 'the editor can take no responsibility for loss or damage to manuscripts' will not be unfamiliar with you."

Quite so! I agree! In modern parlance, *I couldn't agree more!* While highly in favour of those reasonable precautions he mentioned, I deny that the careless insertion of an inadequate piece of cardboard, in place of my own, enclosed with a stamped, addressed envelope, is either reasonable or precautionary. That, in a word, sums up my difference with Lord Darwen.

Thus began and thus ended my dealings with *John o' London's.* Today, as the result of my experience with this publication, I find myself unable to work up any enthusiasm for it.

Some years later, exactly the same sort of thing obliged me to close my file with *The Field,* never to be re-opened. The matter ended with Oh! such a rude letter from me to the editor, and Oh! such a rude letter from the editor to me!

Some months ago, I complained to Mr. John Adams, who succeeded Frank Whitaker as editor of *Country Life,* about the damage done to a large number of prints, attributable to the same cause. He promptly apologised and, without any demur, sent me as promptly my cheque to cover the cost of having them re-made. He had known my work too long, as also my meticulous methods of packing and posting, to have had any doubt as to where the responsibility lay.

I mention these none too auspicious occasions as examples of the trials and tribulations the writer has to endure and, indeed, usually endures without protest, being too poor, or perhaps ambitious, to do otherwise, too afraid of offending, like most people 'in business' in our cringing society.

Most readers have the notion that all this writing business is 'money for jam'. Admittedly, there is quite a lot of money in it for the jam of a few superficial people—people publicly exposed as having been guilty in a really big way, co-respondents, divorcees, whores, and the like, preferably those in 'society' settings or with 'society' connections. But today, owing to the economic and sociological changes demanded by an affluent, undiscerning, and largely illiterate society, serious writing is a more precarious calling than ever. Journalism and, to a large extent, publishing have become a veritable dog-fight, accentuated by fatuous film-star values and radio standards, and mass circulation subrequirements. This is obvious from the most cursory glance at the literature now displayed on bookstalls.

These superficial but all-powerful forces are compelling the writer to conform to the commercial requirements of radio, television, and press. This means in effect that his freedom of expression is waning, and the number of people interested in literature as such continues to decline. Of the three general groups into which authors may be divided —those whose private means enable them to disregard financial recompense, those who are part-time, and those who are professionally full-time—the last mentioned is already shrinking rapidly.

With, perhaps, half a dozen honourable exceptions, weeklies and monthlies of a thoughtful character, striving against ever-rising costs to maintain some literary, artistic, or production standards, and even standards of integrity, are having the most tenuous existence. Casualties among them are constantly occurring. Mass communication is bringing about the eclipse of the few remaining literary publications providing a venue for serious criticism and for the new work of young and unknown writers.

Newspaper and magazine proprietors, as well as publishers, are now in a sort of super-market of their own, in their own rat-race. The Fleet Street World of today is one where dog eats dog and rat eats rat, in the ordinary course of things, often without being the least ashamed of it.

For the same reasons, the personal author publishing with the personal publisher is virtually a relationship of the past. So you see how fortunate I account myself in having found in Michael Joseph the kind of publisher I wanted for this book, as also for at least two subsequent volumes to which he and I are already committed.

The spell of my Golden Lamp of so long ago still holds. Dog-fight or rat-race? Call it what you like. If one be compelled to participate in any race whatsoever, there's no other in which I ever seriously wanted to run.

CHAPTER TWENTY-ONE

A Word for the Classics

THE MORE earnestly and industriously I plied my craft, the more I became absorbed in words, and in the precise and proper use of them. The more, also, I recognised what I owed even to my not too profound knowledge of the Classics. I began to realise how justified had been a particular Latin master at George Watson's College in his constantly encouraging his pupils to contradict immediately anybody referring derogatorily to Latin and Greek as the Dead Languages—dead, as if they were mere dodos. Today, although not quite in the form in which Caesar wrote his *Commentaries* and Homer the *Iliad*, these ancient tongues, he insisted, were more alive—more extensively drawn upon —than at any time in man's history.

That thought has abided with me as one of the most inspiring and rewarding of my life.

The Latin Languages—French, Italian, and Spanish in particular —where would they be but for their Latin origin? he used to ask. They are essentially Latin.

Having dealt at some length with this topic in one of my earlier books, roughly twenty years ago, I must write sparingly on it now except, perhaps, by way of recalling a few amusing classroom anecdotes belonging to the period immediately preceding the First World War, when the Classical masters at Watson's took great pride in their Latinity. Indeed, it is generally conceded that the Scots, for some centuries now, have maintained a preëminence in Latin. Their record in this field dates from about 1582, the year in which George Buchanan published his *Rerum Scoticarum Historia*.

Not so long ago, and in furtherance of this tradition, the headmistress of George Watson's Ladies' College and the headmaster of George Watson's Boys' College, both of whom I knew, conducted entirely in Latin their correspondence on matters scholastic. The headmistress, I should add, found further opportunities for this exercise in her dealings with a prominent official of the Scottish Board of Education. She always communicated with him in Latin, *by postcard!* Can you imagine this sort of academic tenacity anywhere in the world except between two Scots?

At Watson's I had come under the Classical influence of two masters, both of whom, in their resentment of what we might call the Dead Languages Theory, spoke or read aloud to us passages of Latin and Greek in order to illustrate their splendour, the splendour that was Rome and Athens. Afterwards, by way of good measure, they would throw in a few Classical tags for the picking up. There was Uncle Shaw[1] who, in his lifelong endeavour to make Latin *live*, might suddenly point a finger at one of his pupils and say, *Puer! aperi fenestras!*

("Ah'll mak' the Latin a livin' language for ye afore Ah'm deid!" some ungrateful boy away at the back of the class might be heard to whisper.)

If the pupil so addressed failed to understand what had been required of him, it certainly wasn't Uncle Shaw's fault.

He might then turn to the Lord's Prayer: *Pater Noster—qui es in coelis—Sanctificetur tuum . . .*

(Whispered comment from some Protestant back-bencher: "Bloody Papist!")

We all knew perfectly well, of course, that Shaw was as Protestant— indeed, as Presbyterian—as they make them. But, as R.L.S. put it, scratch the Scot, and you will instantly find below the surface a theologian. On an occasion such as this, the dullest Edinburgh schoolboy felt himself called upon to take up arms to defend the Reformation!

Then we had at Watson's the Classics master known as Jimmie Allan. A cut above his colleagues, he showed this superiority by wearing a morning-coat and a lum-hat. His inferiors contented themselves with plain lounge-suits and bowlers. Jimmie was truly in the hierarchy of Edinburgh schoolmasters in that he was also an esteemed boarding-house-keeper. He conducted his large home in South Oswald Road as a boarding-house for Watsonians whose homes lay in distant parts. Though punctilious in his Latin and Greek, he was apt at times to be a little provincial in his English. 'What way' was a favourite opening of his when he meant 'why' or 'how'.

Jimmie Allan to boy endeavouring to sneak unnoticed into classroom: "What way came you late to school this morning?"

Timid boy, pretending to be unaware of Jimmie's predilection: "Up the front steps, sir."

Jimmie Allan to the dour and backward Alasdair Alpin Mac-

[1] Alexander MacKintosh Shaw, 1881-1960. The euonym, Uncle, became attached to him the day he began his career at Watson's in 1903. He retired in 1940.

Gregor, about to expose to his master just how much or how little Latin homework he had done the night before: "Are you prepared, boy?"

MacGregor to the fearsome and formidable Jimmie Allan: "Well, I looked it over, sir."

Jimmie to MacGregor, about to receive a swift bang on the side of his head that sent him spinning with smarting cheek and tingling ear: "You mean you—you—eh—you OVERLOOKED it!"

A day or two might pass before there intervened a little further relief from textbook monotony. What could we remember of those Classical tags, without at least a few of which no lad dared consider himself educated? How soon could we recite, as to the manner born, one or more of those Greek epigrams Jimmie Allan regarded as an essential part of the schoolboy's Classical knowledge?

"MacGregor, those two epigrams inscribed in the Temple at Delphi—."

"Certainly, sir! Γνωθι σεαυτον: Know Thyself, and μηδεν ἄγαν: [Let there be] Nothing in excess."

"My boy, you speak like a native! I congratulate you! At this rate of progress you will be able to give me the longest word in the Greek Lexicon—the word for a fish-pie."

Up went that terrific word on the blackboard. That terrific fish-pie with all its putrescent ingredients. Score: 171, Not Out, as I see from my Liddell & Scott! I could not fail to observe, however, that even Jimmie Allan, for all his Classical scholarship, had to copy it from some printed matter abstracted from a waistcoat pocket, and held as inconspicuously as possible in the left hand to assist the hesitant bit of chalk already between finger and thumb in the right.

My dipping into Aristophanes a few years afterwards familiarised me with that celebrated, though much shorter, example, of which I ought to have reminded him before he died:

ὀρθρο-φοιτο-συκοφαντο-δικο-ταλάιπωροι πρόποι

early-prowling, base-informing, sad, litigious, plaguy ways.

Who would be so bold as to deny that all this Classical sense and nonsense did anything to equip me for the craft I so soon was to adopt? I knew that one day, if I returned from The Trenches, I should want to pursue more closely than ever the craft of words, whether or not I could ever again take up Latin and Greek where I left off in 1915. I knew also that there was literature in the *Odyssey* to which, one day, I would have to return. Even Jimmie Allan had made *that* clear when, with subtle aposiopesis, he read aloud, from his own free translation, that memorable passage in regard to Penelope and her suitors:

And—eh—they murmured among themselves—eh—which of them should be her bed-mate.

Naughty old man, we whispered to one another. Notwithstanding, had we been less terrified of his powerful blows, we would have rewarded this *tour de force* of his with a resounding cheer.

There were many examples of the way in which even my smattering of the Classics was to enrich my mind, my vocabulary, my vision and, therefore, my writing. By the time I had imposed upon myself the discipline of learning, each day, four new words from the English Dictionary, I realised how much more difficult this would have been without a working knowledge of Latin and Greek, and perhaps a few words of Hebrew. My French helped too, though it has never got much beyond the schoolboy stages.

As my writing developed, so did my familiarity with my tools, namely, words and ever more words, and all manner of punctuation and other symbols, every one of which has its precise use or uses. I examined them closely in the light of my Golden Lamp, long after Miss Aitken and any other lodger she had were a-bed and a-slumbering. I scrutinised them as they began to fall so fluently, so *currently,* from my untiring pen.

Most arguments about words could be settled by Miss Aitken herself, to whom a copy of *Chamber's Dictionary* was as important as was her Bible. These two substantial volumes rested upon one another in her kitchen, always ready to hand, always constantly in use.

One of her students, stuck in his studies, entered the kitchen one afternoon. He was sorely perplexed. Recourse to a good dictionary was not the sort of thing in which he indulged. He asked Miss Aitken the meaning of the word, Paraclete.

"And you, a theological student!" she shrilled at him.

"Don't go and ask *him!*" I now overheard him say when it appeared as though Miss Aitken were coming to consult me.

"Why not?" she enquired. "What for no?"

"Because he's sure to know!" was his objection.

Miss Aitken appreciated the point immediately, and shrieked in amusement. Over the supper-table in the kitchen a few evenings previously, she had lip-read a heated argument between three of us, during which the enquirer about Paraclete had denounced the Classics as a waste of time. We had had an evening on the Dead Languages Theory.

The exquisite word, Paraclete, had come into my life at George Watson's not long before I left it to enlist. The occasion was memorable. I was still in the early stages of Greek when παρα turned up. By way of demonstrating how extensively it is used as a prefix to English words, the master supplied his class with a string of them at random. "When you get home," he then said, "turn up any English dictionary, and you will find scores of others. Any boy like to mention another?"

Silence reigned. The master's list seemed to have exhausted all his pupils could think of. In a foolhardy moment up went *my* hand. I thought I would risk it. "Paraclete, sir!" I announced. He was amazed.

"How did you come upon *that* word, MacGregor?"

"It was the last word of the first line of a hymn we had in church last Sunday," I replied. "It's the Greek for the Holy Ghost—the Comforter—according to St. John. It's in John Mason Neale's translation of a 13th-century hymn, sir."

I quoted for his further edification that first verse, which I had memorised:

> *Come, Thou Holy Paraclete,*
> *And from Thy celestial seat*
> *Send Thy light and brilliancy.*

It was obvious instantly that I could not have hit upon an exanple more acceptable and agreeable, since this particular master was a prominent member o' the kirk. I was afterwards to learn that this lucid moment of mine provided the only really searching topic of conversation in the staff-room at Watson's for some days.

Would it interest you to know who the master was on that occasion? —on that final opportunity I was ever afforded of redeeming myself a little, before going off to the war? He was that fine scholar and Classicist, the late William Fyfe, father of my school-friend, David Maxwell Fyfe, better known as Viscount Kilmuir, Lord High Chancellor of Great Britain from 1954 until 1962, when, as an Earl, Big Business claimed him.

It was David's father who introduced me to certain Classical concepts I have carried with me all through life—to ροδοδακτυλος ἑως, for example. Homer's rosy-fingered dawn.

CHAPTER TWENTY-TWO

The Precarious Profession

MY POEM, *The Deserted Garden,* reprinted hereunder, was the first thing I ever wrote in my life with a view to its possible acceptance for publication. Written at Bivouac Farm in 1917, during an ominous lull immediately preceding the disastrous Third Battle of Ypres, I managed to post it to a London newspaper. The censors on the Western Front, not regarding it as something that might be of use to an enemy, allowed it through. So it duly appeared. I cannot recall my ever having been paid anything for it, however. In any case, in what form could a contributor from the desperate Ypres Salient have suggested to a newspaper editor that he might make payment, especially at a time when we were killing and been killed off like those proverbial flies? Having regard to the colossal casualties we were suffering on this sector of the Western Front, a poet's chance of survival was so slender at that time as to justify any editor's assumption that a contributor would probably have been a fatal casualty ere his poem could appear.

That, perhaps, this poem of mine merited some further recognition did not occur to me until 1921, the year before it was included in *Poems to Today*[1] along with works by others of my generation who so recently had been involved in war—Edward Wyndham Tennant, Edward Thomas, Robert Nichols, Julian Grenfell, Charles Hamilton Sorley, to mention but a few. Since then, it has appeared in a number of other anthologies of English verse published abroad— in French and in Italian anthologies, for example, and in the Tauchnitz edition of English Poetry, published in Leipzig.

At the time it was written, I may well have been under the influence of the tattered copy of Palgrave's *Golden Treasury* I carried in and out of The Trenches, and actually managed to bring home— to hospital. The setting and circumstances are recorded thus in my war diary:

[1] Second Series, published for the English Association by Sidgwick & Jackson in 1922.

"Sunday: I am on gas-alert in a deserted garden a stone's-throw in front of the platoon's billet at Bivouac Farm, just behind the lines at Ypres, where we are resting before being thrown into a battle. Remember, one stone left standing upon another out here often goes by the name of a farm. The garden is overgrown and, of course, deserted; and I have been crawling inconspicuously among its blighted bushes during a lull in the straffing, picking their few solitary currants and lingering rasps. The few birds seem to chirp and twitter incongruously. How can they sing in all this sadness, with impending death and destruction on a colossal scale awaiting, alike, ourselves and the Germans, on every hand? The only rose unblasted hangs its head for shame. After the bombardments of recent days, the calm is uncanny, portentous, sinister. Its soundlessness is broken only by the buzzing of insects in flight, manoeuvring or alighting near one. I must try to reduce this scene to verse, though I may never live to complete it, or see it published. I've never felt inspired to do anything like this before."

If merely as a matter of literary coincidence, compare this with the following passage from Sir Osbert Sitwell's *Laughter in the Next Room*:[1]

"It was about this time, during my second period in The Trenches, that a development had occurred, so important to me that, though I remained for another three years in the army, it altered the whole course of my life: it was during one of the brief spaces of rest, in a billet not far from Ypres, that I wrote my first poem . . ."

I wonder just where! I may well have known it.

THE DESERTED GARDEN
Bivouac Farm, Ypres,
July, 1917.

I love this garden, for you used to play
    About its haunted shadows long ago:
The years glide by in waves of blossom gay,
    And tides of jewelled snow.

Each summer brings the drowsy bees that doze
    Among the lazy flowers till you return:
Around your arbour the clematis grows,
    And red carnations burn.

[1] Published by Macmillan in 1948.

Your spirit ever haunts my memory,
　　As some faint echo when the hour is late:
The tall white hollyhocks wait dreamily,
　　Beside the crooked gate.

And jessamine that twinkles in the light
　　Still watches idly through the window-pane;
While scented stocks do weave their spell each night,
　　In case you come again.

The silent trees remember, for they cast
　　Their form, just where your footsteps seem to lag:
The honeysuckle spreads its trailers fast,
　　And the old palings sag.

Nor do the pensive columbines forget,
　　Because they still unfold their pretty flowers:
The fragrance of devotion lingers yet,
　　Across the listless hours.

There is no stir; the eager moments fly,
　　Breathless as embers dwindling on the gloom:
No leaf dare fall; the shadows loiter by
　　Like gnomes about my room.

Above the lattice where the roses cling,
　　The fire-flies dart as they did long ago:
My heart would break if any bird should sing,
　　Or if the wind should blow.

　　　　　　　　　　　　Alasdair Alpin MacGregor.

　　The Golden Lamp was now to illumine many a fevered sheet of
paper, scribbled and scrawled upon like those Frederick Victor Branford used to leave lying about at Miss Aitken's when beating out his
sonnets. I know it is popularly and pleasantly believed that all great
poetry results from inspiration so complete and immediate that the
person thus inspired sets the whole thing down on paper in a
few minutes, making thereafter no more than a few minor alterations.
Known instances of this are very rare. That which comes to mind is
George Matheson's hymn, *O Love that wilt not let me go*—the purest
poetry, written within a few minutes, under exceptional emotional
distress.
　　The merest glance at extant originals of great poems refutes absolutely the belief that they were written right off the reel, as the saying
goes. Were one also afforded access to the waste-paper baskets into

which poets have flung their *pre*-originals, it would be refuted even more. All great poems, like all great prose, are usually the result of enormous correction and revision, often entailing days, and even weeks and months, of worry and distraction.

Anyhow, the reception now accorded *The Deserted Garden* started me off in the direction in which so many writers start, but which, before long, economic necessity compels them to abandon. One must, indeed, have substantial private means to be able to devote oneself to the writing of poetry. In no way unaware of this, I began writing poems furiously. When I had completed about forty, published about thirty here and there in various periodicals, and succeeded in the meantime in getting some of them into subsequent anthologies, I realised I would have to turn any literary talent I might have possessed toward something less exacting, more acceptable, and somewhat better paid. I know not in the least what sort of payment is made nowadays for poetry; but I can hardly believe that, with the serious decline in recent years in the number of periodicals where a poem might receive hospitality, the rates of payment can be much better than those obtaining in the early 1920s, when *I* strove to add my reluctantly accepted or wholly rejected quota.

At that time *The Glasgow Herald* carried a daily feature known as the Casual Column, the top item of which was always a poem by some contemporary aspirant. Roughly half of my publishable poetry output appeared originally in that column, and at the standard rate of seven-and-six per poem. When at last I managed to get one into *Chambers's Journal,* and found that the rate was One Guinea a poem, *The Glasgow Herald* received thereafter only what *Chambers's Journal* declined.

Many a pint of oil travelled up the wick of my Golden Lamp before my total earnings from poetry amounted to five pounds! This was in the days when certain newspapers and magazines were good enough to announce in such literary hand-books and year-books as gave details of their scope and purpose:

"Payment by arrangement. *None for verse.*"

That immediately discouraged prospective contributors like me who fancied they had a few salable verses to dispose of.

Since literary work brings in so little in the material sense, people ask why one should be so foolish as to persist with it. Most people's criterion of values is marketability; and, since poetry has virtually none, except in autograph form when the poet has been dead a century or two, and something he starved to write is exploited in a sale-room, they cannot understand anyone who responds to the urge to write it.

How better can one deal with this aspect of things than by quoting the words with which Sir Egerton Brydges prefaces Pickering's edition of the poetical works of William Collins?[1] To the question, *Cui bono?* —what is the moral use of poems such as Collins's?—Brydges, in alluding to "the most uncertain and deplorable of all professions, that of literature, for a subsistence," replies in a manner at once impressive and memorable. His words should be quoted by every struggling writer embarrassed by the question Brydges answers for him:

> Whatever refines the intellect improves the heart; whatever augments and fortifies the spiritual part of our nature raises us in the rank of created beings . . . To embody, in a brilliant manner, the most beautiful abstractions, to put them into action, and to add to them splendour, harmony, strength, and purity of language, is to complete a task as admirable for its use and its delight, as it is difficult to be executed. No one can receive the intellectual gratification which such works are capable of producing without being the better for it. The understanding was never yet roused to the conception of such pure and abstract thinking without an elevation of the whole nature of the being thus roused. The expression of subtle and evanescent ideas, carried to its perfection, is among the very noblest and most exalted studies with which the human mind can be conversant."

Who would wish to improve on that? There, in a few sentences, the materialist receives an immortal answer.

Those who share the notion that poetry is solely a matter of sudden inspiration have the same sort of notion about prose. Skilful writing they regard as emanating from a gift with which people are born, whereas it is nothing of the kind. It is the result of years of practice and painstaking application, and often of much hardship, if not actually of privation. Rarely does anyone except the professional writer realise that writing, like any other art, has to be learnt slowly and painfully, and that, even after years of intensive application to it, one still feels very much in the apprenticeship stages of one's craft. *Vita brevis, ars longa,* or, as Hippocrates realised twenty-four centuries ago, ὁ βίος βραχύς, ἡ δέ τέχνη μακρή·

As Dan Chaucer put it when translating this Greek aphorism ten centuries later, *The lyfe so short, the craft so long to lerne.*

Despite years of experience, the right word or phrase seldom falls automatically into place, but has to be sought for, and thereafter

[1] *An Essay on the Genius & Poems of Collins,* published in London by Pickering in 1855.

adapted and inserted as a part of one's continual and laborious correction and revision. In the process, of course, the writer cannot avoid becoming engrossed with words as such. Everything about them grows increasingly important. Their origin, form, and length, their colour and tonal qualities, their physical appearance, as it were, their order of arrangement, their musical values, their assonance or dissonance—all these have to be weighed, since they influence so subtly the precise meanings one may wish to attach to them. Each and every one of them must fit into a picture or pattern, which the writer will also strive to tender in rhythmic sequence. Once the critical writer has arrived at this stage in his development, he finds that no language lends itself to so great a variety in texture as English; and how rich in all these qualities is Spenserian English, as I discovered quite early in life from a tattered copy of *The Faerie Queene* I took to The Trenches with me!

Under the benign spell of my Golden Lamp, and never unmindful of Victor's early literary influence upon me, I found myself dedicated to what one might term epeology—to the veritable worship of words, as words. After so many years' indifference to the canons and conventions of good writing, they suddenly began to mean everything to me. With constant application to their meaning and usage, I worked hard to enhance my vocabulary. It was at that time an ambition to be able to state clearly the meaning, and possibly also the derivation, of every word in *Chambers's Twentieth Century Dictionary,* excepting words concerned primarily with scientific matters. With this end in view, and with Miss Aitken at hand to examine me as one would a schoolboy in regard to his home-work, I assiduously applied myself to its learnèd pages, mastering from them a few new words per day. Thus, by the time I was twenty-five, I had familiarised myself with almost every non-scientific entry in that estimable repository of learning and scholarship.

In 1952, this publication, which had now become as indispensable to Miss Aitken as to myself (she used it constantly when reading through my typescripts and correcting my proofs, or when working at her cross-word puzzles), was superseded by the New Mid-Century version, edited by William Geddie. Was it not William and his brother, Liddell, who, in their excellent editorial judgment, advised Messrs. W. & R. Chambers in 1924 to accept for publication my very first book? The Geddie brothers had been associated with this publishing house during most of their lives. It was with Liddell, however, that I had the closer contact, for, when he succeeded the late Charles Edward Stuart Chambers as editor of *Chambers's Journal,* there then passed to him the pleasure of accepting or rejecting the articles I began to submit so frequently to that monthly of long-standing merit. Founded in 1832, it ceased publication with the December issue of 1957.

I also had something to do with William Geddie. To him I submitted from time to time, in my enthusiastic epeolatry, words, together with their meanings and derivations, which I thought ought to be included in what is now the current Mid-Century version I mentioned. I am gratified that many of my suggestions were found acceptable, and that thus I may claim at least an infinitesimally small share in perpetuating in a more complete and comprehensive form a publication upon which my life has been so largely dependent. It became increasingly so as my books began to appear in fairly regular succession. The first three of them were to be published by Messrs. Chambers. Indeed, they 'discovered' me, and virtually established me. Through them, my Golden Lamp musings were to be communicated to tens of thousands of readers all over the world. For several years every issue of their *Journal* contained a full-page advertisement of my books. This publicised my name all over the English-speaking world, and even beyond.

When the current version of the Dictionary appeared, I happened to be busy with notebook and camera among the Aborigines at the Red, Dead Heart of Australia. It could have been out no more than two or three months when I saw a couple of copies standing in the window of a general store in Alice Springs. The sight of them there, so far from Edinburgh, elated me enormously. I entered the premises to buy a film in order to provide myself with a pretext for saying something about the Dictionary. And what do you think I said—to the manager? Something like this: "I'm immensely interested to see that Dictionary in your window, adding a touch of Scottish scholarship to your buckets and pails and bins. I happen to be an author. The publishers of that Dictionary were my first publishers. I was brought up on their famous Dictionary—supped it with my porridge. Among the books in our home, only the Bible took precedence. And—believe it or not—the form in which it now stands so conspicuously in your window contains words which might well have been omitted *but for me!*"

You cannot imagine the wonderment with which this declaration of mine was received at the arid heart of this continent. My *locus standi* in Alice Springs improved quite perceptibly thereafter.

An interest in words inevitably fostered a corresponding interest in phrasing, in figure of speech, in quotation, in "apt alliteration's artful aid," and suchlike. Gradually one acquired a technical knowledge of one's language and of its mechanism, and an anxiety to learn how to manipulate every subtlety of expression, every shade of meaning, every nuance. Such figures of speech as enantiosis (the rhetorical term applied to the expression of an idea by the negation of its contrary) now began to force their attention upon me. I had once heard my father say something like *He's no fool*. The oddness of such expressions aroused my curiosity. "But who said he was a fool, father?" I enquired in my illiteracy. This mode of expression I was afterwards to identify as enantiosis, having found this word in the dictionary when enjoying a little serendipity.

The significance of just the right word in the right place, I make bold to say, passes unnoticed by most readers. This aspect of careful writing can be appreciated only by those in a position to read slowly and primarily for pleasure. Such care as is employed by fine writers means nothing to the rapid and superficial reader. That most people who read do so superficially is assuredly shown in the nature of the books, newspapers, and magazines boasting the greatest circulation.

Those who regard writing as a serious and subtle art recognise how the proper use of words is really a matter of marksmanship—that every word, every sentence, every paragraph, has been carefully aimed to hit its mark in relation to the whole. Allow oneself the exercise of substituting, in a poem or in a beautiful piece of prose, a phrase or a sentence of one's own, or even a word, and see how unsuitable is the best one can devise! It's like interfering with a delicate and intricate piece of mechanism. Remove a wheel or a pawl in favour of another which isn't exactly the same, and it no longer functions.

So now I was to find myself possessed of a compelling sense of vocation, actuated by an ardent ambition to master those technicalities of an art which would give me the fullest self-assurance that I knew not merely what I was writing about, but also that I was writing intelligently and, above all, intelligibly.

Yet, of what proportion of writing can it be said that the choice and position of every word, of every piece of phrasing, of every symbol of punctuation inserted, have been matters of separate consideration?

Few realise that it takes years of application and self-discipline to learn the splendid management of a long sentence. This explains why comparatively few professional writers ever feel themselves qualified to attempt one, and therefore confine themselves to staccato writing in short sentences frequently possessing no verb.

A pre-requisite of good literature is that studious leisure which so few writers can afford, since few have private means, or can enjoy the relaxation which, though it could never make dull people interesting, might do something to prevent interesting writers from becoming dull.

The commercially successful writer is usually the enemy of fine writing, which means so little to the great mass of readers, interested as it is in the indifferent literature of sex and crime. In these days, when most minds, like most commodities, are mass-produced, and ideas (if such one dare call them) are disseminated throughout society with unremitting persistence by such conveyor-belt means as gigantic newspaper combines and pressurised wireless and television systems, there seems but slender hope for the survival of faithful craftsmanship in anything. Fine writing is very much a craft which superficial, mass-produced reading material must render largely extinct before long.

You may follow more closely what I mean when I cite an author like Somerset Maugham as being among the arch-enemies of fine writing. His enmity, he tells us in *The Summing Up,* is attributable to his incapacity:

"I discovered my limitations, and it seemed to me that the only sensible thing was to aim at what excellence I could within them. I knew that I had no lyrical quality. I had a small vocabulary; and no effort I could make to enlarge it availed me. I had little gift of metaphors. The original and striking simile seldom occurred to me. Poetic flights and the great imaginative sweep were beyond my powers . . . I knew that I should never write as well as I could wish, but I thought with pains that I could arrive at writing as well as my natural defects allowed. On taking thought it seemed to me that I must aim at lucidity, simplicity, and euphony. I have put these three qualities in the order of the importance I assigned to them."

No effort Somerset Maugham could make to improve his vocabulary was of any avail. This seems to me an astonishing statement. The quiet and studious reading of other authors' *fine writings* would have helped him, as it assuredly helped *me*!

Of course, the novelist is not usually afflicted with qualms of artistic conscience. On the contrary, the cruder, the better. This partly explains why I have never been able to generate much enthusiasm for fiction, so much of which appears to me to be variants of the themes of love and violence—the sexual affairs of people, at least one of whom must be married in order to provide the adored ingredients of intrigue and all the concomitant flapdoodle I, in my rather naïve way, find rather boring. Others find it so all-absorbing as to render them unaware that sexual intrigue isn't the *whole* of life.

"Stay me with flagons!" one feels inclined to implore. "Comfort me with apples, for I am sick of love!"

Having said all this, I must be careful to add as a safeguard against the likelihood of wrath to come, that a work of fiction *can* be a work of art.

*   *   *

Of my abandoning, in favour of prose, my somewhat puerile attempts to write poetry, I was reminded by something I read a year or two ago by John Betjeman, something in the nature of a review of recently published volumes of poetry. What he wrote truly epitomises the experience of all who hopefully have sought to travel in this precarious realm. As he pointed out, the writing of a poem takes a long time. "There is the original impulse to write it, the line that flashes in at the right place with the right word in the right order. The rest of the poem is long, hard work—giving the whole thing form, and making the other lines of the poem as good and inevitable-sounding as that which provided the original inspiration . . . You might say that, for many modern poets, five good poems represent the work required for one average-length novel. Few poetry books consist of less than thirty poems. They are a man's life-blood poured out on paper."

I was indeed fortunate to have discovered this for myself as early in my literary career as 1922, by which time I had collected, in what I had hoped would have been regarded by some publisher as publishable form, thirty poems of my own, but no publisher would look at them, although one of them did say that he might consider the matter if ever I managed to publish reasonably successfully something in prose. The ambition to place everywhere I could as many articles as possible now obsessed me. My Golden Lamp would have to inspire me to get down on paper material more acceptable, and therefore more remunerative, than poetry. Before long, I was to experience something of a sensuous delight known to those prolific writers of an earlier age, whose quills glided over their pages at a speed wellnigh incredible to those of us who, in the later stages of composition, employ shorthand and typewriter. Though I now use a typewriter every day of my life, seldom travelling afield without one, my delight, for years, was transmitted through a Waverley nib inserted in a glass pen of jade green an old friend had sent me from Malaya. That nib was to slip across the page, line after line, as if animated by some force not wholly attributable to myself. Once into its stride, the words fell behind it as do the miles behind aircraft flying at optimum speed.

For all this, I cannot claim that in taking up the pen I ever experienced Victor Hugo's thrill as of taking a beautiful woman in my arms. Indeed, there have been times when, with the increasing encroachment of new ideas for magazine articles and books, the physical act of writing has become tedious and irksome, if not even painful on occasions. The hand's struggling to keep pace with the mind—with the swiftly evolving process of brain—tends to irritate one when engaged in literary composition. This in certain circumstances has been my own experience, especially when, in response to some powerful im-

William Roughead,
W.S., at Brodick in
1921

Walter MacPhail
(1867-1941)

*Photograph by Drummond
Young, Edinburgh*

Photograph by T. & R. Annan, Glasgow

Neil Munro (1864-1930)

pulse, I have been impatient to get something down on paper, and realised that there could be no respite, no peace of mind, until it *was* on paper, even in a form necessitating radical alteration later. My physical task throughout the years might have been alleviated a little, had I not waited until I was over fifty before I allowed a fountain-pen to displace the Waverley nib to which I had been thirled since schooldays.

Anyhow, my literary output now increased in the ratio in which it failed to find acceptance. Yet, I had only to recall my father's years of warning that, if I insisted on following any literary bent I may have imagined myself endowed with, it would mean years of laborious application with little or no financial return, and that, even if ultimately successful from a literary standpoint, I could never hope for anything but the most precarious existence. The dustman, he would say, maintains a higher standard of living on his wages than most people aspiring to authorship can hope for on the royalties from the sales of their books. This, contrary to popular belief, is terribly true. I had written several books and published innumerable articles, many of the latter in some of the world's most estimable journals and magazines, before I felt myself justified in believing that economically I at last was even as well off as the dustman. Usually one has to be prepared to slave away at book-making for years, without even such financial recompense as would keep salt to one's kail, to achieve even the faintest scintilla of success.

I used to think that, if only I had imposed upon myself that discipline attributed by Pliny to the Greek artist, Apelles—*Nulla dies sine linea:* Never a day without a line—I would by now have thrice the number of books to my credit, though they might not necessarily have been of any literary value. The pen constantly in the hand can sometimes be nothing but a bad, and even dangerous, habit! Where *I* was concerned, the habit was acquired by what my father used to refer to as 'casual scribbling'. I began to pore over those snippets of mine, as he called them, "not as a formal study, but as a pleasing diversion at spare hours," just as Dr. John Wallis, Isaac Newton's eminent predecessor in the realm of mathematics, pored over arithmetic. Whereas Wallis was able to extract the square-root of a number consisting of 53 digits, and announce to a stranger the following morning the answer to 27 places, the result of my lucubrations lay on my bedside table for Miss Aitken to see for herself when she brought me an ever-increasing morning mail of rejected MSS.

As my father was always impressing upon me, for all the recognised glamour of authorship, for all the esteem in which it has been held throughout the centuries, what father, with even the most elementary knowledge of the economic implications, would encourage his son to

H

take professionally to the pen! Fathers are usually too well aware, instinctively, that, as Isaac Disraeli remarked, the pursuit of authorship as a career insulates the author—the *true* author—from society because of its inherent exactions. Furthermore, it subjects him to much discouragement, and correspondingly little remuneration.

It is as true in our own day as in Disraeli's that, even the most successful author fails to obtain any equivalent for his life's labour. "Authors themselves never discover this melancholy truth until they have yielded to an impulse, and adopted a profession, too late in life to resist the one, or abandon the other. Whoever labours without hope—a painful state to which Authors are at length reduced—may surely be placed among the most injured class in the community. Most Authors close their lives in apathy or despair, and too many live by means which few of them would not blush to describe."[1]

The list of those aspirants to celebrity in literature who have participated rather in its misfortunes is a long one. The annals of literary calamity are vast. How many fathers have declared, like my own, that they would do everything in their power to prevent a son's devoting himself to literature? Remember how the scholarly Cowley expressed himself in the preface to his *Cutter of Coleman Street* (1641), in regard to those who, like himself, devoted much of their time to writing poetry: "If I had a son inclined by nature to the same folly, I believe I should bind him from it by the strictest conjurations of a paternal blessing." How thankless a task he found serious literature may be judged from the sentence with which he concludes this same preface: "This I do affirm, that from all which I have written, I never received the least benefit, nor the least advantage; but, on the contrary, have felt sometimes the effects of malice and misfortune!" Notwithstanding, his dust reposes between that of Chaucer and Edmund Spenser.

Yes, I was thoroughly warned by my own father, and, indeed, by others of his generation who had tasted that bitterness to which the reading public remains indifferent. For all this, however, I have been more fortunate than many a more deserving author. Do you recall the melancholy confessions of Tobias Smollett in this connection? "Had some of those who were pleased to call themselves my friends been at any pains to deserve the character, and told me ingenuously what I had to expect in the capacity of an author, when I first professed myself of that venerable fraternity, I should in all probability have spared myself the incredible labour and chagrin I have since undergone."

How many authors have been so impoverished that only through the generosity of some friend or admirer, or possibly a charitable pub-

[1] *The Calamities & Quarrels of Authors*, by Isaac Disraeli, London, 1859.

lisher or bookseller, have they received even the dignity of an identifiable grave? How many have perished immaturely in striving to exist on what the pen could earn them? I believe that the story of those who, so full of promise and romance, came to London from Scotland alone, in search of literary fame, during the last two hundred years, but died early in poverty and obscurity, would provide material for a long and tragic narrative.

Despite such discouragement, one goes on hopefully. This is certainly not the sort of journey R.L.S. had in mind when he held it was better to travel hopefully than to arrive. Recalling his own early literary disappointments, he must have longed to 'arrive' in the sense in which we are concerned here. His first paid contribution to literature was the essay, *Roads*. This, after rejection by the *Saturday Review*, was accepted by *Portfolio*, then edited by P. G. Hamerton. It appeared in the December number, 1873. The following year there was published the first of Stevenson's contributions—twenty-five in number—to the *Cornhill Magazine*. With these he made his first mark as a writer.

Though I would never encourage any young person to adopt literature as a means of livelihood, the young aspirant who has met with nothing but rejections may find a little consolation when he realises that R.L.S. was 23 before he ever received a farthing for anything. Even *I* did better than that, although I can never expect to achieve through my writings anything of the immortality he so deservedly enjoys.

In all probability, the copy of *The Golden Lamp* you are reading at this very moment has been borrowed from some library. It will earn me a royalty of about 2/6. If it be a library copy, hundreds will read it, like yourself, for that solitary half-crown. In the light of the preceding pages, and of those which now follow, you may well see the injustice to authors of the present library system.

CHAPTER TWENTY-THREE

The Editor Regrets . . .

LONG BEFORE I had Robert Louis Stevenson's example as a pretext for what many are apt to regard as eccentric behaviour, I had formed the habit of making notes on things, usually on the spot—

> *A chiel's amang ye, takin' notes,*
> *And, faith, he'll prent it!*

So wrote Robert Burns of Captain Grose and his peregrinations through Scotland.

My own note-taking may well record small things. But how important are one's collection and recollection of just those small things when it comes to putting together a volume such as this! Was it not that dedicated observer, W. H. Hudson, who liked to regard himself as a traveller in the small things of life, realising how tremendous they often are?

So far as my own note-taking is concerned, I have always pursued the practice with confidence ever since my discovery that Stevenson had established a truly literary precedent. "He's an awfu' laddie for speirin' questions aboot a'thing," the Roaring Shepherd of Swanston said of him; "an' whenever ye turn yer back, awa' he gangs an' writes it a' doon."

I am always sympathetic when I see someone else jotting down something *ambulando,* whether on the edge of the pavement, or in bus or train. Very few do; and the very many who don't are inclined to regard as a bit 'touched' those who do. I constantly take notes in this way in my desire to translate into the printed and published word whatever I see, hear, taste, touch, or smell. Miss Aitken thoroughly understood the significance of this. In fact, she herself frequently noted things down in this way. "A'thing is grist tae the mill, laddie," she used to say when she observed me putting down in a notebook or on a scrap of paper something that had occurred to me.

For years there stood upon my mantelpiece at Liberty Hall a coloured reproduction of a garden and thatched cottage. It was mounted on an upright piece of cardboard roughly whole-plate in size. A collapsible strut attached at the back enabled one to stand it up, with just that little bit of backward tilt one remembers about those special portrait photographs then so common on sittingroom mantel-pieces and grand pianos. It reached me from an anonymous hand that had written on the back "In gratitude for 'Poems of Today', page 58". The envelope containing it bore the Torquay postmark. Be-yond that, I know nothing of its sender. When I came south to London I brought it with me, along with such of my household gods as had sentimental value. Where it is now, I cannot say. Gone, I expect, with the accumulated junk of years when we were blitzed in Chelsea. But, if it exist no longer in its material form, it survives in another and very real form.

Returning late one evening to the inspiration of my Golden Lamp, my eye rested on this quite humble production, and I fell to musing, to pensiveness, to wistful reverie. Removing it from the mantelshelf and placing it on the table under the Golden Lamp, I took paper and pen and wrote, in about twenty minutes, an article of 900 words. Giving it the sentimental title, *My Dream Garden*, I immediately typed it, modestly placing at the end of it "A. A. MacG.". In the small hours I crept out with it to the nearest pillarbox. Believe it or not, it appeared eight or ten hours later in *The Edinburgh Evening Dispatch*.

In referring to an old scrapbook in order to re-read *My Dream Garden* after the lapse of nearly forty years, I saw exactly why it found immediate acceptance. It contained all the romantic ingre-dients for which most editors are eternally looking. It had a lily-pond and an iris-pool, a summerhouse and a toolshed, nesting birds in an-cient oaks, thatched eaves, a bucket-and-chain well, any number of bees seeking nectar, and the introduction, at least twice, of 'old-world', an adjective then very much in vogue on sentimental occasions. On the whole, it was an improved prose version of the garden now gleaming under my Golden Lamp.

The reception accorded this rather mawkish effort was so unex-pected and, indeed, so encouraging, that I ransacked my brains and my notebooks with a view to an immediate follow-up. This was pub-lished within a day or two—a slightly longer article on Hebridean Pirates. I now suggested on a typewritten postcard, stamped and ad-dressed to myself, six tentative titles for contributions. This went with a covering letter inviting the editor of *The Dispatch* to run his pen through such as he thought might not be worth considering, and then post the card back to me. It arrived in a day or two. *No title had been scored out!* This astonishing invitation kept me very busy for a week or ten days.

Meanwhile, I had no idea what remuneration to expect; and, since *The Scotsman* group of papers (which then included the now defunct *Dispatch*) paid its wretched contributors at the end of each quarter, I was kept on tenter-hooks for several weeks, especially as I had been warned by an author friend that the group's rates of payment were notoriously low.

When at last my cheque came, I found I was being paid a flat rate of a guinea per contribution, irrespective of length or quality. Through lack of experience, I did not know then whether this was good or bad payment, even having regard to the considerably lower cost of living in the early 1920s.

I know of some worse instances of financial remuneration, of course. That which comes to mind is Cutcliffe Hyne's (1866–1944). The creator of Captain Kettle received from Charles Dickens, eldest son of the novelist of the name, and editor of *All the Year Round* in succession to him, One Guinea and a complimentary letter for a contribution of over 12,000 words. Think of that!

Then there is the case of A. A. Milne. One day, after much perseverance, a certain stamped, addressed envelope did not come back as expected. Soon afterwards Milne was feverishly delighted at finding his initials printed under his first contribution. At the end of the month, to his grim disappointment, he was sent, in respect of it, a cheque for 15/–. A little later he received a further cheque for 16/6 as payment for no fewer than three contributions to *Punch*. "It didn't seem to make sense," he remarks in his autobiography. But he was slightly consoled at the outset when told that he should regard as more than adequate reward the honour of being allowed to appear in so splendid a journal! That's precisely what I was told when I hinted to those concerned that the value of my contributions to *Chambers's Journal* might be assessed a little higher!

My old and valued friend, Mrs. Burnett Smith (Annie S. Swan), told me shortly before her death what *she* received in her early strugling days as an author. I had confirmation of this the other day on seeing a reference to a letter she wrote about 1906 to Catherine Robertson Nicoll, commenting on her just having heard that 60,000 copies of the sixpenny edition of *Aldersyde,* her first novel, had been sold in a few months. "All I received for it was £50, about twenty years ago!"

One could extend indefinitely the list of writers, some of them quite famous, who fared even worse than this.

Finding my payments from Edinburgh's newspapers none too sustaining, I turned my attention to Glasgow's. I began with attempts

to contribute to the Weekend Page of *The Glasgow Herald*. Apart from
the poems mentioned earlier, my success in this sphere was short-
lived, and for the following reason. Having noticed on that page an
article by a rival, dealing with a folklore matter, I wrote to ask the
reason why an article I myself had submitted a month or two previously had been rejected. I pointed out that in the meantime my article had appeared elsewhere, and that the errors it contained, together
with the fanciful inventions I had permitted myself, now appeared in
The Glasgow Herald. A clear instance of plagiarism, I declared!
And there ended my literary career with *that* paper!

But I had another string to my Glasgow bow in *The Glasgow
Evening News*, the editor of which, at that time, was my father's friend,
Dr. Neil Munro, already the author of a host of delightful volumes, and
of some very fine poetry. Nepotism, therefore, rather than merit, ac-
counted for the publication in his columns of the quite trivial typescripts I sent him. My first remuneration from this paper took the
form of a half-guinea postal-order, and a cheap fountain-pen which I
was never able to use except when displaying it in a bragging way as
something the great Neil Munro had sent me.

Under Neil's distinguished editorship, *The Glasgow Evening News*
became one of the finest evening newspapers in the United Kingdom.
Its Saturday Supplement, which he introduced, and to which from
time to time he invited me to contribute, was widely recognised in
British journalistic circles as a literary institution of exceptional
brilliance.

This paper ceased publication in January, 1957, after a run of almost ninety years. During the last few years of its existence, it had
been running at a substantial loss. Its disappearance brought to an end
the protracted newspaper war in Glasgow, where three evening papers,
each conducted at a loss, were competing fiercely with one another
for an aggregate readership of roughly 615,000.

My own humble associations with the Glasgow *News* terminated as
long ago as 1930, the year of Neil Munro's death, at the comparatively early age of 67. His departure was something I felt very deeply.
"Put away paper and books and pen," said Sir Arthur Quiller-Couch
(1863-1944) thirty-six years earlier. "Stevenson is dead; and now
there is nobody left to write for." That is exactly what I myself felt
on learning of the death of Neil Munro.

I wonder how many pints—nay, gallons—of the midnight oil were
consumed by that Golden Lamp of mine in my prolonged and frantic
efforts to obtain even sufficient recognition by editors to enable me
merely to survive! I might have eight or ten articles out at a time,

which meant that every few days I received the same number of rejection slips—"The Editor Regrets . . ."

I knew, of course, that he didn't regret in the least. This was but an additional reason why I resented them so much. A notebook recording the whereabouts and rejections of my typescripts now became essential, so that, as they were rejected, I could provide other editors with the opportunity of adding to my ever accumulating rejections slips.

Then, one day, in fingering my way through a heap of returned MSS., I discovered that they added up to one less than the number in circulation. Caution was now exercised: the missing MS.—well, it would probably turn up all right with the next post. And, if it didn't, something very strange and unusual had happened. You might actually be going to see it in print, which meant that at last you had broken through, though only to a mild extent. Thus your endeavours to adopt a literary career went on, for a year or two more, with perhaps a slight improvement in the number of your acceptances. But this was offset by your increased output, and a proportionate increase in the number of rejection slips which in due course reached you.

For some time I collected all those painfully impersonal slips, believing that one day they might be preserved by some literary institution as Variations on a Theme, since the wording in which regrets accompany such rejected MSS. is a study in itself, an art of its own.

Many a struggling writer has saved up his slips—for a while, anyhow. I know that Neville Cardus did, until his bundle became unmanageably thick. That was in the days, as he himself tells us somewhere, when it was impossible to get into print unless one could write reasonably good English, either as an occasional contributor or as a reporter. Editors are less particular on that score nowadays; and so are publishers. The reason for this is too obvious to require explanation. Today, one doesn't need to be able to write at all in order to find acceptance. On the contrary, the better you write, the lower are your prospects of acceptance—and conversely, of course.

Some rejection slips are more imposing than others, as if designed to impress their import so firmly on the would-be contributor's mind as to discourage him from making further futile attempts. I have by me at the moment an imposing example from *John Bull* which accompanied the return of the only article I ever submitted to it:

The Editor thanks you
for submitting the enclosed contribution
but regrets that it is unsuitable
for publication in
John Bull

A not infrequent variant of this distressing theme runs as follows:
"*The Editor expresses his regret that he is unable to use the enclosed contribution, which he returns with thanks.*"
Of course, some of the more Cadogan journals and magazines have their own special rejection formulae. Take *The Times*, for example. It is considerate enough to send you a letter marked *Private & Confidential*. Until you have received a few of these, you are apt to be taken in by this gentlemanly ruse, believing the letter contains an invitation to —to contribute something. But the letter, on the contrary, runs undeviatingly as follows:

> Dear Sir,
> The Editor asks me to acknowledge your letter of such-and-such a date, which has been carefully noted.
> Yours faithfully,

Carefully noted, mark you! Not really the least ambiguous, once you've had a few of them. You then suddenly realise that this is *The Times's* euphemistic way of announcing that the proposal you have submitted is already in the editor's wastepaper-basket.

As you become a little better known through the publication of a few snippets here and there, a touch of courtesy begins to creep into things. Point-blank, anonymous refusals by printed rejection slips give way to fatuous, signed letters explaining why the material you have submitted is being returned to you. I think that, of all the editorial people I have dealt with in the last forty years, those connected with the late *Everybody's Weekly* have been the most resourceful in compounding pretexts for declining both contributions and suggestions relating to them. Let me cite a few examples from my collection:

> "I regret to say that I am not in a position to say 'yes' to your suggestion."
> "Unfortunately, I do not think that the manuscript you have so very kindly sent me quite fits in with what I want."
> "Thank you for your letter. I can only say how sorry I am that you have felt we have meted out rather bad treatment to you of late." (The rejected MS. usually follows this precursor by the next post.)
> "Thank you exceedingly for giving us the opportunity of using this article, but I'm afraid it is not suitable."
> "Your article is awaiting my decision, and I hope to read it in the course of a few days."

(A sure sign that it's on its way back!)

I

"Of course, you should have received ten guineas, and I apologise for the mistake. As a matter of fact, I blame myself entirely for
not having given proper instructions to our Accounts Department.
However, I will read it at the earliest opportunity, and then get in
touch with you again."

(Such courtesy invariably presaged the return of my MS., not
quite so precipitately as on occasions when no such letter was being
sent you. Part of the courtesy consisted of waiting a couple of days
longer than usual before favouring you with a further rejection slip.)

I wonder what proportion of writers has persevered for five or
even ten years before ever receiving a slip worded: "With the Editor's
Compliments," attached by a tiny pin to a little cheque! I wonder, too,
how many authors, even after they have published a few reasonably
successful books, are apt to feel as did Horace Walpole when he said
"I have taken a thorough dislike to being an author!"

That section of the public reading serious authors' works virtually
for nothing through libraries has no conception of the incredibly long
hours they work for twenty-five or thirty years, and at very high pressure, before they feel themselves sufficiently experienced and established to slacken a little and, perhaps, indulge in a modicum of leisure.
For older authors this is rarely possible, unless they possess private
means. An author writing to *The Daily Telegraph* a year or two ago
put his position very clearly when he stated that, in order to maintain
a standard of life built up as a result of thirty years' intensive applica-
cation to his craft, he was obliged to work longer and harder than
when younger, and consequently better able to withstand the pressure
and anxiety.

Not the least disconcerting treatment meted out to writers like me,
who illustrate their own work, is the condition in which, nowadays,
rejected material reaches him. Bad enough having it rejected; but,
when it comes back in a grubby condition, stamped with the bottom
of wet teacups, clarted over with lipstick, stuck to the gummy flap of
the envelope, the poor author finds himself fighting against insuper-
able odds. Often the top page of his typescript is heavily scored with
a serial number and a date imprinted indelibly with a sharp, rough
pencil that no amount of rubbing will erase. So he must needs re-type
it if he mean to submit it elsewhere. The edges of his pages are often
creased, frayed, and sometimes even torn. So, likewise, are the edges
of the proposed photographic matter he has sent in for illustrative
purposes. His photographs, though received in perfect condition,
together with properly cut cardboard and envelope for return in due
course, get metal clips inserted so ruthlessly as to convince the already

frustrated recipient that their purpose was to see that the photographs really got torn a bit, or at any rate so deeply impressed as to be rendered useless. Worst of all, rejected photographs are frequently returned, not with the protective material with which they were submitted, but by the insertion of a flimsy piece of cardboard protecting only *part* of the photographic surface. This means that the unprotected part gets bent over and cracked in the post. Editors like to blame the postoffice: photographers like me, with a library of several hundreds of subjects, blame the editors, and beg of them to see that no protective cardboard at all is better than a piece not covering the entire photograph. The other day I was fortunate enough to find an editor who, without arguing about this, sent me a cheque for some pounds in respect of returned photographic material damaged in transit through this sort of thing. The pounds helped with the replacement of the damaged prints; but they did not compensate for the time lost in looking out negatives, typing out precise masking and other instructions, captioning, writing yet another letter, and posting.

Had it not been for Miss Aitken's tolerance and encouragement, I would, of course, have been a literary casualty within a year. Nobody lacking the care and consolation she bestowed upon me in those early struggling days could have survived with the pen still defiant in his hand. Unlike most landladies, she was exceedingly well read. After her day's work, she spent two or three hours in serious reading. The rate at which she got through the daily papers was remarkable, often noticing in them items pertinent to myself or to my work that had escaped me. "Ay, laddie, ha'e ye no' got eyes in yer heid?" she would ask when she came rushing in upon my Golden Lamp soliloquies to draw my attention to something I had missed.

She was excellent at proof-reading; and I seldom submitted for publication an article she had not revised. When I completed a typescript, I laid it as a matter of routine on the kitchen table, that she might go through it leisurely. If I returned at night after she had gone to bed, I found it lying on my pillow, with little slips of paper inserted where she had discovered mistakes in spelling or in grammar, and other inaccuracies. When proofs arrived, she always liked to see to the first revision of them.

Incidentally, when not occupied in these ways, she worked at crossword puzzles, picture puzzles, literary problems, and the like. On several occasions she won substantial money prizes. These she shared with me, for it was agreed between us that we halved whatever we won in this way. She was consistently the more successful; and I benefited accordingly.

And how Miss Aitken and I argued as to whether a particular solution in some weekly publication should be this or that! When the issue containing the correct answers relating to some such competition was due, she sent Ruairi round to the newsagent's to collect it. That he had duly returned with it became audibly evident when I heard a shrill voice, followed by urgent footsteps. "Ye see, ma laddie, if ye hadna stopped me frae puttin' in yon word last week, Ah wud ha'e got aboot £40 as ma share o' the prize-money!"

There was one notorious instance when I persuaded her to alter something. Had she refused to do so, she would have been the only entrant with an entirely correct solution. This would have brought her the entire prize-money, which on that occasion amounted to £500. As she was one of several with only one mistake, she had to be content with her proportion. I felt very ashamed of myself over this.

CHAPTER TWENTY-FOUR

Walter MacPhail

●●

DOWN THERE, in Edinburgh's busy Market Street, are the offices of *The Edinburgh Evening News,* the *Evening Dispatch's* powerful rival. Mr. Walter MacPhail, its pawky, rotund, and immensely jovial editor, I knew well by sight from the time of my earliest struggles and schemings to get my rather amateurish work published. Few Edinburgh citizens didn't know his kenspeckle figure, for he was truly one of our city's 'characters', one of her peripatetic memorials. Six days a week he might be seen trundling across the Meadows toward Gladstone Terrace and his home in the adjacent Mayfield district, always carrying in each hand a strapped bundle of new books for review purposes. He looked very editorial.

One day, accompanied by Ruairi, I called on him at his office in Market Street, and was agreeably surprised to discover that he knew who I was. He had seen me scampering with Ruairi on the Meadows, and had made it of his purpose to identify us. Very unexpectedly, Ruairi and I were shown into his formidable presence. He addressed me straight away as Aaleestar, his own Scots rendering of my Gaelic Christian name. I ought to mention that he spoke 'The Doric' exactly like Miss Aitken. His editorial associates, so many of whom I was to know intimately in subsequent years, assured me that this was a pose of his. Be that as it may, he never failed to make himself understood in it.

"Well, noo, Aaleestar! Whit can we dae for ye?"

"I've brought an article you might like to consider for your Saturday Page."

Rather timidly I proceeded to abstract from a pocket a typescript of about a thousand words, and handed it to him as he swung to and fro in his editorial chair—the first I ever saw, with or without an editor in it. He no more than gave a quick glance at the title I had given my proposed contribution.

"Lord's Sake, Aaleestar! Wha in 'The Name' wants tae ken aboot Mediaeval Markets & Fairs? Oor readers want 'human interest', no' a lot o' mediaeval noansance. That sort o' thing is a' richt for

Chambers's; but it's no' damned guid for *The Edinburgh Evening News*."

"What do you mean by 'human interest', Mr. MacPhail?" I enquired in my naïvety.

"Wattie's ma name, Aaleestar! A'm Wattie tae ma freens. Human interest! Seager! [calling out to his assistant editor in an adjoining room] Here's a laddie edicated at the University; an' he doesna ken the meaning o' 'human interest'! What'll we dae wi' 'im? You college boys are no blest wi' muckle in the way o' wit, wi a' yer graand degrees! Awa' hame an' write me an article on yer dog. Bring it doon tae me here by ten tomorrow—aboot 900 words—an'—wait there a minute!"

Mr. MacPhail wandered off to see about something equally agreeable. "A've made an appointment for ye at ten in the mornin' wi' oor photographer. He'll tak' the dog's fotty. So ye'll ha'e a fine splash in the paper a' tae yersels."

I rushed home to Miss Aitken with these tidings. She was beside herself with joy. 'Ye'll ha'e tae be up in the mornin' afore yer claes [clothes] are on, ma certie!" she remarked.

Ruairi and I duly kept our appointment. I handed the editor my typescript; and he escorted us by winding ways to the photographic department, where Ruairi was dealt with by flashlight. We left Mr. MacPhail to his leader-writing, and anxiously loitered outside in Market Street until noon, when the first edition of *The News* was due to appear. Soon the newsboys were dashing through the city with their quotas, carrying before them a poster that read:

STORY OF A
HEBRIDEAN
COLLIE
by
ALASDAIR ALPIN
MACGREGOR

Purchasing straight away a dozen copies of this issue, I hastened home with them to Miss Aitken, together with a poster, its printer's ink barely dry. We pinned that poster to a shelf in the kitchen at Liberty Hall. There it remained for many a day.

Thus was inaugurated many years' happy associations with *The Edinburgh Evening News*, and the most understanding and amusing editor I have ever had. Walter MacPhail was certainly the most democratic in my not inconsiderable experience of editors. There was absolutely no side—no swank—about him. Incidentally, I have maintained, in one way or another, my contact with this paper, though he died as long ago as 1941.

On referring to my scrapbook I see that my next contribution to it dealt with our window-boxes at Liberty Hall. It contained a great deal of poetic exaggeration, of flowery hyperbole thoroughly soaked in 'human interest'. In glancing through it, I see mention of three things which were no exaggeration, namely, our wallflower display in the late springtime, our sweetpeas in summer, and our festoons of nasturtiums in early autumn.

For a while my sundry contributions to the Saturday Page of this paper brought me about £6 a month. A belated appeal to Mr Mac-Phail for some small improvement in my rate of remuneration fixed it at Two Guineas per article. This represented an increase of roughly 50%. The frequency with which my articles appeared in this paper over a dozen or more years enhanced my literary reputation with a considerable section of the Lothian population which otherwise might never have heard of me. Its circulation in Fifeshire did the same there. I once innocently remarked to MacPhail that I had received a couple of appreciative letters from *News* readers in Fife. "D'ye no' ken, Aaleestar, that there's scarcely a hoose in the Kingdom o' Fife that doesnae get oor paper?" I felt mildly rebuked.

Walter MacPhail, J.P., was born in Edinburgh in 1867. At the age of fourteen he began his journalistic career as an apprentice with *The Edinburgh Courant*. At that paper's demise he went for a short spell to a paper in the Lake District. In 1886 he returned to his native Edinburgh to become a reporter on its *News*. In 1913 he became its leader-writer. Six years later, he was appointed editor and managing editor. When he left us in the autumn of 1941, at the age of seventy-four, he had served with this paper for fifty-five years. His funeral to our Grange Cemetery was attended by a mighty concourse from all walks of life, since no man of his generation in Scotland had sponsored so many deserving causes, and done so much to plead the case of the poor and oppressed. When one reads the snobby and fatuous obituaries now so prominent a feature of journalism, and then turns to the press tributes to Walter MacPhail, one instantly recognises how deeply the contributors of them assessed the sterling human qualities of the man we had known.

MacPhail was assuredly an individualist, and the last of our great editors in Scotland. He did an immense amount for his native city, and was infinitely more deserving of its Freedom than all the political mis-chiefmakers and successful self-seekers for whom such recognition is usually reserved. His contribution to literary wit was immense, his pawky humour proverbial. They permeated everything he touched. They were seen very frequently in the Editor's Postbag, where he allowed his readers to divest themselves of their weirdest conceptions, and ask the silliest questions. The latter MacPhail sometimes dealt with himself, without disclosing his identity. In an endeavour to relieve the boredom of wartime news items, he gave us of his best. Here is his account of a bore-absorber: "A friend back from London tells me he saw a man going along Oxford Street with a large placard dangling in front of him: 'For sixpence I'll listen to your bomb story'."

One of Walter MacPhail's recreations as listed in *Who's Who* was typical of him—"dodging bores".

Of the fifty or more editors with whom I have had dealings over the years, he was, with perhaps the exception of Neil Munro, the most approachable. I shall always remember him with affection, and admire him for his enormous industry. His capacity for work was astounding, his judgment of men and affairs shrewd. Behind that pawky humour of his lay something sound and sincere.

CHAPTER TWENTY-FIVE

Behold the Hebrides!

AN EARLIER chapter contains a mention of my first book, *Behold the Hebrides!* As the circumstances of its acceptance and publication were, perhaps, the most momentous of my life, it would seem apposite that I should conclude this first volume of our Trilogy with a résumé of them, in spite of Disraeli's remark that the author who speaks about his own books is almost as bad as a mother who talks about her children. How true this can be! I have listened to mothers: I have also listened to authors, as they expatiated on the superlative qualities of their literary offspring. But, since I now find it a little incumbent upon me to relate just how *I* first slipped into authorship, I trust the reader may excuse me if, now and again, I appear to lapse into that state of parental egotism and ecstatic adoration in which parents recount the most trivial sayings and trifling achievements of their children, so often boring, if not indeed embarrassing, their listeners.

If there be one concatenation clinging more tenaciously to memory than another, it is that which ultimately linked my earliest appearances in print with fully-fledged authorship. I recall every link in that chain with remarkable clearness. I had no more than graduated when the Muse took possession of me. Its symptoms I ought to have recognised immediately, for I had been brought up by a father who, with paper and pencil always ready to hand, was continually browsing among his books and manuscripts. Scribbling had been a hobby of his during the greater part of his life.

A prolonged sojourn with cousins in the Outer Hebrides provided me with ample 'copy', so that, throughout the ensuing months, I was feverishly occupied in writing innumerable articles, and in sustaining innumerable rejections. To succeed at all in literature, as you now realise, one has to slough those spells of despondency so apt to overcast one's existence when the first post each morning consists of little but returned MSS., and the second brings those posted a little too late to catch the first.

However, when I had managed, by one artifice or another, to get roughly a score of them published, it occurred to me that, if suitably arranged and somewhat amplified, these snippets, as my father derisively termed them, might be publishable in book-form. With this end in view, I had a discussion with a certain John Fisher, a partner with Robert Grant & Son, Edinburgh's well-known booksellers, then established at 126, Princes Street.[1] This firm had just launched out into publishing new Scottish books. Fisher was responsible, incidentally, for the publication of those volumes by the Rev. T. Ratcliffe Barnett, already mentioned.

One afternoon Fisher and I, seated in a Princes Street tea-room, surveyed the prospect of his publishing in book-form somewhat amplified versions of my published snippets. "Let us adjourn to the fresh air," he said, "and discuss the proposal more rationally." So we betook ourselves across West Princes Street Gardens to a seat on the steep, grassy slopes under Edinburgh Castle. There we went into matters seriously. It was resolved that forthwith I should put a selection of my published articles together in some sort of sequence, enlarge them, type them, and add a preface. A day or two later I took to Fisher what I believed to be a publishable proposition. Indeed, I already felt myself a potential author.

Need I say that I paid frequent visits to Robert Grant's during the next few days to ascertain, at the very earliest possible moment, whether he meant to undertake publication? Finally, Fisher told me that, owing to other commitments, he could not do so that year, BUT —and this is the most significant 'but' that has ever come my way— but that, in the interval, he had had a telephone conversation with Mr. George Morris, managing-director of W. & R. Chambers, and that Mr. Morris would be pleased to have me call that very afternoon with my typescript. "See that you take Ruairi with you!" Fisher added. "He

---

[1] When in Edinburgh a few weeks prior to the publication of the book you are now reading, I called on such survivors of my bookseller friends as had helped me in my early, struggling days. At the Edinburgh Bookshop, in George Street, I saw John Young, one of the first bookman acquaintances of my life.

"What are you smiling at, John?" I asked. "I haven't told you anything very funny—yet!"

"When I saw you enter, I suddenly remembered a little incident regarding your father, an incident still recounted in the book trade in Scotland. You know, of course, that I began my career as a bookseller with Robert Grant at 107, Princes Street. In 1922, when the business was in process of being transferred to 126, your father thought he ought to go along and inspect our new premises, and see whether he approved of them. He entered in his old military way and addressed the foreman fitter. 'What's your name?' he asked. 'Campbell,' replied the fitter. 'TRAITOR!' roared Colonel MacGregor, and indignantly strode out."

may well help you to get your book accepted!"

This sounded too wonderful to be possible. Too fantastic! The historic and honourable imprint of W. & R. Chambers! Good Gracious Me! I had been familiar with it virtually all my life. It appeared on many of my school-books, and on that indispensable Dictionary. It also appeared on the *Journal,* then read in cultivated homes throughout the entire English-speaking world.

I rushed back to Miss Aitken with this news. Was it possible that these rather slight things, contrived in the gleam of my Golden Lamp, might be accepted?

I brushed our black-and-tan Ruairi until his coat glistened, and then set off with him and my manuscript for 339, High Street, Edinburgh, where Messrs. Chambers's premises were in those days. On arrival I intimated my appointment with Mr. Morris, then very much . 'the big noise' in Auld Reekie publishing circles.

"The dog will be all right here," suggested a subordinate when on the point of conducting me from the front office to the mighty presence in a remote room at the back of those rambling premises.

"Oh, no!" I protested. "The dog must accompany me! You see, he's very much part of the plan! An integral part, in fact!"

Ruairi and I were now shown into the first publishing *sanctum sanctorum* we ever had the privilege of entering. Therein sat the portly Mr. George Morris, moving to and fro in semi-circles on a swivel chair by his desk. I handed him my typescript. Without as much as glancing at it, he slammed it down with emphasis on a desk bestrewn with MSS., letters, and sundry papers to a depth of several inches.

"Well, now," he began, and in a tone that almost extinguished hope in me, "what reason have you to suppose that the great British book-buying public is likely to be interested in this work of yours? You understand, of course, that we're not in publishing for the good of our health! Doubtless, Mr. Fisher will have told you *that!*"

Gathering together my flagging wits, I strove to convince him that this proposed book of mine was destined, above all others, to be an unqualified success. Indeed, a best-seller!

"But you see," he continued, "every author believes this of his own book. I've been interviewing authors for half a century, and never yet met one who didn't. You would have me understand that you're leaving with me the typescript of the finest piece of unpublished literature in existence? Eh? Ah! I know you authors. You have such extraordinary ideas, but so little business sense."

The awkward hiatus that followed this crushing reception narrowed appreciably when Ruairi, meanwhile lying in the knee-hole of Mr.

Morris's desk, as he did in that of my own, responding to an almost inaudible snap of fingers, emerged a little to examine the situation, resting his chin on Mr. Morris's knee, and looking up at him in a very pleading way. Yes, I could see he had pleaded all right, in his own silent manner. "Mr. Morris, you *will* accept Alasdair's book, *won't you?*"

"What a beautiful collie!" observed this somewhat mollified man of affairs. "What do you call him?"

"Ruairi" I answered. "It's the Gaelic for Roderic. I brought him as a puppy from the Hebrides; and—and—and there's a chapter on him in my proposed book. And—and—and a photograph of him among my proposed illustrations."

This happy turn of events evoked from Mr. Morris a dawning interest in my typescript, which, up till now, had lain completely ignored. He stretched forth his hand and grasped it with an air of resolve. I maintained a discreet silence. Turning to the chapter on Ruairi, he began to read through it. He then glanced at the photograph accompanying it.

"That's interesting!" he remarked. "Is this by any chance the dog we read about in our *Evening News* some little time ago?"

"Yes, it is! The very dog!"

"What else does your book contain of interest?"

"Oh! it's all frightfully interesting, Mr. Morris, frightfully interesting! And, by the way, an abbreviated version of the final chapter has been accepted for publication in your own *Journal*."

"In *Chambers's Journal*, do you mean?"

"Yes, indeed!" I was swift to reply, realising that its acceptance for publication in a monthly as established and esteemed at once conferred upon me a not altogether negligible status as a writer.

"Ah! That certainly improves matters. We'll write you in the course of the next few days."

As Ruairi and I rose to quit this truly august scene, the door opened, and in walked Charles Edward Stuart Chambers, the editor of *Chambers's Journal*, bearing in his hand something highly acceptable —a cheque for Nine Guineas! Shall I ever forget it? The biggest sum I had ever received for anything I had written hitherto. My article was appearing in the impending issue of the *Journal*.

"We hope to see you both again," said Mr. Morris of the large, beetling eyebrows, as he deferentially bowed Ruairi and me to the door. This parting observation of his implanted in me some slender hope. When black-and-tan Ruairi and I found ourselves on the pavement of the High Street once more, I gave him a very special word of thanks for his having acquitted himself so memorably. We now hurried home across the Meadows to Liberty Hall to relate to Miss Aitken all that had happened.

"Eh! sodger!" she shrieked at the dog as we entered. "An' did ye behave yersel as befits a gentleman, and mak' a graand impression on a' thae big bugs in the auld Hoose o' Chambers?"

As I was now in too unsettled a condition to remain indoors, I set out on my bicycle for Portobello, three or four miles away, to inform my father of this interview, conveying Ruairi with me on the carrier I had designed for him, and in which he travelled many hundreds of miles during our excursions together. Between father and son there now took place a conversation like this:

Son: "I've just been to see the managing-director of Chambers, in the High Street. I left a typescript with him."

Father: "A typescript! Of what? Not those snippets of yours we see from time to time?"

Son: "Yes, father, those very snippets!"

Father: "Well, my boy, I admire your industry. But don't get it into your head that one becomes an author quite so easily. If publishers won't look at my beautiful Gaelic lyrics, you can hardly expect them to publish your snippets. I don't want to discourage you, of course. Only, be more than prepared for a rejection, and then you won't be disappointed."

Son: "But, father, you don't seem to realise that, whereas most people can at least *read* my snippets, comparatively few can make anything of your beautiful Gaelic lyrics."

Publishers, as a race, are notorious for the time they sometimes take in arriving at a decision about accepting or rejecting a manuscript. They occasion authors much anxiety and frustration in consequence. However, so far as Messrs. Chambers were concerned I had but a few hours to wait. That evening, when Ruairi and I returned home to Gladstone Terrace, Miss Aitken, in great excitement, greeted me with: "Eh, ma laddie! A letter frae Chambers! It's ben there, on the kitchen mantelpiece, atween the gas-bracket an' the tea-caddy!"

"How do you know it's from Chambers?" I asked.

"Guid gracious! Isn't the imprint on the back o' the envelope? It cam' by hand a couple o' hoors syne."

"Open it and tell me what it says," I added, as I seated myself by the kitchen table, in too much of a dither to attend to it myself.

"Wait till I get ma spec, then!"

She opened the letter and, holding it up to the gas-light, began to read it aloud. "Eh, ma certie!" she screamed, in bending down to address Ruairi. "Yer maister's going tae be an author! Ye'll ha'e tae scoot awa' back tae Portobello wi' him at ance, and tell his auld faither. Off ye gang, the twa o' ye! Won't the auld man be prood o' 'um noo?"

And that is how I came to know that W. & R. Chambers had accepted for publication my first book, *Behold the Hebrides!*

Though it was already nearly 11 p.m., Ruairi and I were soon a-wheel again. Downhill by the King's Park and Duddington we sped to the seashore at Portobello, by which my father then lived. He was just undressing by his bedside as we arrived. I ushered the dog into his room ahead of me, and then followed a second or two later.

"What in the name of God has happened?" he asked, as the dog approached him. He thought we had had an accident with the bicycle, and that the dog had returned to report it.

"Something extraordinary has happened, father," I gasped. "Something *very* extraordinary. Chambers have accepted—my BOOK!!"

"Accepted those snippets, as I call them? Those snippets, when no publisher will look at my beautiful Gaelic lyrics? What *is* publishing coming to?"

"Yes, those very snippets," I replied.

"Great God in Heaven! Wonders will never cease! This is the best news I've had since my marriage to your mother blighted my life! What terms are they offering you?"

"An initial royalty of 10% of the published price on every copy sold, or Fifty Pounds down for the Rights."

"Take the Fifty Pounds!" my father urged. "You may never earn *five* in royalties."

My father got into his dressing-gown. We re-kindled the sittingroom fire, and celebrated my success with—lemonade. We sat down to consider this entirely gratifying situation. In support of his advice that I should sell the book outright for the sum offered, he proceeded to recite classic examples of famous books that had brought their authors next to nothing. True, the opportunity of laying my hands so readily on the sum offered was tempting enough, especially when one recalled R.L.S.'s ecstasies on receiving from Messrs. Cassell an offer of but twice that amount for the book-rights in *Treasure Island*—"A hundred pounds, all alive O! A hundred jingling, tingling, golden, minted quid!"—and that Kegan Paul & Co., in paying him a paltry twenty pounds for the copyright of *An Inland Voyage*, were not at all sure that the sales would even cover their production costs. Indeed, part of the first small edition of this latter work was actually remaindered.

"Think of the notorious rejection of books which afterwards became famous!" my father began. "Publishers, with their stereotyped regrets, returned the manuscripts of Conan Doyle's *Sherlock Holmes*, Blackmore's *Lorna Doone,* Carlyle's *Sartor Resartus,* Kipling's *Plain Tales from the Hills,* Stanley Weyman's *House of the Wolf,* Thackeray's *Vanity Fair,* Rider Haggard's *Dawn,* Mrs Stowe's *Uncle Tom's Cabin.* And, yet, apparently without much effort, you, an unknown writer, can find a publisher who offers you Fifty Pounds for these snippets!"

Of my father's recital on this truly auspicious occasion of famous rejections, I was reminded a few years ago by the letter George Bernard Shaw wrote in 1881 to Messrs. Smith, Elder, & Co., the celebrated London publishers of the time, offering his recently completed novel, *Love Among the Artists,*[1] which they turned down. Shaw, on his 92nd birthday, 67 years later, commented upon this: "My first books—five novels—were referred to every publisher of any standing in London, and to some in America. ALL were rejected."

The setting in which I announced to my father this first acceptance brings to mind that in which Joseph Severn conveyed to *his* father the news of *his* first triumph, immediately he learnt that he had been awarded the Gold Medal of the Royal Academy. Into his father's bedroom he, likewise, rushed.

"What in heaven's name is the meaning of this intrusion?" demanded Mr. Severn, in sitting up in bed to take stock of the situation.

"Father!—The—Medal!—President!—Mr.   West!—Not—for twelve years!—They've given it to me!"[2]

I think I may have been a little less incoherent than this when Ruairi and I returned to Portobello with similar news.

You cannot imagine Mr. Severn's astonishment, since Joseph, in his father's view, was as unlikely to reflect credit on him as Alasdair had been in the view of the critical Colonel MacGregor. Just as Joseph had knelt down by his father's bedside to thrust half-a-pound of gold medal into his hand, I bent down over my father's to thrust into *his* hand a scrap of paper weighing but a dram or two. Its weight mattered not. Its brief sentences carried all the weight required. Mere physical contact with this half-sheet of notepaper assured him of the veracity —nay, of the reality—of my utterance as I entered his bedroom. You must understand that by now he had lost his reading sight, although he could still see comparatively well for other purposes.

In the small hours Ruairi and I returned to Liberty Hall to find Miss Aitken waiting up for us. "Ah couldnae gang tae ma bed till Ah heard yer auld faither's reactions. Ma certie! He must be gey pleased! A'm that excited masel that sleep wes never farther frae me. Did he advise the Fifty Pounds?"

---

[1] Now published by Constable.

[2] *Against Oblivion,* by Sheila Birkenhead (Cassell, 1943).

"I'm afraid he did," I replied. "But I must obtain a second opinion before deciding."

Acting on her advice, I hastened to Glasgow the following day to consult Neil Munro, bearing Messrs. Chambers's letter with the urgency of a royal courier. Neil and I lunched together. Showing him the letter, I explained my quandary. He suggested my asking Messrs Chambers how many copies they proposed as a first printing. "If they agree to print 2,000 or over," Neil counselled, "take the 10% royalty."

Mr. Morris promptly replied that the first printing would be a minimum of 4,000 copies. Having already been told that the published price would be 7/6, I now knew where I was. Assuming Chambers print 4,000, I said to myself, and, in spite of their reputation, sell no more than half that number, the position would be:

$$10\% \text{ of } 7/6 = \text{Ninepence.}$$
$$\text{Ninepence} \times 2,000 = £75.$$

That is to say, half as much again as the Fifty Pounds.

A day or two later, accepting a royalty of 10% of the published price on the first 4,000 copies sold, and 15% thereafter, I signed with Mr. Morris my first Publisher's Agreement. It was the simplest Agreement I have ever signed. It consisted of no more than three clauses typed on a half-sheet of notepaper, duly stamped and signed.

A few months afterwards I handed to my partially blind father something larger than Severn's gold medal. It was the first copy in existence of *Behold the Hebrides!*—the First Fruits of my Golden Lamp. It had a Foreword by Lord Alness, the Lord Justice-Clerk. The printer's ink was scarcely dry. That was in 1925. My father was then nearly 78. "I am prouder of you for having achieved this than I can say," he sobbed. "Wolfe, you remember, said he would prefer to have written Gray's *Elegy* than to have taken Quebec."

When I received my first cheque from Messrs. Chambers, my father was quite overcome. "Your having earned even five pounds from literature means more to me than if you had come by a hundred thousand in some other way."

The first two months' sales brought me more than twice £50. The following year's brought thrice that sum. For more than a dozen years, this naïve and quite flimsy volume went on selling. In all, I had several hundreds of pounds from it.

So little had I auspicated any literary proclivities in my early years that my father could never have imagined the day would come when he and I were to share, in the world of letters, an interest that was to be the means of effecting the most complete understanding between a father and son who, hitherto, appeared to have given one another a good deal of pain. My backwardness, on the one hand, had occasioned him years of despair: his thoughtless cruelties, on the other, had brought me corresponding years of physical torment and mental anguish. All this was now resolved. Literature, by some odd accident, had provided the basis for reconciliation.

"*Rien ne réussit comme succès,*" as Dumas discovered. Nothing succeeds like success. My father was continually quoting these words in slow, husky, gruffy tones, the better to emphasise them, whenever I announced yet another forthcoming book, or somebody mentioned to him that he had been reading an article of mine somewhere.

Of course, a first success is apt to engender a magic conviction in one's own literary ability and stability. I had to guard against this, and realise that my literary struggles were by no means over. But they were substantially alleviated.

Epilogue

••

As I HAVE shown in our opening chapter, the felicity of those introductory weeks at Miss Aitken's was the first thing of its kind ever to reach the realm of acute perception where *I* was concerned. However, the duration of that felicity was, alas! all too brief. Eight or ten intensely happy weeks at the most, I should say. Like all truly good things, it diminished and faded away, to be all but erased from memory by the sordid and saddening realities of the years which were to follow.

This foretaste of Paradise came to an end, very definitely and poignantly, with my discovery of something which was to destroy any hope of true happiness I might otherwise have found. That discovery related solely to the practice of experimentation upon living, sentient animals, and the suffering it entails for them—a practice now so universally and so legally established, approved, defended, and recklessly endowed.

The impact all this denoted knocked the bottom out of any deep concern I may have entertained hitherto for the supposed wellbeing of human society. It extinguished in me just that flickering ray of hope for mankind which had survived my spell in The Trenches of Flanders, of Artois and Picardy.

But, if the hope had now vanished, conviction had taken its place: I was absolutely and resolutely certain that by no honourable standards could vivisection be justified. I saw in a flash what Alfred Russel Wallace meant when he said: "So long as vivisection is legal, our legislation against cruelty to animals is the most barefaced hypocrisy." I instantly realised this vile practice to be the modern version of that execrable sum of human villainies, as John Wesley described the slavetrade. Even if I could have found any reason for being unsure or ashamed of my feeling in this matter, it would have vanished immediately I discovered into what brilliant company I had strayed, and how readily one could compile, from literature alone, a catalogue of the condemnatory pronouncements upon it by the truly great, ignor-

250

ing for the moment of the published strictures of men prominent in medicine and surgery. Let me quote, a little at random, half a dozen that come to mind:

"I believe I am not interested to know whether vivisection produces results that are profitable to the human race or doesn't. To know that the results are profitable to the human race would not remove my hostility to it."—*Mark Twain.*

". . . The Queen has seen with pleasure that Mr. Gladstone takes an interest in that dreadful subject of vivisecting in which she has done all she could, and she earnestly hopes that Mr. Gladstone will take an opportunity of speaking strongly against a practice which is a disgrace to humanity and Christianity."—*Queen Victoria, in a letter to Gladstone, dated April,* 16, 1881.

"Vivisection is a crime . . . The human race must repudiate such barbarous practices."—*Victor Hugo.*

"My own life has been one of great bodily suffering, and I am, therefore, well acquainted with pain of this nature. But all the many and various physical torments I have undergone are as nothing when compared with the mental suffering which has been caused me by the knowledge of the practices and principles of vivisection . . . Will any *physical* benefit which the vivisectors may ever wrest for mankind from their mangled, poisoned, crucified, or scalded martyrs ever compensate us—the men and women who think and feel as I do—for all the hideous mental pain their deeds have caused us? . . . Do they prate to me about science and health when they have made the whole earth a wilderness for me, and my whole life one long struggle and protest? Every moment of my waking hours is absorbed by the warfare against this great wrong. My very sleep is rendered fearful by visions of its horror. Who or what is to compensate me for this?—*Anna Kingsford, in a letter to the press.*

"The thought of their sufferings penetrates with horror and dismay into my soul, and in the sympathy evoked I recognise the strongest impulse of my moral being, and also the probable source of all my art."—*Richard Wagner, in a translated letter on vivisection to Ernest von Weber.*

"I would rather submit to the worst of deaths, so far as pain goes, than have a single dog or cat tortured on the pretence of sparing me a twinge or two."—*Robert Browning.*

It may be some small solace that so many of this calibre have expressed their abhorrence in terms forceful and unequivocal; but, of course, we haven't, as yet, saved one victim one twinge of pain. For myself, I am pretty much in Anna Kingsford's position. My constant awareness that this shameful business is going on, and increasingly so, all the time, all over the world, has overshadowed my days—which means, of course, that those responsible for it are also responsible for having made pretty unbearable the lives of such as are capable of thinking and feeling and perceiving beyond their own personal and immediate selves.

So my Happy Day had gone from the shining fields, never to return with anything of its first joyous intensity. That peace at eventide, induced by the glow of my Golden Lamp, had been disrupted for ever. No longer could I smell, without a twinge of pain, the blossom at Grantchester I so recently had lived with, nor yet the narcotic whiff of that new-mown hay which first reached my nostrils from Edmund Gosse's verses propped up against my knees on a coloured counterpane, the very pages engoldened by my Golden Lamp. "The mowers all are gone, and I"—well, need I explain further?

In 1929 I returned my graduation diplomas to the Principal and Vice-Chancellor of Edinburgh University, the late Sir Alfred Ewing,[1] as a protest against my Alma Mater's extensive vivisectional activities. I asked that my name be deleted from the University's records; and at the same time I challenged any vivisector, man or woman, to debate with me, publicly, either the moral or the scientific justification for the acts they are licensed to perform. Professor Crew, of the department of genetics at Edinburgh, was being widely acclaimed just then for his having succeeded in turning cocks into hens, and hens into cocks, and making hens crow! All very edifying—all very elevating—you must agree!

Sir Alfred acknowledged my protest courteously. He regretted my attitude, and pointed out that statutory regulations did not provide for

[1] This distinguished physicist and engineer was born in 1855, and died in 1935. Between 1914 and 1917 he was in charge of the Admiralty Department dealing with enemy cipher, when he became celebrated as The Man in Room 40. As an authority on magnetism and on the physics of metals, he was far ahead of his time in the field of nuclear science, and certainly one of the first to state publicly its appalling implications.

As President of the British Association in 1932, he expressed a view for which I have always respected him. It was to the effect that he believed mankind was not yet good enough to be entrusted even with such knowledge about the atom as he and his colleagues possessed.

Ewing's physicist successors, instigated by Roosevelt and Churchill, with Attlee as a consenting party, dropped the highly improved results of this knowledge upon Japanese mankind, and then unashamedly tried and executed others for Crimes Against Humanity.

the removal of my name in the manner I had requested. In the course of subsequent correspondence with the Registrar, when I sought to be spared posted information relating to statutory meetings of the General Council, prospectuses of university literature, and the like, I suggested that regulations empowering the University to accept large endowments unquestionably involving countless animals in indescribable suffering should be amended to enable an alumnus, who felt exceedingly strongly on matters of this kind, to sever his associations in a statutory manner. My request was granted; and my association with Edinburgh University, except where a few of my professors and contemporaries were concerned, came officially to an end, there and then.

Much else came to an end at the same time. A bit of my livelihood went literally overnight when the ungallant Sir George Waters, then editor of *The Scotsman*, wrote me that my action had rendered impossible our continuing as editor and contributor. When I responded by saying that I must needs give to the import of his letter what publicity I could, and at a public meeting I was due to address in Edinburgh, he wrote me further that the letter I had received from him was *his*, and not *mine*, and that my reading it publicly might very well involve me in legal trouble over copyright.

All this is as long ago as 1929. Only once since has an article of mine appeared in *The Scotsman*; and that was in connection with the bi-centenary celebrations I attended in 1958 at Ticonderoga, in New York State.

When my father died in 1932, papers like *The Glasgow Herald* devoted as much as half a column to his quite unique career. *The Scotsman* completely ignored his passing, although he had spent the last twenty of his 84 years in the city where it is published, had been a frequent contributor over the years, and was a well-known character there.

It is a popular fallacy that editors must necessarily be people of sterling character and integrity, a race sacrosanct and apart, whereas there is no reason for supposing them to be a whit better or worse than other folk. My own experience of editors during forty years' dealings with them hasn't been too bad on the whole. In a few cases it has been exceptionally agreeable. Retirement or demise in these cases has usually been to my disadvantage, however. Editorial chairs are apt to find very quickly occupants who know not Joseph, and wouldn't have much time for him anyway, owing to the impersonal and mechanical relationship between editor and contributor which, in the last decade or two, has invaded journalism, like everything else. An age of take-over bids has no room for the courtesies, civilities, and considerations of former years.

The dirtiest trick an editor has ever played in my knowledge was played by an Edinburgh editor during the Second World War, when domestic help was scarcely available at any price, and elderly house-holders consequently found themselves in dire straits. The wife of the editor I have in mind was in such straits when, for some reason or other, her domestic staff left. Anxious to be neighbourly, an octo-generian couple of the old and honourable school, who lived close by, and whom incidentally I had known since my boyhood, sent their two maids over to the editor's house one day to help out his comparatively young wife, having been informed by the editor himself of her domestic predicament. She promptly offered them higher wages which they, as promptly, accepted. So the old couple was left without help, and had to fend for itself throughout the most difficult period of the war. In this caddish manner the editor was relieved 'for the dura-tion' of all household chores. This left him free to pursue his patriotic part in the interests of the war in which, according to his editorial columns, we, in a life-and-death struggle against evil and uncharitableness, were so honourably engaged!

My University protest received so much press publicity (though ignored by *The Scotsman*, certainly so far as its readers were con-cerned) throughout the country—and, indeed, all over the world—that it seemed unlikely to escape my father's notice in one way or another. If he did not actually see for himself that I had committed academic suicide, somebody was bound to mention it to him. When he first learnt of it, he was greatly perturbed. By the time I saw him, how-ever, he had accepted the situation with astonishing equanimity. Some-one had accosted him in the street to congratulate him, rather than me, and at the same time to tell him something I myself had not known, namely, that in 1885 John Ruskin resigned the Slade Chair of Fine Arts at Oxford as a protest against exactly the same thing. In the course of a speech dealing with experiments on living animals, delivered at Oxford on December, 9th, of the previous year, Ruskin stated:

> "*These scientific pursuits were now defiantly, provokingly, in-sultingly separated from the science of religion; they were all carried on in defiance of what hitherto had been held to be compassion and pity, and of the great link which bound together the whole creation from its Maker to the lowest creature.*"

Since that suicide of mine, the abhorrent practice of vivisection has increased enormously. According to a recent White Paper, over 4,000,000 animals are now being used annually in Britain alone in experiments by vivisectors licensed under the Cruelty to Animals Act of 1876. These are the numbers *admitted*. I believe the actual numbers to be considerably higher. After all, to the vivisector, 20 or 120 rats or mice, or whatever they can lay their hands on, doesn't make much difference; and it certainly assists those who breed and sell them commercially for this purpose. There's never any shortage of living material, though I *have* known vivisectors to complain publicly that at times they had experienced a falling off in the number of victims procurable, owing to the wicked activities of people like me!

I, for one, have no difficulty in believing that those who get themselves licensed to do this sort of shady thing cannot have much compunction about being accurate when they come to making their Home Office returns of the numbers of victims they have been responsible for.

In any case, why bother about numbers? The practice is as legal as it is remunerative. The higher the numbers, the more profitable. You see, there is no limitation upon the *numbers* of animals used.

I might mention that, of the 4,000,000 animals cited, 3,500,000 "did not require anaesthetic". But who said so? The victims? The sufferers?

Indeed, no! The men—*and* women—who, having hurt, mutilated, and diseased them, without reference to their consent, have always arrogated to themselves the right to say it for them, supported by such self-confessed cads as the late Dr. Halliday Sutherland, whom I knew. "Halley" himself describes in one of his books how, for experimental purposes at Aberdeen, he lured, trapped, and stole people's cats in the grounds of the fever hospital there. "The thought of stealing never troubled me," he writes, apropos this caddish conduct.

But for protests from members of the nursing staff, he would have enlarged these unprincipled activities of his. His blatant confession makes it difficult to assume that his abandoning Presbyterianism for the permissive Path to Rome, which he adopted with such a mighty fanfare, improved his standards of integrity.

Then, of couse, he got himself seriously involved with Dr. Marie Stopes as the result of this change-over, and the casuistry he now exhibited. If man survive (and I sometimes think it would be quite a good thing if he didn't), Halliday Sutherland will be entirely forgotten, as are all superficial apostates. Marie Stopes, on the other hand, may well be canonized. Many, of both sexes, have been so elevated for less.

Most people are wholly indifferent to all this sort of thing. They, and the effete churches they attend, thoroughly enjoy the notion that animal experimentation is necessary to progress. A scientific necessity and, therefore, a practice the morality of which must never be questioned. As Bernard Shaw put it, there is nothing nowadays people will not believe if only it be presented to them as science, and nothing they will not disbelieve if it be presented as religion. H. G. Wells and his followers had much to do with the widespread acceptance of his un-questioning faith in science—in 'science', I should write—irrespective of all moral considerations.

With the growing weight of vivisection upon my conscience, with this ever-gnawing awareness of something very wrong and terrible and unjust, I already had come south to London, inspired not as was Dick Whittington with the desire to amass a fortune, nor yet attracted by the prospect of taking a hand in that digging for gold in its streets, but to pursue my life in surroundings less conventional and provincial, less circumscribed and nationalistic. Nationalism, since my days in The Trenches, I have regarded as an accursed thing. It constitutes, in my view, the central weakness of so-called Christian society, the canker at the heart of the Christian Church throughout Christendom. In my own lifetime the Christians, in Christ's Name, for nationalistic ends, have made war more violently and destructively upon one another than any other believers in anything, anywhere in the world. I hold that the more nations—and organised religions—the greater the likelihood of human disorder.

Except for lengthy periods spent overseas, then, my home for thirty-five years or thereabouts has been in London. For this, I have always been truly thankful. Notwithstanding, in reflecting on my arrival here, I cannot but see myself a little in the light in which Dr. Johnson saw poor William Collins when *he* first reached London—"A literary ad-venturer, with many projects in his head, and very little money in his pocket." I certainly was full of projects; but I was, perhaps, a little more favourably placed where money was concerned. I had to my credit three books, each of which was still earning me appreciable royalties.

The painter, Sir James Lavery, recalling Whistler's having dedi-cated *The Gentle Art of Making Enemies* to the rare few who, early in life, had rid themselves of the friendships of the many, claimed that in London one can be of that rare few more easily than anywhere else on earth. I believe this to be so. Lavery himself, by the way, professed to having lived forty years in Cromwell Place without knowing even his nextdoor neighbour.

"When a man is tired of London, he is tired of life." Thus wrote Dr. Johnson to James Boswell, nearly two centuries ago. Despite the many regrettable changes London has undergone even during my own rela-tively short, but by no means uneventful, stay in it, I regard my living there as an incalculable privilege. London furnishes a mental climate and a stimulus I find essential to my wellbeing.

Of course, I would not deny that I am free to get away from it whenever I want to, or feel I must. A second home, in Hampshire, beautifully Georgian, with a walled garden, colourful and fruitful, gets me out of London fairly frequently. Nevertheless, I am seldom sorry to get back to London. If it should ever come to your knowledge that I have left it for good, you will know that I am very tired, indeed, of life!

In saying this, however, I would not have you think that I am unmindful of what I owe to my long and personal associations with Edinburgh and the Lothians. They are still very much an integral part of my better self.

But what has happened to my Golden Lamp? *That* I would certainly like to know. Can it be gathering dust in some old Edinburgh junk-shop? Can it be lying, unwept and unhonoured, on some Lothian scrap-heap? Unhonoured and unwept, I fear, wherever it may be.

But no longer unsung . . .

Index